The
OXFORD
Children's Book of
Science

Charles Taylor ◆ **Stephen Pople**

The
OXFORD
Children's Book of
Science

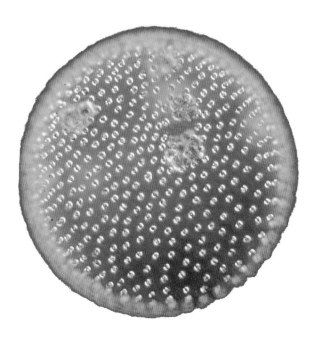

Oxford University Press

Oxford University Press, Walton Street, Oxford,
OX2 6DP

Oxford New York
Athens Auckland Bangkok Bombay
Calcutta Cape Town Dar es Salaam Delhi
Florence Hong Kong Istanbul Karachi
Kuala Lumpur Madras Madrid Melbourne
Mexico City Nairobi Paris Singapore
Taipei Tokyo Toronto

and associated companies in
Berlin Ibadan

Oxford is a trade mark of Oxford University Press
© Charles Taylor and Stephen Pople 1994

ISBN 0 19 910036 5

A CIP catalogue record for this book is available
from the British Library

Printed and bound in Great Britain by
Butler & Tanner Ltd, Frome and London

CONTENTS

ALL IN THE MIND
Senses, illusion, and science
6–11

IMAGES IN VIEW
Forming images with light and
other types of radiation
12–19

A COLOURFUL WORLD
Sensing, mixing, and using colours
20–29

SOUNDS OF MUSIC
Sounds high, low, loud, quiet,
and combined
30–39

PASSING IT ON
The secrets of plant and animal
communication, and data handling
40–47

MATERIALS UNDER THE
MICROSCOPE
The world of atoms and the
materials they make
48–55

GROWING AND
CHANGING
Cells, DNA, and the secret of life
56–63

MADE WITH SUNSHINE
How living things depend
on the Sun
64–71

A LOT OF ROT
Rotting, preserving, and recycling
72–81

Photo right *An aurora borealis (northern lights).*

Facing title page *'Manny', a fully articulated
mannequin used to test space suits and other
hazardous-environment clothing.*

Title page *A colony of* Volvox, *a water-living
organism, magnified 250 times.*

CUSTARD, GLUE, AND CONCRETE
Chemistry in action around the home
82–87

A MATTER OF CHANCE
Events possible, probable, and improbable
88–93

HOLDING THE WORLD TOGETHER
Atoms and the fundamental forces of nature
94–105

THRILLS AND SPILLS WITH g
The effects of gravity and acceleration
106–111

FLIGHT AND FLOW
Air pressure and its effects
112–117

FLOATING AND SINKING
The ups and downs of boats, balloons, fish, and divers
118–125

MOVING MACHINES
Forces in action, from levers to robots
126–133

THE HUMAN MACHINE
Using, powering, and controlling the human body
134–143

ENERGY FOREVER
Where energy comes from, what it does, and where it goes
144–151

HOT STUFF
Heat on the move and heat in store
152–159

SHOCKING BEHAVIOUR
Producing and using electricity
160–169

QUICK AS A FLASH
Radiation in action: light and the electromagnetic family
170–177

TIME ON YOUR HANDS
Forward to the future and back to the Big Bang
178–185

GLOSSARY
186–187

INDEX
188–191

ACKNOWLEDGEMENTS
192

ALL IN THE MIND

*W*e experience the world through our five senses –
sight, hearing, touch, taste, and smell. But it is the
brain which has to interpret the signals, and sometimes it
can be deceived. However real the world may seem,
it is full of illusions.

Right The Indian rope trick, being demonstrated in1935. First, the rope is thrown up into the air, then the boy climbs up it. The illusion works because the brain expects the rope to be flexible, and does not even consider the possibility that it might be rigid.

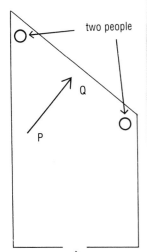

two people

P Q

viewing point for illusion

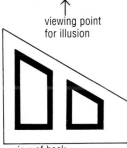

view of back wall in the direction of PQ

Left In the distorted room illusion, identical twins appear to be different sizes. However, it is the room which is abnormal, not the twins. You can see the actual shape of the room in the diagram **above**. The twin on the left looks smaller because she is much further from the camera. The illusion is helped by the distorted paintings on the back wall and floor which make you think that the wall is normal.

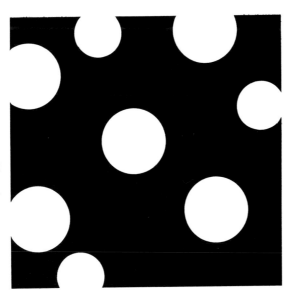

PERCEPTION AND DECEPTION

Seeing depends on three things – the presence of light, eyes to collect the light, and a brain to interpret the signals from the eyes.

Most light has a two-stage journey to reach our eyes. Starting from the Sun or a lamp, it falls on different objects and is then scattered by them so that some light ends up in the eyes. This scattered light carries with it a kind of code containing all the information needed for us to imagine what the objects are like. The word 'imagine' is used deliberately here, because that is just what the brain has to do. However, the process is more usually called perception.

It is easy for the brain to imagine things incorrectly, even though the eyes are working properly. Sometimes it can happen accidentally. For example, sitting in a café with a large mirror covering one wall, you may think that you are looking at real people on the other side of the solid wall, even though they are only reflections. Sometimes the brain can be tricked deliberately. This is called deception. Examples include optical illusions and conjuring tricks.

Above There appears to be a white triangle lying over this picture, but it is not really there. Your brain perceives the gaps and assumes that they must be made by a triangle.

Left Stare at this picture for 10 seconds without moving your eyes, then look at a piece of white paper. You should see dark dots where the white ones were.

JUGGLING THE JIGSAW

The nine diamond-shaped pieces of this jigsaw can be put together in several different ways. In grouping 1, the picture looks like three cubes, each coloured differently. In grouping 2, the areas of light and shade are different for each cube. The brain is confused and finds this picture disturbing. In grouping 3, the picture looks like three identical cubes. Here, the brain accepts that the colour differences are due to light and shade.

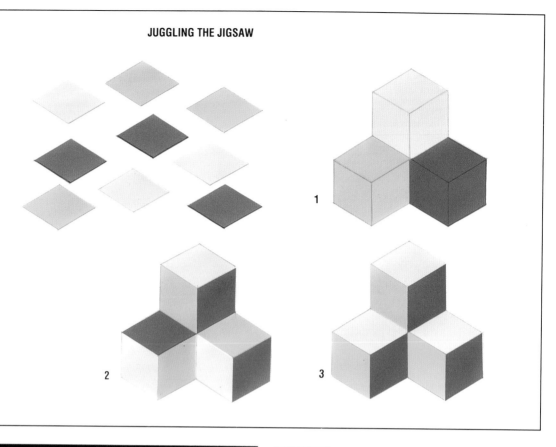

Right The person in the box seems to have been cut into three pieces. Now the magician is adding to the audience's amazement by sliding the centre section out of the box. As in all illusions, what the brain imagines to be happening is quite different from what is really taking place.

DIFFERENT DECEPTIONS

In some optical illusions, the brain is fed with correct information but it jumps to the wrong conclusion. The distorted room in the photograph on page 6 is like this. In reality, it is an odd-shaped room, with one corner much further away from the camera than the other. But you are not used to seeing rooms like this, so you imagine that the room is rectangular in shape. Your brain tries to build the most likely picture out of the information supplied. Other examples of the brain doing this can be seen in 'Juggling the jigsaw' at the top of the page.

Some optical illusions work because the eyes become tired. This happened in the example on the previous page when you stared at the white dots on the black background. The light-sensing cells on the back of your eyes soon became tired by the bright, white parts of the image they were picking up. So, when you looked at a piece of plain white paper, the tired cells gave a much dimmer picture than the others. As a result, you saw dark dots where there had been white ones.

There is another kind of optical illusion in which the brain is so used to a particular thing happening that it perceives something that is not really there at all. The triangle illusion on the previous page is an example of this. The brain needs a convincing explanation of the gaps in the picture, so it imagines a white triangle.

If your brain is upset in some way by a fever or by drugs, then it can imagine all kinds of strange things. These sensations are called hallucinations. You experience similar effects whenever you are dreaming. The brain imagines events that seem real, even though your five senses are largely out of action.

Illusions can happen with other senses as well as sight. Compared with many other animals, humans have a rather poor sense of smell, but we do have a very good memory for smells and find it easy to imagine them. The sight of a cooked meal or even a picture of a cooked meal can, briefly, trigger the sensation that you can smell the meal.

SOUND ILLUSIONS

The brain can play tricks with hearing. Sometimes people imagine sounds that are not really there – for example, a doorbell ringing. Sometimes, they can fail to hear sounds that are there, although the signals are reaching the brain. This can be an advantage. For example, if you are concentrating on learning the words of a play, you may be completely unaware of the sound of a loud, ticking clock in the room.

People who live near railway lines do not always notice the noise of passing trains. This, too, is because the brain has developed the clever trick of ignoring sounds that do not not seem important. This trick probably evolved long ago to aid survival. For early human hunters, it was vital to hear the animal being hunted, and not to be distracted by other noises. It was equally important for the hunters to hear animals that might be hunting them!

Below Many creatures have a much better sense of smell than our own. Using the featherlike antennae on its head, this male atlas moth can sense the presence of a female several kilometres away. It does so by detecting tiny traces of chemicals called pheromones which are given off by the female to attract a mate.

HOT AND COLD ILLUSION

Telling hot from cold is not always as easy as you might think. Put hot, but not scalding, water in one bowl, cold water in a second bowl, and warm water in a third. Place your left hand in the hot water and your right hand in the cold water. Keep them there for about 20 seconds, then put both hands in the warm water. Your left hand will tell you that the water is cold and the right hand that it is hot.

Another important feature of the brain is how quickly it can recognize sounds. Think of how many different voices there are in the world, yet you can instantly recognize a friend's voice on the telephone, even if you have not heard from them for a long time. This ability of the brain causes problems for impressionists on stage and TV. They have to create the illusion that some well-known person is speaking, but the audience finds it easy to tell if a voice is not quite right. Often, the impressionist uses facial expressions and body movements so that the brain will accept a slightly wrong voice.

SECRET PROCESSING

Many sense signals are processed by your brain without your being aware of them. For example, if someone is speaking in a large room, you seem to hear each word only once. Yet the sound is reflected from the walls and ceiling, so it arrives at your ears by many different routes and at slightly different times. The brain works on the principle that, if the same thing is heard many times in rapid succession, then it is probably meant to be heard only once.

The brain carries out another processing trick as well. When it works out the delay between each sound, it tells the subconscious mind the size of the room. You can try the effect for yourself. If you are taken into a hall, room, or cupboard with your eyes shut, you can guess its approximate size by listening to noises made around you.

Each image on the back of your eye takes a fraction of a second to die away, so you cannot always detect rapid changes. Here is an experiment which demonstrates the effect. Cut a disc of stiff white card. Draw a bird on one side and an empty cage on the other. Attach two elastic bands to the card to make a 'whizzer'. When the card spins round fast, the bird will appear to be inside the cage.

BIRD IN A CAGE

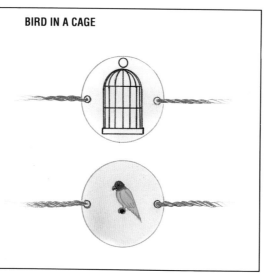

TOUCHING IMPRESSIONS

A sense of touch is very important, and without it you would quickly injure yourself. You have to rely on touch to tell you how hot or cold things are. Touch sends signals back to the brain to tell you how hard your grip is when picking things up. Without this feedback, objects would either get crushed or be dropped. Touch is also needed so that you can control a pen or pencil when writing or drawing.

Your sense of touch depends on the nerve endings in the skin. Its sensitivity varies for different parts of the body. Many people think that the fingertips are the most sensitive, but you can easily prove that this is not the case. Stand in front of a mirror and touch your hair very gently with one finger. You can hardly feel the hair with your finger, but the very slightest movement of your hair will be sensed by nerve endings in your scalp.

FALSE IMPRESSIONS

The signals that come from our senses depend on what happened immediately before. For example, warm water feels hot if your hand was cold before you touched it. A smell seems much stronger when you first come across it. And if you move from bright light into a darkened room, the room may look pitch-black until your eyes get used to the gloom.

Everyday life is full of false impressions like this. Some can be dangerous. When drivers slow down after hours of fast driving on a motorway, they may feel that their speed has reduced to no more than a crawling pace, but they may still be travelling far too fast for ordinary roads.

Not all false impressions cause problems. Indeed, some experiences in modern life depend on them. Cinema and television both rely on the fact that the eyes go on seeing things for a short time after they are no longer there – an effect called persistence of vision. As a result, we are not conscious that separate still pictures are being flashed on the screen one after another. Instead, we get the sensation of a moving picture.

SENSES AND SCIENCE

Our human senses allow us to experience the incredible variety of the world around us, but they are not always a safe and reliable guide to what is really happening. In poor visibility and without a compass, people in open country or at sea can travel round in circles for hours without realizing it. And in cloud, and without instruments to provide an artificial horizon, pilots can be in a dive or even upside–down while still believing that they are flying straight and level.

Scientists use measuring instruments to extend the range of the human senses. With these, they can probe deeper, look further, estimate more accurately, and detect things which would otherwise be invisible to the human eye. But they must still be aware of how the brain can misinterpret signals, otherwise wrong conclusions can be reached. That is why they repeat experiments many times and cross-check their results by doing them in different ways. Scientists rely on many instruments, but there is one that they rely on more than any other – the human mind.

Above This drawing by M. C. Escher is full of illusions. All the objects in it seem to fit with their immediate surroundings, but the whole picture is a mass of contradictions which the brain finds disturbing.

IMAGES IN VIEW

We are surrounded by images of all kinds –
in mirrors, through lenses in binoculars and
microscopes, on television and computer screens.
But although these image-forming systems are
different from each other, they all use the same
scientific principle.

SEEING WITH MIRRORS

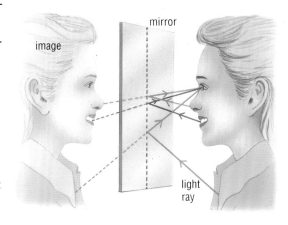

An ordinary mirror is one of the simplest image-forming systems. It is just a flat piece of polished metal or glass coated with a thin layer of silver or aluminium. The metal surface reflects light. When light rays falls on it, they bounce off, and the direction in which the light is travelling is changed.

Your eyes and brain are used to working out where something is from the direction of the light received. So if a mirror changes this direction, your brain is fooled into thinking that the object you are looking at is behind the mirror. That is where you see an image.

Above Light is reflected by the mirror to the eye. But the brain thinks that the light has travelled in straight lines and imagines the image to be behind the mirror.

Right A funfair mirror has a mixture of concave and convex surfaces. The final image depends on which part of the mirror is being used.

Above In the concave (curving in) side of a spoon, your image is small and upside down. If the spoon is moved much closer it is large and the right way up. In the convex (bulging out) side, the image is always small and the right way up.

Left Three ways of making images. The two air traffic controllers are making an image of the aircraft on the runways with their eyes. They are also seeing the images on the electronic screens made by the radar system. And the whole picture has been recorded on film by a camera.

Bending Light Beams

The direction in which light is travelling may be changed when light moves from air into water or glass, or vice versa. In a vacuum, light travels at a speed of about 300,000 km every second. Its speed is almost the same in air. But as soon as it enters a transparent material like water, plastic, or glass, it slows down. In glass, light only travels at about 200,000 km every second. If it enters the glass at any angle other than square on, its direction is changed because one side of the beam enters the glass and slows down before the other. This makes the beam swing round. The effect is known as refraction.

Looking at the beam carefully shows you that individual colours are bent by different amounts. This is because the slowing down of the light is greater for the blues and greens than it is for the reds and oranges. If the glass slab is in the form of a triangular shape, called a prism, the light is bent as it goes in and again as it comes out. This means that spread of colours is even greater. The spread of colours is called a spectrum (see page 21).

Below Light travels a little faster in hot air than in cold, so patches of hot air can act like lenses and bend the light. But these lens-like patches are irregular and constantly moving, so an image seems to shimmer, as seen here when Concorde takes off.

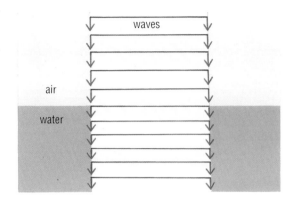

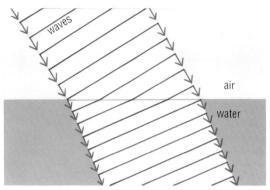

Above Light travels more slowly in water than in air, making the wave crests closer together (top). If the waves hit the water at an angle (bottom), those hitting first slow down first, so the whole wave bends round. The bending effect is called refraction.

Above We know the girders in pylons have sharp edges. Because they look fuzzy here, the picture must be out of focus.

Right The apparent size of pylons or poles depends on how far away they are. The closer they are, the larger they look.

concave lens

convex lens

Above A concave lens makes the light spread out and allows a short-sighted person to focus on something further away. A convex lens concentrates the light and allows you to see clearly something very close to the eye.

A CLOSER LOOK

When you look at something, its apparent size depends on how far it is from your eyes. For example, you may know that two houses are the same size, but if one house is a long way away from you, it will appear much smaller than the other house. By contrast, the closer something is to you, the bigger it looks.

If something is very close to your eyes, it will look huge, but it will also look fuzzy because your eyes will not be able to focus on it. Short-sighted people can hold things very close and still see them clearly. A magnifying glass works by making your eye behave as though you were short-sighted – the object can be held closer to your eye than normal, and so it appears bigger than normal. A microscope is a collection of lenses that makes objects look even bigger than does a single lens.

EYES AND CODES

You use your eyes as information-gathering devices. During a meeting, a speaker may be explaining something in words, but at the same time, she is also exchanging other types of information with her audience.

During the meeting, the speaker may notice that one person has a black eye, another has had her hair cut, and a third is staring out of the window. The audience may notice that the speaker has new shoes, a pile of notes on her table, and keeps looking at her watch. These, and many other pieces of information, are being exchanged without interrupting the speaker's voice or the audience's understanding of what she is saying.

When the speaker and the audience are looking at each other, they are exchanging information using light. If there was no light in the room, or if everyone closed their eyes, the exchange of information would stop.

When light strikes things in a room, it bounces off them in many directions. In other words, it is scattered. It is also changed, so that it now carries information about the colour, shape, and texture of the things which scattered it. When the light enters your eyes, the information is then changed into nerve impulses. This is the form in which it can be handled by the brain.

So the light entering your eyes is really a kind of code sent out by the things that scattered it. To produce an image, this code must be decoded by your eyes and brain.

These two steps, coding and decoding, happen in every kind of imaging system.

LOOK SHARP

When you use a projector, the picture on the screen is a magnified image of a colour slide or piece of film. To begin with, the picture is not always clear. You have to focus it by moving the lens in or out until it is sharp. When focusing the picture, what you are really doing is making the image look like you think it should look. If the picture is of something never seen before, then focusing can be difficult. This often happens when powerful microscopes are first tried out on new materials.

If a projector has no lens, the light from the slide is scattered in all directions and you only see a fuzzy patch of light on the screen.

The information about each point on the slide is spread over the whole patch. The job of the lens is to gather together the information about each point on the slide and focus it on the right place on the screen. In other words, its job is to decode the information so that it is in a form which makes sense to you.

A lens is one way of decoding scattered light, but there is an even simpler way. Just put a tiny pinhole in a piece of card or foil. Although light from the slide is scattered in all directions, the pinhole only lets through those rays which will end up at the right places on the screen to form a picture. All the rest are blocked. The main disadvantage of the system is that nearly all the light is cut out, so the final picture is very dim.

Below With this electron microscope, the operator can see the image through one of the windows (seen glowing green), but the image is also shown on the video screen (in blue). The researcher is studying the virus which causes hepatitis B. The virus particles can be seen on the screen.

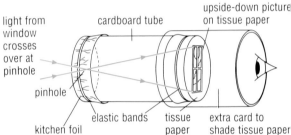

light from window crosses over at pinhole

cardboard tube

upside-down picture on tissue paper

pinhole

kitchen foil

elastic bands

tissue paper

extra card to shade tissue paper

Above A pinhole camera which you can make yourself. This one does not take photographs, but if you point it at something bright, like a window on the other side of a dark room, you will see an image on the tissue paper.

IMAGES WITHOUT LIGHT

It is not always light that carries the information needed to make images. It can be ultrasonic waves, X-rays, beams of electrons, microwaves, and radio waves. These different sorts of rays and waves are called 'radiation', because they 'radiate' from their source. Radiation does not only mean the dangerous radiation from nuclear reactors.

UP TO THE LIMIT

It is not possible to make images of absolutely anything. Scientists cannot, for example, make a light-gathering microscope that would magnify millions of times. Or, to be more accurate, they could, but the picture it would create would be a fuzzy blob.

So there is a limit to how much you can magnify with light. The reason is complicated, but it is linked with the wavelength of the light. Light travels in the form of tiny waves (see page 172), and its wavelength is the distance from the crest of one wave to the crest of the next. A wave can only carry information about things that are bigger than its wavelength. Light has wavelengths of less than a millionth of a metre, so no matter how good your microscope is and how much it magnifies, you can never see things that are smaller than a millionth of a metre.

If this puzzles you, imagine trying to sign your name with a wide paint brush. The result would be just a formless blob. Trying to form an image with waves that are longer than the size of the object is like trying to sign your name with too wide a brush. This limitation on the size of the object that can be imaged also applies to all types of radiation.

If you want to look at things smaller than the wavelength of light, a beam of electrons can be used instead of light. But ordinary lenses will not work with electrons; they cannot decode the information. Also, electrons can only travel in a vacuum (completely empty space). In an electron microscope, the whole apparatus, including the thing being studied, is inside a tube from which all the air is removed. The 'lenses' are cylindrical electromagnets with a fine hole down through the centre that focus the electron beam. The electrons fall on to a screen and produce a highly magnified picture. The code has been decoded.

SCANNING

With a lens or a pinhole camera, every part of the image is formed at the same time. In other words, all the information is decoded at once. But lenses and pinhole cameras are not suitable for all kinds of radiations. Sometimes, to code information, a process called scanning is used.

Television, radar, and many medical images use scanning. It is especially useful when the picture has to be transmitted along a cable, or by radio waves. First, the picture is divided up into small bits in a regular way.

Right This fearsome-looking creature, shown about 25 times its real size, is a grain weevil. The yellow part is the grain of wheat in which it was born. The picture was taken by a scanning electron microscope with colour added by computer.

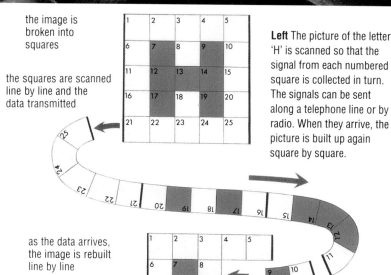

the image is broken into squares

the squares are scanned line by line and the data transmitted

as the data arrives, the image is rebuilt line by line

Left The picture of the letter 'H' is scanned so that the signal from each numbered square is collected in turn. The signals can be sent along a telephone line or by radio. When they arrive, the picture is built up again square by square.

These bits are sent to where the picture is needed, and then put together again as a picture. In practice, a picture might be divided into more than a million pieces. If the picture is of something moving, like a television picture, each set of pieces might have to change 25 times every second!

RADAR

In radar systems, pulses of microwaves are used to detect aircraft or other objects (see page 174 for more on microwaves). The pulses are sent out in a narrow beam by a radar dish. If they strike an aircraft, they are reflected back to the dish. The closer the aircraft, the less time the pulses take to return.

The image on the radar screen is formed by scanning. As the dish sweeps round, the image is built up by a moving line on the screen.

MEDICAL IMAGING

In hospitals, there are various machines which use scanning to form images of the insides of people's bodies. Several different types of radiation are used.

Ultrasound scanners are used to form images of unborn babies in the womb.

Below Ultrasonic waves are scattered by bones more than by liquids. In this ultrasound scan, a baby can be seen inside its mother's womb after about 16 weeks' development. The head is on the right and the legs on the left.

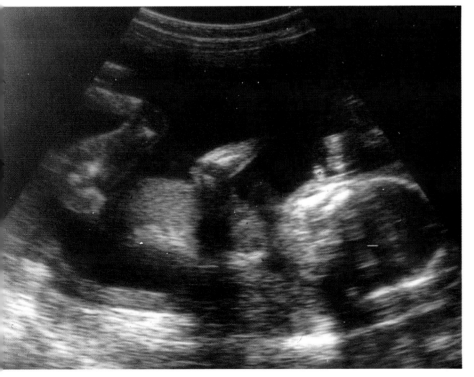

Above A radar dish rotates to scan the sky round an airfield. The orange box sends out and receives back the microwave signals that are focused into a beam by the large reflector.

Ultrasound is sound of a frequency which is too high for the human ear to hear. It can be reflected by different layers inside the body. Ultrasound waves are much safer for unborn babies than X-rays. X-rays can harm a developing foetus.

CAT scanners use X-rays, but give a much more detailed picture than an ordinary X-ray photo. In a CAT (Computerized Axial Tomographic) scanner, a thin 'slice' of the patient's body is X-rayed from different angles. A computer collects the information from this scanning process and puts it together so that an image of the 'slice' appears on a screen.

SEEING ATOMS

Light waves are too large to make images of things as small as atoms.

X-rays have wavelengths that are short enough to make images of atoms, but there is no direct way of decoding the information because there are no lenses which will focus X-rays. To get round this problem, a technique called X-ray diffraction was developed. A tiny piece of the substance being studied is placed in a beam of X-rays. This produces a pattern of scattered waves – the coded information – which can be photographed.

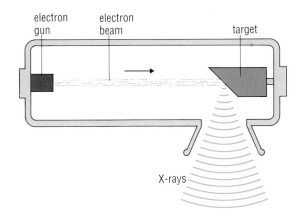

Above In an X-ray tube, electrons emitted from the gun are attracted to the target by a high voltage (20,000 volts or more). They hit the target so hard that its atoms become excited and emit X-rays.

As the pattern cannot be decoded directly, scientists have to embark on a complicated piece of detective work to deduce what arrangement of atoms could have made it. It was indirect image-making like this that led to the discovery of the double helix of DNA – the molecule of life (see page 56).

HOLOGRAMS

A photograph of an object gives you a flat picture, but if a hologram is made of the same object, a 3D picture can be produced. This means that the image has depth, so you can see round its sides as though it were solid and really there.

Some holograms only give an image when laser light is shone through them; others give an image when they reflect ordinary light. The holograms printed on credit cards are like this.

To make a hologram, single-colour light from a laser is needed. The laser beam is split into two halves. One half shines on the object, which reflects the laser light. This mixes with the other half (called the reference beam), making patterns called interference fringes. The hologram is a photograph of these patterns. It does not look anything like the original object – in fact the fringes on the hologram plate are too small to see. However, the hologram contains all the information needed to produce an image when laser light shines through it or light is reflected from it.

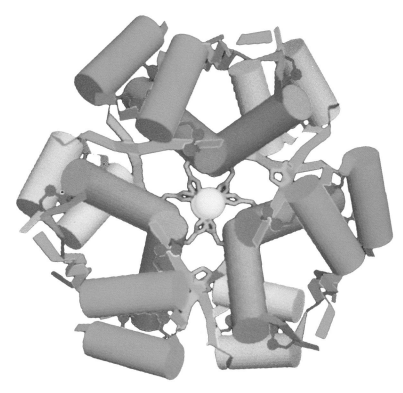

Above Computer images play an important part in scientific research. Instead of building actual models, a computer can be used to imitate a 3D model which can be turned and viewed from any angle. This is the structure of the hormone that controls the production of insulin in the body.

Left This boy is viewing another kind of visual model – a 3D image formed when a cylindrical hologram is illuminated by laser light.

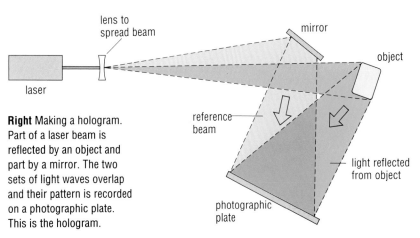

Right Making a hologram. Part of a laser beam is reflected by an object and part by a mirror. The two sets of light waves overlap and their pattern is recorded on a photographic plate. This is the hologram.

A COLOURFUL WORLD

The world around us is amazingly colourful. Yet,
incredibly, we see it with eyes which are sensitive
to three basic colours only. But colour is more than
decoration. Animals and plants rely on it, and scientists
can tell a great deal about materials by studying it.

We take colour very much for granted, but without it the world would look a much duller place. It would be like black-and-white television.

About 1 in 12 boys and about 1 in 200 girls are colour-blind. This does not mean that they see in black and white. Colour-blind people see many colours, but they confuse certain ones, particularly red and green.

COLOURS FROM WHITE

The light that we get from the Sun is white. But white is not a single colour. In 1666, Isaac Newton used a glass prism to split sunlight into a range of colours called a spectrum. In doing this, he was able to show that white light is a mixture of all the colours of the rainbow. Raindrops can act like natural prisms, so if there is sunshine and rain, a rainbow may be formed.

Here is a messy way of forming your own rainbow! Standing with your back to the Sun, use a hosepipe to make a fine, spread-out spray in front of you.

Below A rainbow over mountains in Arizona. Raindrops, acting like tiny prisms, are splitting the sunlight into its different colours and reflecting them back. As the Sun is behind the camera and the rainbow appears to extend to the ground, the rain must be falling between the camera and the mountains.

MAKING A SPECTRUM

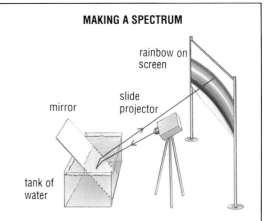

Above A piece of card with a narrow, horizontal slit in it is used as a slide in a projector. The beam is aimed at a mirror placed at an angle in the water. The water between the mirror and the water surface acts like a prism and forms a spectrum on the screen behind the projector.

Below How a glass prism forms a spectrum.

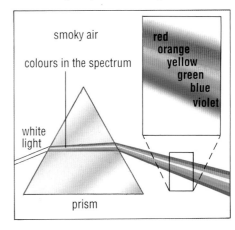

There have always been arguments about how many colours there are in the rainbow. Often people claim there are seven: red, orange, yellow, green, blue, indigo, and violet. They remember them with this sentence: Richard Of York Goes Battling In Vain. The first letter of each word stands for a different colour.

In fact there are millions of colours in the rainbow, but we only have names for some of them. For instance, we call two of them red and orange, but in between there are dozens of shades which we have to call reddish orange, orangey red, very orangey red, and so on. For simplicity, we usually use just the six or seven colour names. There are also colours which you cannot find in the rainbow, like cerise and magenta. These can be made by mixing coloured lights, or by taking away some of the colours from white light.

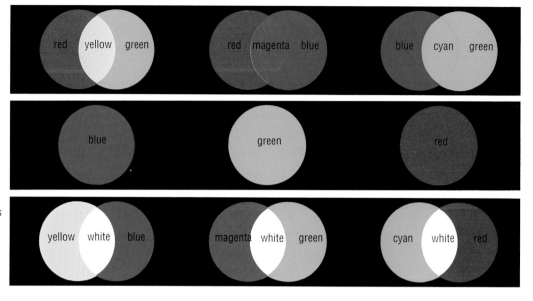

Add two primary colours and get a secondary colour.

The third unused primary colour is called the complementary colour.

Add the secondary colour and its complementary colour and you see white.

Above When light beams are mixed, the colours are added. Equal amounts of any two primary colours (red, green, and blue) give a secondary colour (yellow, magenta, or cyan). But by mixing three primaries in other proportions, almost any colour can be made.

MIXING COLOURED LIGHTS

To see the effects of mixing coloured lights, beams of different colours can be overlapped on a white screen. Mixing red and blue light gives magenta, mixing green and blue light gives a greeny blue colour called cyan, and mixing red and green light gives yellow. If red, green, and blue are mixed, the result is white.

As light is being added to light, the colours red, green, and blue are often called the additive primaries. It sometimes surprises people that red added to green gives yellow, but that usually means that they have confused mixing lights with mixing paints.

Lights need not be mixed in equal amounts. For instance, if bright red light is mixed with dim green light, the mixture will be orange, not yellow.

If two primaries are mixed, for example red and green, the result is called an additive secondary, in this case yellow. The unused primary, in this case blue, is called the complementary colour. Adding the complementary to the secondary gives white. Another way of looking at it is to say that taking away blue from white gives yellow, taking green from white gives magenta, and taking red from white gives cyan. Yellow can be called 'minus blue', magenta can be called 'minus green', and cyan can be called 'minus red'.

SEEING COLOURS

The eye is rather like a camera, with a lens system to produce an image. Instead of a film at the back, there is a very sensitive screen called the retina. This contains four kinds of light-detecting cells.

Right A section through a human eye. The retina, which is like the film in a camera, has an image on it. In the retina, there are millions of light-sensitive cells, some of which respond to colour (red, green, or blue). There is a watery fluid between the retina and the lens, and a jelly-like fluid between the lens and the cornea.

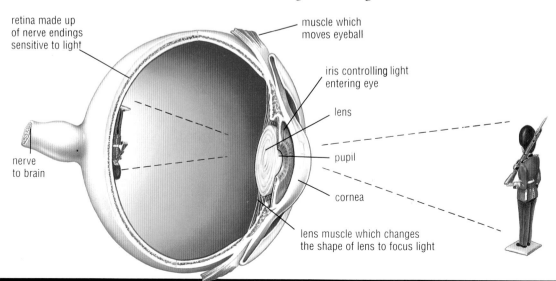

One kind, called rods because of their shape, are simply sensitive to light and dark. They are the ones that show detail when there is not much light to see by. The others are called cones, also because of their shape. There are three kinds of cones, each sensitive to a different colour: one to red light, one to green, and one to blue. So, if you are looking at a yellow daffodil, the red and green cones will be sending signals to the brain, and the blue ones will be resting. Rods and cones are called receptors.

HOW THINGS GET THEIR COLOUR

In a stained-glass window, the chemicals in the glass absorb some of the colours in white daylight, and let others through. For example, in a part that appears yellow, the blue is absorbed, in the part that appears blue, both the red and the green are absorbed, and so on. Scientists call this 'selective absorption and transmission' because selected colours are absorbed by the glass, while the rest are let through or transmitted.

COLOUR BEFORE YOUR EYES

You can find out more about the colour-sensitive receptors in your eyes as follows. Paint or stick a patch of colour (about 75 mm square) in the middle of a sheet of black paper (about 150 mm square). Place the black paper next to a sheet of white paper of the same size. Now stare hard at the coloured patch while you count up to 20. Then stare hard at the middle of the white paper.

If, say, your coloured patch is green, the green receptors on the retina in the green part become tired, but the red and blue ones will not. None of the receptors in the black part of the image become tired. So, when you look at the white paper, the shape of the green patch will look magenta ('minus green'). If the patch were yellow, you would see blue, and so on.

In a yellow flower, there are chemicals that absorb the blue light but reflect red and green. The red and green mix to give the yellow. In a green leaf, the red and blue light are absorbed, and the green reflected. These are all examples of selective absorption and reflection: selected colours are absorbed, while the rest are reflected.

If you look at a scarf which appears magenta, then the dyes are absorbing the green, while the red and blue are reflected.

Left White light from the Sun shines through a stained-glass window in the church of St Martin of Tours, Basildon. The chemicals in the glass absorb some colours and allow the rest to pass through, so the light falling on the floor and walls appears coloured. For example, in the parts that are coloured green, all the red and and some of the blue light is absorbed, and a mixture of green with a little blue passes through.

MIXING PAINTS

When you paint with poster colours, they appear coloured because of selective absorption and reflection. But if you mix red and green you will not get yellow as you would when mixing lights. Instead, the result will probably be a muddy colour. This is because the red absorbs some green and blue light, while the green absorbs some red and blue light. Between them, the two paints absorb so much light that there is very little left to reflect.

If you wash your brushes at the end of a painting session, the water always ends up the colour of mud. The reason is not difficult to find if you think about how colours are absorbed. For example, if red and green are mixed, the red paint will absorb blue and green light, while the green paint will absorb red and blue light.

This means that, if the brush-washing water has red and green in it, all three additive primary colours are absorbed, but more green is absorbed than the other two. 'Minus green' is magenta, so the result is a very dark colour with a slight magenta tint – in other words, a muddy purple. As you wash your brushes, each colour absorbs more and more of the light, so the resulting mixture looks very dark.

When mixing paints, one way to avoid ending up with dark colours is to use the additive secondary colours. If you use magenta, yellow, and cyan paints, each one absorbs only one primary. So, for example, mixing magenta and yellow ('minus green' and 'minus blue') will give you quite a bright red; magenta and cyan will give blue; and cyan and yellow will give green.

Artists who use oil colours or acrylic paints have a trick to help get round the difficulty of the very dark colour mixes. By adding white paint, they can, in effect, put back some of the light taken away in the first place. For example, if red and blue paints are mixed, the result is a very dark purple. But if white paint is now added, you are putting back all three primaries, and can get a good magenta shade. That is why, if you look in an artist's box of oil paints, you will always find a big fat tube of white.

COLOUR PRINTING

Printers can produce a full-colour picture by printing three single-colour pictures on top of each other, together with a black-and-white picture to improve the quality. Our eyes have red, green, and blue receptors. However, the coloured inks used by printers are not red, green, and blue. They are yellow, magenta, and cyan. In other words, they are 'minus blue', 'minus green', and 'minus red'. The printing process works as follows.

Imagine that you want to photograph a full-colour picture and print it in a book using coloured inks. First, a 'black-and-white' photograph is taken with a blue filter over the camera lens. When the film is printed, the parts of the picture which gave no blue light come out black, the parts which gave only blue come out white, and the parts which gave some blue come out in shades of grey.

Below Some of the results of mixing paints. Red paint absorbs blue and green light, and blue paint absorbs red and green light. So when red and blue paints are mixed, some of all the colours is absorbed, but more green is absorbed than anything else. The result is the complementary colour of green, which is magenta ('minus green'). But it is a very dark colour. If the paint is opaque (not clear) like oil, acrylic, or poster paint, it can be made lighter by adding white.

YELLOW   MAGENTA   CYAN   BLACK   ALL FOUR COLOURS

This first picture is printed using yellow ink, so that the black parts are yellow and the white parts are white. The picture is actually made up of thousands of tiny yellow dots on the white background.

Next, a photograph is taken with a green filter over the camera. Its 'black-and-white' picture is printed on top of the first one, using magenta ink. Finally, a third photograph is taken with a red filter over the camera lens. Its 'black-and-white' picture is printed over the other two, using cyan ink.

We can check that the process really does produce the right colours, as follows.

Suppose there is a yellow flower in the photograph you want to print. The yellow flower reflects both red and green light, but not blue. So it will be printed yellow in the first picture, white in the second picture, and white in the third. Yellow shows through, so the printed flower really does look yellow.

Now suppose there is a green leaf in your photograph. The green leaf reflects green, but not red or blue. So it will be printed yellow in the first picture, white in the second, and cyan in the third. The yellow ('minus blue') ink mixed with the cyan ('minus red') ink absorbs all colours except green. So the printed leaf really does appear green.

Finally, suppose there is a black vase in your photograph. Black absorbs all light – in other words it does not reflect red, green, or blue. So this time, all three colours, cyan, magenta, and yellow, will be printed. Between them, you might expect them to absorb all the light. In fact the inks do not absorb all colours completely. Instead, the result is a dark, muddy brown. Printers need something else to give them really dark blacks, so they print a fourth 'black-and-white' picture, using black ink, on top of the other three.

COLOUR TELEVISION

Colour television uses additive colour mixing of the primary colours red, green, and blue. The screen of a colour TV is covered with thousands of tiny strips or dots which can be made to glow in different combinations. Some glow red, some green, and some blue. In a red part of the picture, only the red strips will be glowing. In a yellow part of the picture, red and green strips will be glowing, and in a white part, all three kinds will be glowing. Because the strips are so small, several of them cover each of the sensors in the eye, so the colours are mixed additively.

It seems amazing that all the colours of tropical fish or birds can be made just from three types of coloured strips on a screen.

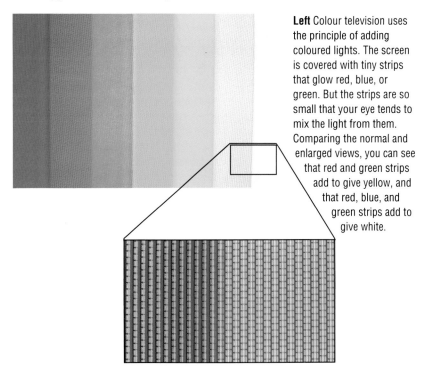

Above To create the full-colour picture at the end, four separate pictures were printed on top of each other. The first was taken through a blue filter and printed in yellow ink, the second through a green filter and printed in magenta, and the third through a red filter and printed in cyan. The fourth picture was taken without a filter and printed in black ink.

Left Colour television uses the principle of adding coloured lights. The screen is covered with tiny strips that glow red, blue, or green. But the strips are so small that your eye tends to mix the light from them. Comparing the normal and enlarged views, you can see that red and green strips add to give yellow, and that red, blue, and green strips add to give white.

In fact, your television picture is a kind of illusion. Although the television engineers might think they are producing the miracle, most of the work is being done by your brain! It is the brain which is having to take the three kinds of colour information and imagine them as a full colour picture. Someone who had not seen television before would probably find it very difficult at first to understand the picture.

THE STRANGE EFFECTS OF COLOURED LIGHTS

Most things appear coloured because of selective absorption and reflection. Normally we see things in daylight – in other words, with white light falling on them. But if the light falling on them is not pure white, then their colours may appear different. Think for example what will happen if you look at three shirts, red, green, and blue, which have yellow ('minus blue') light falling on them. The red shirt will look red because it has some red light to reflect, and the green shirt will look green because it has some green light to reflect. But the blue shirt will look black because it has no light to reflect.

Many streets are lit by sodium lights. The light they give out is yellow, but unlike most other yellows, it is not only 'minus blue'. It is minus everything except for one single narrow yellow bit of the spectrum. It contains no red, no green, and no blue. This can have a very strange effect on people's faces. The red of their lips looks black, and so does any red in the cheeks. This produces a very sickly appearance.

Lights with a slight tint do not give such dramatic effects, but they can upset our perception of colour. That is why, when you are buying clothes, it is important to look at them in daylight before choosing. The artificial lighting in shops is not pure white.

COLOUR IN PLANTS AND ANIMALS

Colour plays an important part in the natural world. Birds use their colours to attract a mate. Flowers are coloured in order to attract insects which carry pollen between them. Coloured berries are easier to see in the winter, and caterpillars or insects with a nasty taste are often highly coloured to warn off birds or animals that might eat them.

Below Sodium street lights give an extremely pure yellow light with no red or green. Our eyes normally expect yellow to be a mixture of red and green. In sodium light, any object that is red cannot find any red light to reflect, so it appears unexpectedly dark.

Other animals use colour in their camouflage to prevent themselves from being seen. The tiger has stripes which make it difficult to see when stalking through long, waving grasses. The leopard has spots which can be mistaken for the dappled sunlight through the trees, and chameleons can assume the colour of their background in order to 'disappear'.

Some fish and lizards can change colour completely. Their skin provides a background colour, but there are small cells dotted all over it which are of a different colour. When the animal changes colour, these cells are suddenly increased in size, and so their colour becomes mixed with the background colour.

Of course, humans can also change colour, but in a less dramatic way. Some of us blush when embarrassed, go pale with fright, and turn a little green when sick. Exposure to sunshine can also alter skin colour.

It is surprising how strongly colour can affect us. If you walk into a room with pale blue walls you probably feel quite relaxed, whereas red decorations can make you feel more tense. This might be because blue reminds you of the sky on a summer day, but you associate red with fire or blood.

Above This deadly arrow-poison frog from Central America is calling for a mate. The brilliant red and blue colours warn creatures that might otherwise want to eat it that it is poisonous.

Left If you look very carefully, you can just make out the shape of this leaf-tailed gecko from eastern Australia. The colour and pattern match the bark of the tree so well that the camouflage is almost perfect.

Above A coral reef in the Red Sea. The stunning colours serve many purposes. Fish may match the coral colours for camouflage, and colours help members of the same species to recognize each other. The intense blue of the water comes mainly from the sky.

We also get used to certain colours and can be disturbed if we see the wrong ones. A plate of brown sausages, green peas, and white mashed potatoes may look acceptable. But if the food were dyed so that you had blue sausages, grey peas, and green potatoes, it would look far less appetizing.

Some colours tend to be linked with moods. In the English language, for example, people are said to be red with anger, black with rage, and green with envy. They are blue if depressed, and yellow if cowardly.

Plants are normally associated with the colour green, so it may come as a surprise to discover that it is green light which is least useful to plants. To live and grow, plants must take in energy from sunlight. They do this by using a substance called chlorophyll which is mainly in their leaves. Chorophyll absorbs red and blue light, but very little green. The green light is mostly reflected. That is why leaves normally look green.

COLOUR CHEMISTRY

Scientists learn a great deal about chemicals by studying how they change colour under different conditions. If a chemical is heated in a flame, the flame shows a colour that is characteristic of the elements in the substance. For example, any chemical containing sodium will turn the flame a vivid yellow (like the yellow of sodium street lights). Any compound containing potassium will give a lilac colour to the flame. A flame test is one of the simpler ways of finding out about a chemical.

Sometimes, scientists need to know whether solutions are acids or alkalis. Chemicals called indicators are useful for this. For example, litmus is an indicator which goes red in acid, and blue in an alkali. With some indicators, a colour chart is used to work out how strong the acid or alkali is.

COLOUR CHEMISTRY IN THE KITCHEN
Put a teaspoonful of blackcurrant juice in a tablespoon of water to make a red solution. If you add this to some ordinary soda, bath salts, or bicarbonate of soda dissolved in a little water, it will turn blue, showing that the solution you have added is alkaline. If you then add some vinegar or lemon juice, it will turn back to red, showing that the solution is now acid. You could try some other cordials or juices to see if they work in the same way.

BUBBLES, FILMS, AND SHELLS

You sometimes see lots of swirling colours on the surface of a soap bubble. These are produced in a quite different way from the colours in a rainbow.

When white light falls on a very thin soap bubble, light waves reflected from the inner surface have to travel a little bit further than those reflected from the outer surface. This means that the two sets of reflected waves are not quite in step. The amount by which they are out of step depends on the thickness of the bubble, the angle at which the light falls, and the wavelength of the light. As different colours in white light have different wavelengths (see page 172), they are out of step at different places on the bubble. Where waves are exactly out of step, they cancel, and that colour disappears. So, at different places on the bubble, you see white minus different colours. For example, one part may look magenta and another cyan.

Below Light falling on a soap film is partially reflected partly from the outer surface and partly from the inner. The reflected beams may be in or out of step, depending on the thickness of the film and the angle at which the light falls.

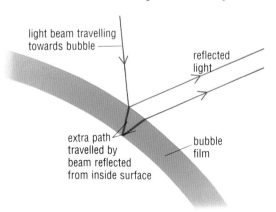

light beam travelling towards bubble

reflected light

extra path travelled by beam reflected from inside surface

bubble film

The cancelling effect of waves is called interference. It also causes the colours when there is thin film of oil or petrol on a wet road. Similarly, it makes the colours on the inside of a sea-shell, which is coated with several thin layers of a transparent material.

If you look at the light reflected from the surface of a compact disc, you will see a spectrum containing all the colours of the rainbow. The effect works particularly well in a darkened room, with all the light coming from one small but powerful source such as a torch or table lamp. It too is caused by interference, but in this case rows of microscopic steps on the CD are reflecting light so that, for certain colours, the waves are in step and reinforcing each other. This is called constructive interference.

With all these effects, it is amazing to think that so many spectacular colours can come from white light.

Below Colours produced when a film of oil floats on water. When white light falls on the film, light of a particular colour reflected from one surface of the film may be out of step with that from the other. If so, the light waves cancel, and that colour is not seen. It is the remaining, uncancelled light that gives the film its colours. The pattern arises because the thickness of the film varies.

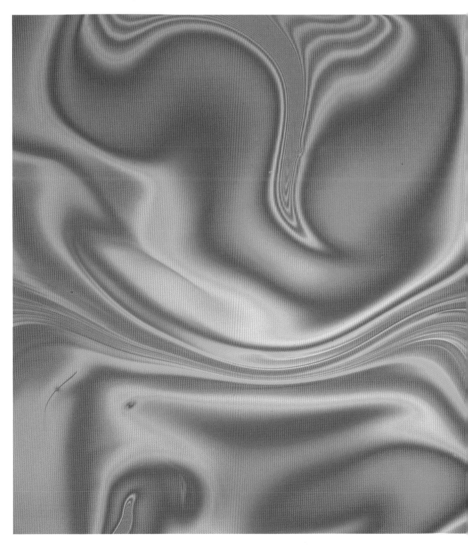

SOUNDS OF MUSIC

Sounds can be as quiet as a whisper or as loud as a jet engine. Whatever the sound, you experience it because tiny pressure changes are reaching your ears. Vibrations cause the pressure changes. If they happen in a regular way, you may hear the sounds of music.

Right Graphs, lasting about 1/15 of a second, showing the changes in pressure made by: **a** clapping, **b** whistling a high note, **c** an insect buzzing, **d** a treble recorder playing a note about an octave lower than **b**, **e** a trombone playing a note three and a half octaves lower than **b**, **f** a bassoon playing a note four octaves lower than **b**. Graphs like this are displayed on the screen of an oscilloscope.

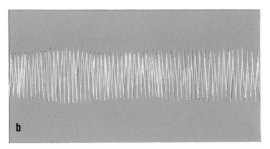

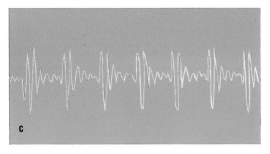

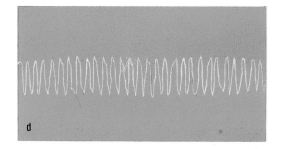

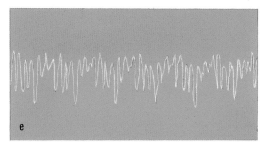

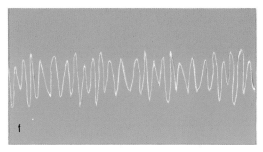

Left In this gamelan orchestra from Bali, many of the instruments are struck with hammers to make sounds like those of bells or gongs. On the left are bronze bowls, each of which gives a separate note, and on the right are instruments that look a little like a xylophone, but the bars are made of hollowed metal.

PRESSURE CHANGES

Sounds are rapid pressure changes that your ears detect. The pressure changes cause tiny movements in the air. For example, if you put your hand in front of a loudspeaker when it is sounding a low note, you will feel the air vibrating.

In normal speech, the pressure changes are only a few parts in a million. To understand how small this is, imagine a party balloon blown up to about 20 cm in diameter. Then imagine pushing the point of a blunt pencil into the balloon to a depth of a few millimetres. You will have increased the pressure in the balloon by a few parts in a million. Of course, if you do this slowly, you will not hear a sound. But if you cause a rapid change in pressure by sticking in a pin, you will certainly hear a bang.

Whether the change in pressure is large or small, it travels out through the air as a wave. However, sound waves do not move up and down like those on the sea. They are compressions which pass from one bit of air to the next in succession.

DETECTING SOUNDS

In sound waves, the first bit of air is squashed. That squashes the next bit, and so on. Each compression spreads out in all directions at a speed of about 330 metres per second, which is the speed of sound in air. Once a compression reaches your ears, the pressure change moves the ear drum, and the mechanism of the ear sends a signal along the nerve leading to the brain. As a result, you hear a sound.

SOUNDS HIGH AND LOW

To study the pressure changes in sound waves, scientists use a device called a cathode-ray oscilloscope (CRO for short). This draws a graph of the pressure changes.

You may have seen oscilloscopes in hospital programmes on television where they are used to watch the heartbeat of a patient. A tiny spot of light travels from one side of a screen to the other. As it does so, it jumps up and down and draws a graph on the screen.

Loudness also affects the shape on the screen. If a sound becomes louder, the changes of pressure are bigger, and the graph has bigger up-and-down movements.

MAKING AND HEARING MUSICAL SOUNDS

To make a musical sound, you have to produce regular changes in the pressure of the air. In order to play tunes, you need to alter the rate at which these pressure changes are made. Scientifically speaking, you have to alter the frequency of the sound waves.

Frequency is measured in hertz (Hz). For example, if something is sending out 440 compressions a second, the frequency is 440 Hz. This corresponds to the musical note A used for tuning.

A common way of producing a musical sound is to use something that vibrates regularly. Twanging a ruler on the edge of a table, twanging a stretched rubber band, bowing the string of a violin, blowing across the neck of a bottle, hitting a bell – all of these set up vibrations which then cause regular changes of pressure in the air nearby. They all make musical sounds.

Above When the first domino in a row is knocked over, it knocks the second over, and so on in succession until all are down. This could be described as a domino wave in which the 'falling over' is passed along the line. In a sound wave, it is a pressure change which is passed from one bit of air to the next.

If a microphone is connected to an oscilloscope, the signals from the microphone can control the vertical movements of the spot on the screen. As the pressure rises and falls, the spot is moved up and down, and a graph of the sound waves is drawn on the screen.

Different sources of sound give different graphs. When an audience claps, the pressure changes follow each other in an irregular way. Sound like this is usually called 'noise'. If the pressure changes are regular, for example, like those of the wings of a bee, the sound takes on a musical pitch. The sound of a whistle is even more musical. It still has regularity, but the pressure changes are smoother and the shape on the screen is more obviously wave-like. A recorder, playing a lower-pitched note than the whistle, gives the same kind of shape, but there are fewer changes every second. With an instrument like a bassoon, you can still see that there is regularity, but the repeating shape is far more complicated.

In general, the more 'reedy' a sound, the more complicated the shape of the wave tends to be.

Above An alpenhorn is made by sawing the bough of a tree in half lengthwise, hollowing out each half, and sticking them together. It is played like a bugle but gives lower, very loud notes.

To make different notes, the frequency of vibration must be changed. With a twanged ruler, you can alter the length that is over the edge of the table. With a rubber band, you can stretch it more.

The higher the frequency of the vibrations, the higher the musical pitch of the note. But there are limits to the notes which you can detect. Your ears and brain start to recognize a vibration as a musical note when the frequency becomes higher than about 25 to 30 a second – the lowest note on a grand piano has a frequency of about 30 a second. The highest frequency that can be heard by human beings is about 20,000 a second, but the top limit comes down as you get older. Many people over 60 cannot hear much above about 10,000 a second.

SOUNDS SHOULD BE LOUDER!

In a world full of noise and bustle, it seems odd to suggest that sounds should be louder, but in musical instruments they often need to be, as the following experiment will show.

Stretch a thin rubber band between your thumbs and pluck it with one of your fingers. You will hear a note but it will be very quiet.

Now hold one end of the band in your teeth and the other over a thumb and pluck it again. You should hear a much louder sound.

In the first case, the band is so thin that it cannot make very large pressure changes in the air. In fact, the air rushes round the band without being squashed very much at all. In the second case, you are bypassing your ears and feeding sound directly to the nerve of the ear through the bones of your jaw and skull.

Like the rubber band in the first experiment, the strings of an instrument like a violin or acoustic guitar produce far too quiet a sound. But the player and the audience cannot bypass their ears by connecting the strings to their teeth, so a way must be found to increase the size of the air-pressure changes. That is why instruments like this have a body – a carefully shaped, hollow box. Violas, cellos, and double basses also have bodies. In pianos and harps, the strings are fixed to a soundboard, which has a similar effect.

The bodies of stringed instruments change sounds as well as making them louder. A badly made violin body may make different notes louder by different amounts, so it is more difficult to play the instrument evenly. The difference between a violin by Stradivari, worth a fortune, and a cheap violin is almost entirely due to the design of the body.

Above A string quartet in 18th-century costume. On the left are two violin players, on the right at the back is a viola player, and on the right at the front is a cello player. Each instrument has four strings. The highest string has a frequency of 660 Hz on the violin, 440 Hz on the viola, and 220 Hz on the cello. The other strings each have a frequency that is two-thirds of the one above them.

Right The concert harp has about 47 strings, each of which plays a separate note. Normally, the strings play notes like the white keys on a piano, but a series of seven pedals can make notes sharper by one or two semitones. One pedal works on all the C's, one on all the D's, and so on. To guide the player, all the C's are coloured red and all the F's purple.

LAZY BODIES

In a stringed instrument, the body takes a little while to start vibrating. It suffers from a kind of 'laziness' which scientists call inertia, and the result is that each note takes a short time to begin. Although this start-up time may be only about 1/20th of a second, it is very important. Each instrument, stringed or otherwise, starts up a little differently, and it is in that first 1/20th of a second that the marvellous computer called your brain recognizes the instrument being played.

What happens as a note begins is called the starting transient. It is the part of the sound that helps you to listen to any particular group of instruments when a whole orchestra is playing. As the sound from each instrument arrives, your brain registers that fact, so that you can then consciously listen to one instrument even though there are many others playing at the same time. The remarkable thing is that your brain recognizes these starting transients so quickly. This is possible only because your brain has already been 'programmed' – you have heard the various instruments before and so can recognize them again.

WIND INSTRUMENTS

In a wind instrument like a flute or a recorder, air compressions are made to rush up and down a pipe. It is the time taken for these compressions to go from one end to the other and back again that determines the frequency of the sound produced. The longer the pipe, the lower the frequency – in other words, the lower the pitch. Different notes are made by 'stopping' (covering) holes in the instrument. This is equivalent to changing the length of the pipe. The more holes you cover, the lower the note.

One of the simplest instruments that uses the air-in-the-pipe principle is a Nigerian one called a shantu. It is made out of a hollow gourd (the dried case of a large fruit), which may be about 50 cm long. The shantu is open at each end, and is played by slapping one of the open ends on the bare thigh of the player. The result is a kind of 'plop' whose pitch depends on the size of the gourd. Although a shantu produces only one note, large numbers can be played together to give a complicated, but musical, rhythm.

In the shantu, each slap causes air compression which runs back and forth perhaps five or six times, so the note lasts only for a fraction of a second before dying out.

Above The cheng originates from China. The pipes have metal reeds which sound when a finger-hole is opened. It is thought to be the ancestor of the mouth organ.

If the note produced by a pipe is to last longer, then more energy must be fed in. But it must be fed in at just the right time. The following example might help explain why. Imagine that you are pushing a child on a swing. If you push just at the moment when the swing reaches its highest point and is about to start back, then a big swing can be built up with very little effort. But if you attempt to push forwards when the swing is moving back, then you are likely to end up on the ground! A build-up of a vibration by successive pushes at the right times is called resonance.

In an instrument like a flute or recorder, the jet of air from the player's mouth hits the opposite edge of the hole and produces an 'edge tone'. You can get some idea of how it works by imagining that the jet of air has to 'decide' whether to go into the hole, or over the edge. If the first bit goes into the hole, the next bit goes over the edge, the next into the hole, and so on. It is this oscillation of the jet that sets up the vibration of the air in the pipe.

Some wind instruments have a reed in them which vibrates when you blow through it or along it. An oboe is like this. The reed acts like a tap. Each time it opens, it lets a little puff of air through. If the puffs come just as the compression rushing up and down the pipe is about to start on its way back, a steady note can be built up. Of course, if the puffs come at the wrong time, then there is no steady note. Instead, there may be squeaks and squawks like those you hear when someone is first learning to play.

You can make a model showing how sound waves travel along a pipe using one of those toy springs that will 'walk' down stairs. Lay the spring on the table and stretch it between your hands. Then move one hand sharply inwards to send a compression along the spring. When it reaches the end, the compression will bounce back.

Below A swing is a good model for resonance. Provided the push occurs at the right moment in the cycle, very little effort is needed to build up a large oscillation. But if the push occurs at the wrong time the swinging soon stops.

Above The shantu is a Nigerian instrument made from a gourd, the hollow dried skin of a fruit. Its single note depends on its size. The instrument is played by striking one end on the bare thigh, so sending a wave up and down the tube.

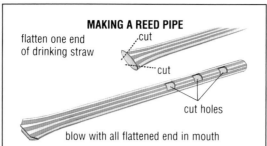

MAKING A REED PIPE

flatten one end
of drinking straw

cut

cut

cut holes

blow with all flattened end in mouth

Cut a piece of straw about 12 cm long and flatten 3 cm of it at one end. This is best done by running it between your thumb and the edge of a blunt knife. Cut off each corner of the flattened end. You now have a reed instrument. To play it, put the flattened end right in your mouth, with your lips tightly round the circular part. Then take a deep breath and blow. By cutting holes near the open end you can make the pipe into an instrument that will play tunes.

THE BRASS FAMILY

Brass instruments such as the trumpet, trombone, and tuba also have air compressions travelling up and down inside them like other wind instruments. But in brass instruments, the energy to keep the sound going is fed in at the right moments by the vibrating lips of the player.

If you take a 3 or 4 metre length of hosepipe and buzz your lips at one end, with a bit of practice you can produce a note. In fact, you can produce quite a few notes! For the lowest note, the compressions are moving up and down roughly like those in the pipe of a reed instrument. But there is no reason why there should not be several lots of compressions moving up and down the pipe at the same time. For example, if the lips of the player vibrate three times as fast, three lots of compressions will travel up and down, and the note produced will have three times the frequency. Notes of two, three, four times the frequency, and so on (called harmonics), can be produced on a brass instrument – more easily than on a hosepipe.

Altering the lip vibrations can only produce a limited number of notes. On a bugle or post horn, these are the only notes that can be produced easily. But the lower ones are a long way apart, so it is not possible to play tunes other than bugle calls.

Instruments such as the trumpet, French horn, and tuba all have valves which, when pressed, add a bit to the length of the tube. By pressing different combinations of valves, you can fill in the gaps between the notes. On the trombone, the length is altered by sliding part of the tube in or out.

Right Trumpets are popular with marching bands like this. A trumpet sounds the notes of a harmonic series like a bugle, but the valves allow the player to 'fill in the gaps' between the lowest notes to make more complicated tunes possible.

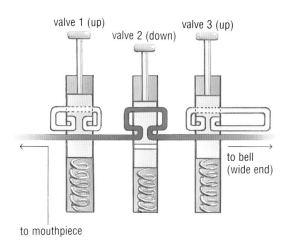

valve 1 (up)   valve 2 (down)   valve 3 (up)

to bell
(wide end)

to mouthpiece

Above A trumpet has three finger-operated valves. Depressing a valve adds an extra length of pipe to the trumpet so that the pitch of the note is lowered. The middle valve lowers it a semitone, the left-hand valve in the picture a tone, and the right a tone-and-a-half.

ELECTRONIC SOUNDS

Just as a string or the air in a pipe can vibrate, so can the current in a circuit. If a changing current is fed to an amplifier and loudspeaker, the cone of the loudspeaker will vibrate and produce a sound.

Some of the earliest experiments on electrically produced sounds were carried out in the 1930s. One system used a metal disc with teeth on it rather like those on a circular saw. The disc was rotated close to a magnet which had a coil wound round it. As each tooth passed closer and then further from the magnet, a varying current was generated in the coil (see also page 168).

Nowadays, we have synthesizers and keyboards which work electronically. In effect, they are computers. They calculate the exact shape of the sound wave required, and then produce it in the form of a varying current which can drive a loudspeaker. Provided the computer is big enough, it is possible to produce almost any sound by this method.

Synthesizers provide entertainment in the home, and are an easy way for bands to play keyboard music without having to transport a large piano. But for scientists, one of the most important uses of synthesizers is in trying to imitate the sounds of real instruments. By doing this, it is possible to learn how the different tones of real instruments are produced. However, synthesizers can sometimes sound too perfect. Our human hearing often seems to prefer real instruments with their minor irregularities.

Below Rock bands rely on electronics to produce their sounds. Signals from the instruments are passed to amplifiers which drive the loudspeakers. In some cases, the signals are also processed by computers to produce a variety of different effects.

ANIMAL SOUNDS

Bees, wasps, and mosquitoes have wings which buzz. But crickets and grasshoppers make chirping noises by rubbing together their legs or wing cases. This way of producing sounds is called stridulation. It is used for communication.

Many insects have ears, though these do not look like our ears, and are often in places which seem strange to us. A cricket has ears on its front pair of legs, a grasshopper has them on its abdomen.

Frogs were probably the first creatures to develop a voice during their evolution. They have a vocal sac which opens into the bottom of the mouth and can be blown up like a balloon. The frog inflates the sac by closing its mouth and nostrils, and blowing.

Across the opening of the sac, there are membranes (thin, stretched skins) rather like the vocal cords in your voice box. As air is blown in and out of the sac, the characteristic sounds are produced. For a similar effect, try trapping two blades of grass between the sides of your thumbs, and then blowing through them. You should be able to produce a sound – though it will be more like a squawk than a croak.

A frog has eardrums, but there is no outer part of the ear. The drums are membranes that lie flush with the surface of the skin.

In birds, the singing organ is called the syrinx. It has membranes across the opening of the windpipe, all of which can be controlled by muscles. Sometimes the notes are produced like a human whistle – though the air is blown through an opening in the membranes rather than through lips. Sometimes the notes are produced by vibration of the membranes, as in vocal cords. And sometimes both methods are used.

Right A hyla tree frog from South America uses the large inflatable sac under its throat to amplify the sound of its voice. Only the males can do this, and their calls can travel up to 10 times further than sounds from frogs that do not have the large amplifying sac.

Some birds can control different parts of the membranes independently, so they can sing more than one note at a time. Birds' ears are roughly similar to those of frogs, but the membranes are under feathers.

Most mammals have ears and voice systems rather like our own. However, most bats have specially shaped mouths and ears for sending out sounds in a particular direction, and then judging where the reflected sounds have come from. They use high-frequency sound waves as a kind of radar to help them to avoid obstacles or to catch flying insects. The sounds are ultrasonic – which means that they are beyond the range of our hearing.

If you watch a horse turning its ears, you can see how it senses the direction of a sound. Although we humans cannot move our ears, we have developed a very clever system for working out where sounds are coming from. When a sound reaches your ears, it may arrive at one of them before the other. Your brain senses the difference and use this to judge the direction of the sound.

Humans have the most complicated voices of all the mammals. The vocal cords produce the basic sounds, but these are modified by cavities in the nose, throat, mouth, and chest. That is why humans can produce such a remarkable variety of vowel sounds.

Below This chart shows the range of frequencies which can come from different animals, instruments, and other sources, and also the range of frequencies that some living things can detect. On the frequency scale, C_4 is 'Middle C', C_5 is an octave above it, C_6 is an octave above that, and so on.

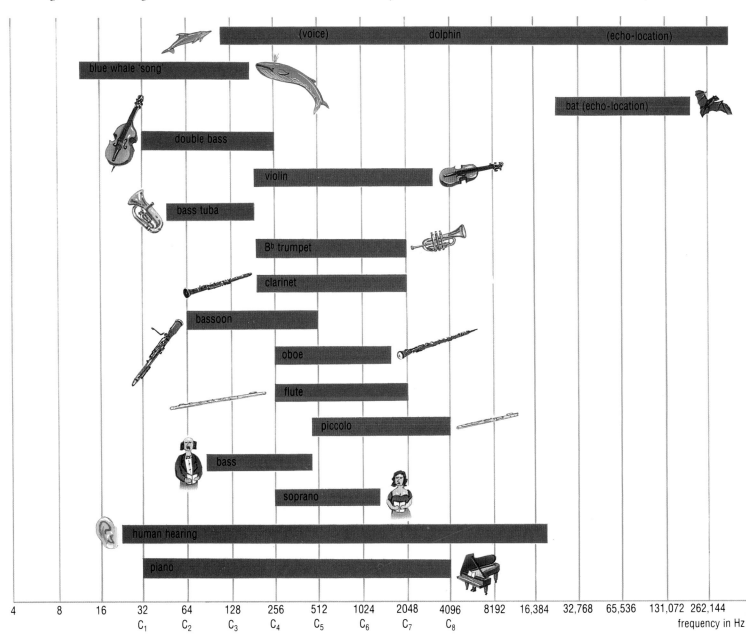

PASSING IT ON

*L*iving things have been exchanging information for millions of years. It has been necessary to ensure their survival. Today we are in the middle of an electronics revolution. This is allowing humans to pass on more information than ever before.

INFORMATION FOR ANIMALS

Animals need to send and receive information. There are four kinds of information that are especially important:

1 How can a mate be found (to ensure that the species survives)?
2 Where can food and water be found?
3 Is there danger around?
4 How can a territory be marked so that a claim on it can be made known to others?

Some animals find out this information for themselves, but there are many examples of cooperation in which animals help each other. The help usually comes from animals of the same kind, but it can also come from those of a different species.

FINDING A MATE

Left One of the most powerful instincts of animals is to make sure that only the genes of the strongest and healthiest animals are passed on to succeeding generations. Here, stags fight for the right to mate with a group of females. The winner will not only mate with the females but also guard them.

For animals, passing on visual information can play a very important part in the process of finding a mate. Often the male is more colourful than the female, and relies on his impressive appearance to persuade a female that he is the one for her. But, especially in birds and fish, the appearance is reinforced by elaborate rituals which look like a complicated dance. For example, a pair of great crested grebes will face each other on the water, raise their crests, and bob their heads up and down and from side to side.

This sort of behaviour is fine once a mate has been located. But before it can happen, the partners first have to find each other, possibly in a thick jungle or in the canopy of a rainforest. Sound plays a large part for many creatures. Frogs and birds can produce very loud sounds which travel a long way. Many mammals have special calls or cries which announce their presence.

Although males may actively search for a mate, females may take part in the search by giving out a special scent when they are ready to mate. The scent contains substances called pheromones which can be detected by males over considerable distances. This process is used by many animals, including insects like moths and ants. It is one of the most powerful of the techniques used to ensure the survival of the species.

Above These Japanese cranes are performing a ritual courtship dance. It will help the female decide whether she thinks the male is a suitable mate.

Above Publicity is not a modern invention. Mandrills have been using their brilliant colours to advertise for millions of years. This one is a male looking for a mate.

When animals mate and have offspring, they are passing on genetic information. Genes are sections of a long chemical code which carries instructions for building a complete living thing (see page 61). A baby receives half its genes from its mother and half from its father. When animals mate, it is an advantage to have partners whose characteristics are likely to produce offspring with the best chance of survival.

PLANTS NEED MATES

Plants must reproduce to ensure that their species survives, but unlike animals, they cannot move about to look for a mate. To overcome this problem, plants have evolved many ingenious ways of getting their powdery pollen containing male sex cells transferred to other plants of the same type so that female sex cells can be fertilized.

Some plants rely on the wind to carry the pollen from the male parts of one flower to the female parts of another. But an enormous number of plants rely on insects to do the job. To ensure that insects perform this service, the plants have to advertise their presence in some way, and produce some kind of reward.

Colour is one of the tricks used to advertize the fact that tasty, sugary nectar is available – apparently free of charge – for insects to collect from inside the flower. Once an insect lands on the flower, it picks up the pollen on its body and passes it on to the next plant visited. Some flowers reflect ultraviolet light, and this is attractive to certain moths.

Scent provides another attraction for insects, which is why some flowers smell so nice. It is far more likely that the scent of flowers evolved in order to attract insects than to give pleasure to humans – though of course that is an added bonus for us.

Below This violet-crowned hummingbird collects nectar from flowers. As it does so, it picks up pollen and passes it on to the next flower it feeds from. When the bird hovers, its wingbeats are so fast that they make a humming sound.

FINDING FOOD

Most animals must find food to survive. Sometimes, they will go to great lengths to avoid sharing it with others. However, some animals will cooperate and communicate in their search for food.

Bees have evolved a very elaborate system of passing on information about the location of food. In a hive, bees perform a dance in which they wiggle their bodies while moving in a particular direction. Using this dance, they can communicate to other bees that there are flowers with a good supply of nectar in a certain direction relative to the Sun. Their movements also give an indication of how far away the supply is.

DANGER AROUND

Many animals have a special call which warns other members of the group when danger is present. This is particularly true of birds, which can produce very loud alarm calls. Near airfields, recordings of bird alarm calls are often played back in order to get rid of flocks that might interfere with the planes. At airfields, humans regard birds as a danger. However, for the birds, the planes are the danger.

Some animals listen for the alarm calls of other creatures to give them warning. Others

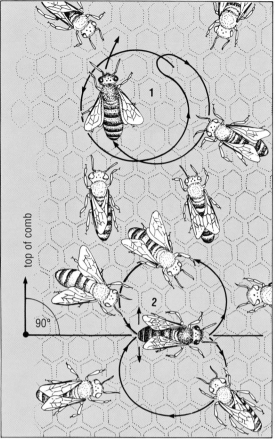

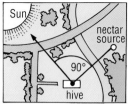

Left and above When a worker bee returns to the hive, she does a dance to tell other bees where to find flowers with nectar in. If the flowers are close, she does a simple, round dance (1). But if they are further away, she does a complicated 'waggle' dance (2). The speed at which the tail waggles indicates the distance of the flowers. In the middle part of the dance, her direction relative to the hive gives the direction of the flowers relative to the Sun.

post sentries to look out for danger and give warnings to the rest of the group. That way, the others can safely concentrate on feeding or drinking. Meerkats are like this. They can stand up almost vertically and swivel their heads through a very wide angle to spot danger approaching.

Left Many animals help each other by giving warning of approaching danger. This meerkat in the Kalahari Desert, southern Africa, has been posted as a sentry to stand up as high as possible. His job is to warn the rest of the group if he senses a predator in the area.

Above Many animals mark their territory with scent. This cheetah is doing so by spraying urine onto a tree. Scent signals can pass on a great deal of information, including the family, age, and sex of the animal, and they may warn other creatures to stay away.

Many animals use their urine or faeces to make scent marks. Others have special glands in various parts of the body. Some deer have glands near their eyes. They can rub these glands on twigs and leave a scent mark that can be picked up by other deer. The large cats like leopards and cheetahs spray their urine on the trunks of trees. Dogs and related animals have anal glands that leave a scent.

Using a technique called gas chromatography, chemists have analysed the chemicals that cause animal smells. There are dozens of these chemicals, and they can communicate a whole variety of messages. They can tell other creatures whether the mark was made by a relation or by an enemy, the sex of the animal, whether it is ready to mate, its rank in the 'pecking order' of the group, and whether it 'owns' the territory or is just visiting.

HUMAN INFORMATION

The human face is very flexible. Also humans have two limbs – their arms – that they do not need for walking. So, from the earliest times, humans were probably communicating with each other by pulling faces and making signs with fingers and hands. Speech soon became important too.

LEAVING A MARK

Animals may use colour, motion, and sound to communicate, but they sometimes need to leave messages which will last a little longer.

Many creatures are fiercely territorial and will go to great lengths to defend their areas against intruders. But to claim a territory, they must mark it in some way. Humans build fences and put up notices. Other animals, of course, need different methods of marking territory. By far the most common is scent–marking.

People like to be clean and fragrant, so they often find it difficult to understand why so many animals seem to enjoy finding the smelliest materials to roll in. But to animals smell is like a visiting card that conveys information.

Above This clay tablet with cuneiform inscriptions came from Sumeria (in present-day Iraq) and is about 4000 years old. It is a receipt for some tools that were borrowed.

These methods of communications could only work when the people involved were fairly near each other. Also, the information received could not be stored. However, both of these problems were solved by the development of writing.

The first writing was probably a series of indentations on a clay tablet. With writing, messages could be sent from one place to another and then kept. Indeed, some of the messages made four or five thousand years ago are still with us today in museums.

Before people can talk or write to each other, there has to be agreement on what the sounds or symbols mean. English-speaking people agree on what is meant by the word 'dog', but French-speaking people call the same thing 'chien'. All communication uses an agreed code, though it may be so familiar that we do not even recognize it as a code.

Our alphabet is itself a code, as are all the other alphabets in the world. Any code can be used for communicating information, provided that the people who are meant to understand it know the secret of the code.

Right There are many different types of writing for passing on information. Here are just five alphabets. They are **1** Greek, **2** Cyrillic (used in Russia), **3** Devanagari (used in northern India), **4** Hebrew, and **5** Arabic.

A SECRET CODE

People can send written information to each other, provided they all agree on what the symbols mean. In this code, each symbol tells you where a particular letter is in the 'noughts and crosses' grid. So, for example, a dot in the middle of a four-sided box represents the 'N' in the centre of the grid. See if you can use the key to work out what the message says.

The key to the code

ABC	DEF	GHI
JKL	MNO	PQR
STU	VWX	YZ

A message in code

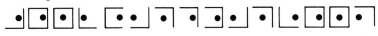

1	ΑΒΓΔΕΖΗΘΙΚΛΜΝΞΟΠΡΣΤΥΦΧΨΩ αβγδεζηθικλμνξοπρστυφχψω
2	АБВГДЕЁЖЗИЙКЛМНОПРСТУФХЦЧШЩЪЫЬЭЮЯ абвгдеёжзийклмнопрстуфхцчшщъыьэюя
3	अ आ इ ई उ ऊ ऋ ए ऐ ओ औ अं अः क ख ग घ ङ च छ ज झ ञ ट ठ ड ढ ण त थ द ध न प फ ब भ म य र ल व श ष स ह
4	א ב ג ד ה ו ז ח ט י כ ל מ נ ס ע פ צ ק ר ש ת
5	ا ب ت ث ج ح خ د ذ ر ز س ش ص ض ط ظ ع غ ف ق ك ل م ن و ه ي

INFORMATION IN STORE

Books store information. Some of the biggest information stores of all are large national libraries like the British Library or the Library of Congress in the USA. But, of course, their information is no use unless you can get it out again. The index of a book is a help, but before you can use the index, you have to find the right book.

In libraries, books are arranged according to a classification system. Non-fiction books like this one are normally given a special code of numbers and letters. The code depends on the subject. Classifying a book is not always as easy as it sounds. For example, should a book about how birds sing be classified under 'Birds', 'Music', or 'Sound'?

Left Books are a useful method of storing and passing on information, provided they are carefully classified so that you can find the ones you want. This is the reading room of the British Library in London.

One of the big advantages of computer catalogues is that the same book can be listed under many headings. An old-style card index would be very large and unwieldy if every book had to appear many times.

Classification does not solve all the problems. If a book has been put back in the wrong section of a library, it can still be almost impossible to find.

THE DIGITAL REVOLUTION

Today, computers handle all sorts of information, including words and pictures, but they were originally developed so that calculations with numbers could be done very rapidly.

Computers work with binary numbers rather than ordinary decimal numbers. In binary counting, there are only two digits, 0 and 1. For example, the numbers 1, 2, 3, 4, and 5 are written in binary as 1, 10, 11, 100, and 101. In electronics, the advantage of binary is that 0s or 1s can be represented by circuits that are either on or off. So, a microchip with millions of tiny circuits on it can store and handle lots of numbers. Using the binary system, numbers can be represented in other ways as well – as sections of cassette tape that are unmagnetized or magnetized, for instance, or as stripes on paper that are black or white.

Below Optical-fibre cables are much more efficient than traditional metal telephone cables. This cable has been split open to show the optical fibres inside. Using pulses of laser light, such a cable can carry thousands of digital messages simultaneously over distances of up to 50 km without the need for amplification.

Bar codes use this idea. Almost every item sold in a supermarket has a bar code on it, and there is also one on the back of this book. Bar codes store an identifying number for each product in binary form. The stripes are arranged so that a change from black to white or white to black represents binary 1. If the stripes stay the same, that represents binary 0. At the shop checkout, a rotating mirror makes a laser beam scan across the bar. The pulses of reflected light are picked up by sensors. These feed signals to a computer which is linked to the till display.

DIGITAL OR ANALOGUE?

Not all measurements and readings are in digital (number) form. For example, many clocks show the time by the position of two rotating hands. Displays like this are called analogue displays. The measurement is represented, not by particular numbers, but by something whose setting can vary continuously. A speedometer reading is analogue; so are the lines of a graph such as those for the sound waves shown on page 31.

Computers can deal with analogue information provided it is first turned into digital signals. For example, sound waves carry analogue information which can be stored digitally on compact disc (CD). In a CD player, a small computer called a processor takes the digital signals from the disc and changes them into the analogue form needed for the loudspeakers.

But why should digital signals be preferred to analogue? A useful way of comparing the two is to think of a message being transmitted over a very poor telephone line with a lot of background noise. If the message is being sent as speech, it may be difficult to recognize the words. But if the message is sent in Morse code as dots and dashes, it is much more likely to get through. Speech is the equivalent of analogue signals, Morse code is the equivalent of digital signals.

Records (LPs) are analogue recordings. The groove on an LP has wavy sides which represent the sound waves. The main problem with a record is that any dust or scratch on the surface will make the stylus jump and produce unwanted background noise.

If a recording is digital, as on a CD, then a speck of dust may still cause a wrong number to be picked up, but the processor can be told to ignore any sudden changes like this. An additional advantage with CDs is that there is no stylus to cause wear. The information, in binary form, is stored on the disc as a series of microscopic steps and flats on the surface. These are read by a laser beam, rather like a bar-code reader.

Most telephone systems now work digitally. Once the sound information has been changed into digital form, it can be sent as a series of electrical pulses along a wire or light pulses along an optical fibre. Over longer distances, radio or microwave links can be used, sometimes via satellite as well. With a fax machine, pictures can be sent by telephone. The picture is scanned strip by strip (see page 17) and the information transmitted as a series of digital signals. The receiving fax turns these into a digital picture, made up of thousands of tiny dots.

It was once said that seeing is believing, but this is no longer true. By digital processing, a picture can be changed completely. A frowning person can be given a smile, colours can be altered, and one person's face can be merged with another's or put onto a different body. All of these are possible without anyone noticing that there have been any changes.

BOOKS ON DISC

Words and pictures from books can be stored in digital form on compact disc. Later they can be retrieved and displayed by a computer. You can even have moving pictures and sound as well. One advantage of the system is the huge amount of information that can be stored. For example, a single CD could hold all the words, charts, and colour pictures in a book like this one, and still have space to spare for another 20 books.

Books are convenient and easy to use; you do not need expensive equipment before you can see what is in them. But the information that a computer takes from a CD can be searched, sorted, sifted, and presented in an endless variety of ways. The only limit is your imagination!

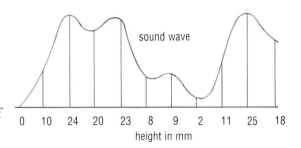

sound wave

0   10   24   20   23   8   9   2   11   25   18

height in mm

Left Analogue signals like this sound-wave graph can be turned into digital signals by measuring the height of the graph at regular intervals. The heights are then converted into a series of binary numbers as below.

Height in mm	Height converted to binary code
0	0
10	1010
24	11000
20	10100
23	10111
8	1000
9	1001
2	10
11	1011
25	11001
18	10010

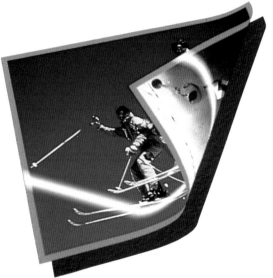

Above Once images have been changed into digital signals, they can be processed electronically to give on-screen pictures which are rolled up, compressed, stretched, or in entirely different colours.

Left The *Oxford English Dictionary* contains more than half a million definitions and over two million quotations. In printed form, it occupies 20 volumes. Yet all its information, and more, can be stored on a single compact disc.

MATERIALS UNDER THE MICROSCOPE

Using microscopes and scientific detective work, scientists have discovered why there are so many different materials in the world. Their results suggest that everything is made of tiny particles which can join together in millions of different ways.

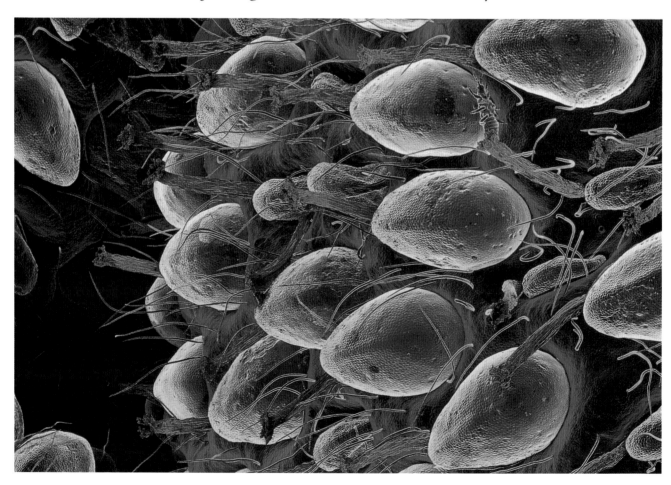

Right The tip of a syringe needle used for injections, magnified about 25 times. This is a scanning electron microscope photograph, with computer-added colours. The orange dots at the end are bacteria.

Far right The same needle magnified about 400 times. The tip of the needle is bent and the bacteria have collected in the bend.

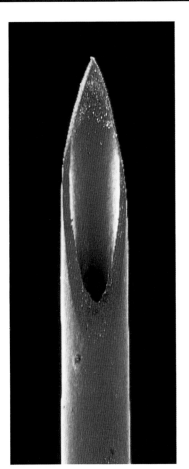
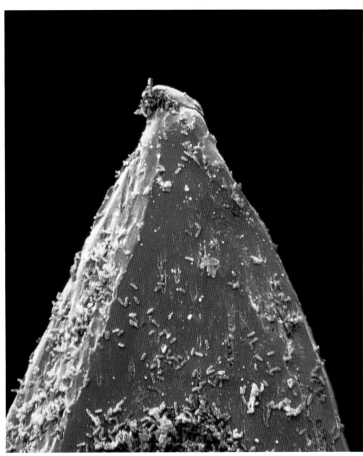

Left Scanning electron microscope photograph of a strawberry magnified about 25 times. Photographs like this are black and white when taken, but colour has been added by computer to make it resemble the real fruit. The oval green shapes are the seeds which are outside the flesh. The styles and stigmas are brownish yellow.

People sometimes divide materials into three groups: animal, vegetable, and mineral. Your body is in the animal group. The strawberry on the opposite page is in the vegetable group. And non-living materials such as metals and plastics are in the mineral group. However, we now know that animal and vegetable materials are related, and made from the same basic particles as minerals.

SMALLER AND SMALLER

The Ancient Greeks wondered what would happen if you kept dividing a substance into smaller and smaller bits. Could you go on doing this forever? Or would you reach a point where no further division was possible? They reached the conclusion that matter must be made up of tiny, indivisible particles, though they had no direct evidence for this.

Modern scientific research supports the idea that matter is made up of tiny particles. These are called atoms, from the Greek word *atomos*, meaning 'indivisible'. However, we now know that atoms can themselves be split into smaller particles.

There are about 100 different kinds of atoms in the world, and substances made from only one kind of atom are called elements.

LOOKING AT DIFFERENCES

Atoms can combine and join in different ways to make the millions of different substances that exist. Atoms of hydrogen are the lightest and atoms of uranium are among the heaviest. A single atom is the smallest amount of an element that you can have.

Even substances that appear different may contain atoms of just one element. For example, diamond is made only of carbon atoms. It is an extremely hard and transparent material; these are two of its properties. When 'cut' by a jeweller, it sparkles in the light.

Graphite is also made of carbon atoms, but its properties are very different from those of diamond. It is a much softer, darker material, used in the lead of pencils. It has different properties from those of diamond because its carbon atoms are arranged differently.

Often elements are mixed together to produce materials with more useful properties. Here are some examples.

Gold is an element. It is a metal which stays bright without being polished. A ring could be made of gold, but gold by itself would be too soft, so a small amount of copper is mixed in to make it harder. The gold is no longer pure, but the ring will not wear down so quickly.

Copper is an element. It is a metal which becomes dull and tarnished when left exposed to the atmosphere. However, mixed with zinc, it makes a material called brass, which is stronger than copper and does not tarnish as badly.

Steel is mainly the element iron, but it is made stronger and harder than pure iron by adding small amounts of carbon and other elements.

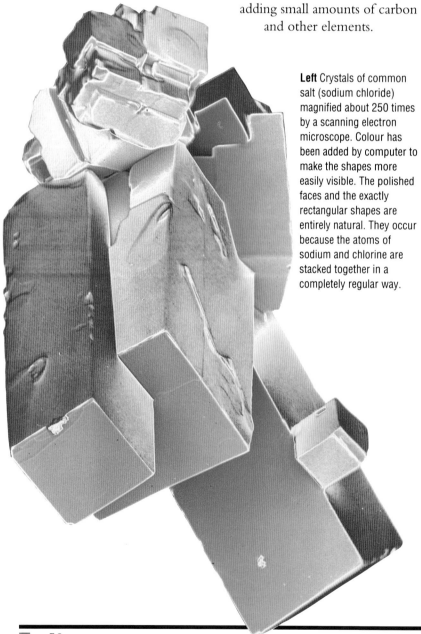

Left Crystals of common salt (sodium chloride) magnified about 250 times by a scanning electron microscope. Colour has been added by computer to make the shapes more easily visible. The polished faces and the exactly rectangular shapes are entirely natural. They occur because the atoms of sodium and chlorine are stacked together in a completely regular way.

Sometimes atoms of different elements combine in tiny groups to form a completely new substance. For example, the smallest 'bit' of water you can have is made up of two atoms of hydrogen joined to one atom of oxygen. This is called a molecule of water. Chemists represent it with a formula, H_2O.

When elements combine chemically like this, the new substance formed is called a compound. Often, it has very different properties from the elements it contains. For example, hydrogen and oxygen are gases, while water is usually a liquid.

Common salt is a compound. It is a chemical combination of the elements sodium and chlorine. Sugar is a compound of carbon, hydrogen, and oxygen. In fact, most of the materials around you are compounds.

HARD AND SOFT

Diamond and graphite are both made from carbon atoms. To find out why they have such different properties, scientists have investigated how the atoms are arranged. It is not possible to see these arrangements using a microscope, but a technique called X-ray diffraction has helped build up a picture.

The technique works like this. A beam of X-rays is shone onto the material. The X-rays bounce off the atoms and make a pattern of black spots on photographic film. From the pattern, it is possible to work out how the atoms must be arranged. However, the analysis is difficult! It is rather like studying the pattern of light spots on the walls and ceiling of a disco, and then trying to work out what the object which is reflecting the spotlight beam must look like. In this case, the answer is relatively simple – a glitter ball with hundreds of tiny mirrors on it. With the X-ray diffraction patterns, the arrangement of atoms that does the reflecting is usually much more complicated.

Computers have greatly speeded up the analysis of X-ray diffraction patterns. However, the arrangements of atoms in diamond and graphite were worked out in 1913, long before computers were invented. In diamond, the atoms are connected in a regular and extremely rigid framework. That is why diamond is so hard and strong.

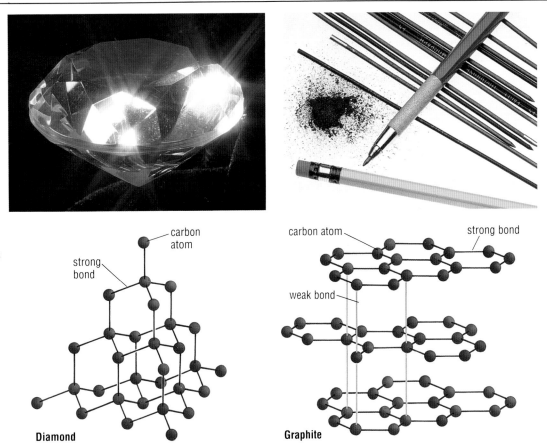

Right The photographs show a single diamond that has been cut and polished by a jeweller, and a collection of pencil leads made of graphite. Diamond and graphite are different forms of carbon. In diamond, each carbon atom is bound to four others to make a strong framework. In graphite, the carbon atoms are arranged in sheets, but these are loosely joined, can slide over each other, and can be pulled apart easily. That is why a graphite trail is left on paper when you pull the tip of a pencil across it.

Diamond

Graphite

In graphite, the carbon atoms are arranged in sheets. Each atom is connected very tightly to other atoms in the same sheet. But the sheets are further apart than the atoms in diamond, and are not tightly connected. As a result, they can slide over each other easily. That is why graphite is so soft compared with diamond. When you use a pencil to draw, sheets of atoms slide off the graphite lead and are left on the paper.

A change between solid, liquid, and gas – for example, turning water into steam – is called a physical change. You still have the same chemical substance. On the other hand, water can be made in the laboratory by burning hydrogen with oxygen. That is a chemical change, which is much more difficult to undo.

FREEZING, MELTING, AND BOILING

Many substances can exist as a solid, liquid, or gas. For example, water is normally liquid, but when cooled, it becomes ice. When heated, it evaporates to becomes a gas called water vapour, or steam. Boiling is a very rapid form of evaporation which, for water, happens at 100°C under normal conditions.

Even a diamond can melt (at 3550°C) and boil (at 4832°C). Oxygen on the other hand is normally a gas, but it becomes liquid at -183°C and solid at -219°C.

Below Icebergs in the Antarctic. In conditions like this, water can exist as a solid, a liquid, and a gas.

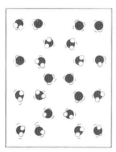

ice (solid water)   liquid water   steam (water vapour)

water molecule

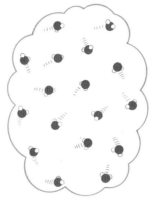

Above Water molecules each consist of an oxygen atom and two hydrogen atoms. In ice, the molecules are held in fixed positions to form solid crystals. In liquid water, they are still close but free to move about. In steam, they are spaced out and move about independently.

Many compounds will not melt because a chemical change takes place before this can happen. For example, if you heat wood, it does not melt – it catches fire instead. Burning is a chemical change which turns the wood into new compounds containing oxygen.

Ice, liquid water, and steam are all made up of water molecules. The difference between them lies in the way the molecules are spaced. In ice, the molecules are tightly held to each other in a regular structure.

Even in a solid like ice, the molecules vibrate. If very cold ice is warmed up, the vibrations becomes more violent until, eventually, the links between the molecules start to break and the ice melts. In liquid water, the links keep breaking and reforming. The molecules are free to change positions, so the liquid can flow.

If liquid water is heated, some of the vibrations becomes so violent that the links are completely broken. The molecules can drift away from each other as water vapour.

MORE METALS

About three-quarters of the elements are metals, though most of these are very rare. Common ones include iron, copper, zinc, aluminium, and lead. Many metals have the following properties, though any one does not necessarily have all of them. When metals are cut, the exposed faces are often shiny. Metals conduct heat and electricity. They usually bend or stretch when forces are applied. And they often make a ringing noise when hit.

Left When ice crystals grow rapidly, for instance when water droplets are blown up through a thundercloud, they take up beautiful shapes like this single snow crystal. Each crystal is different, but all have the same six-fold symmetry. (You can turn the picture round through 60° six times and it will look the same after each turn.)

Right The Eiffel Tower in Paris, built in 1889, is 300 m high. Although made of relatively thin steel girders, its strength is achieved by the way in which they are bound together in a cross network – rather like the way in which the carbon atoms in a diamond are bound together.

ELEMENTS AND ATOMS

Gold is an element which occurs naturally as a pure metal. It can be found in nuggets in the ground. Most elements are found as compounds. For example, copper occurs naturally in a compound with sulphur or oxygen (although it can also be found as a metal). A chemical process is needed to extract the copper from the compound.

Gold atoms do not readily combine with other types. Chemists say that gold is very unreactive. That is why it occurs naturally in a pure form. Copper is more reactive, so its atoms will combine with other atoms to form compounds. But to find out why some elements are more reactive than others, we must look more closely at atoms.

Atoms are extremely small. There are over 10,000,000,000,000,000,000,000 of them in a gold ring! Atoms are made from smaller particles called protons, electrons, and neutrons (see also page 98). The protons and neutrons clump together to form the nucleus (core) of each atom. The much lighter electrons form a cloud round this nucleus, but an atom is mostly empty space! If a whole atom were the size of a football field, then the nucleus would be no bigger than a pea. The electrons would be even smaller – like sugar crystals scattered around the field.

It is the number and arrangement of the electrons which decide what type of atom it is and how it will behave.

In most metals, the atoms are packed tightly together and share their electrons. The electrons are not attached to any particular atom, so some of them can move around easily. Electricity is a flow of electrons, so metals conduct electricity very well.

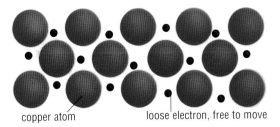

copper atom   loose electron, free to move

Above When metal atoms form a solid, the outer, loosely attached electrons can wander freely among the atoms. When these electrons all move in one direction, the flow is called an electric current.

TABLE OF ELEMENTS

No.	Name	Symbol	State	No.	Name	Symbol	State	No.	Name	Symbol	State
1	Hydrogen	H	gas	36	Krypton	Kr	gas	70	Ytterbium	Yb	solid
2	Helium	He	gas	37	Rubidium	Rb	solid	71	Lutetium	Lu	solid
3	Lithium	Li	solid	38	Strontium	Sr	solid	72	Hafnium	Hf	solid
4	Beryllium	Be	solid	39	Yttrium	Y	solid	73	Tantalum	Ta	solid
5	Boron	B	solid	40	Zirconium	Zr	solid	74	Tungsten	W	solid
6	Carbon	C	solid	41	Niobium	Nb	solid	75	Rhenium	Re	solid
7	Nitrogen	N	gas	42	Molybdenum	Mo	solid	76	Osmium	Os	solid
8	Oxygen	O	gas	43	Technetium	Tc	solid	77	Iridium	Ir	solid
9	Fluorine	F	gas	44	Ruthenium	Ru	solid	78	Platinum	Pt	solid
10	Neon	Ne	gas	45	Rhodium	Rh	solid	79	Gold	Au	solid
11	Sodium	Na	solid	46	Palladium	Pd	solid	80	Mercury	Hg	liquid
12	Magnesium	Mg	solid	47	Silver	Ag	solid	81	Thallium	Tl	solid
13	Aluminium	Al	solid	48	Cadmium	Cd	solid	82	Lead	Pb	solid
14	Silicon	Si	solid	49	Indium	In	solid	83	Bismuth	Bi	solid
15	Phosphorus	P	solid	50	Tin	Sn	solid	84	Polonium	Po	solid
16	Sulphur	S	solid	51	Antimony	Sb	solid	85	Astatine	At	solid
17	Chlorine	Cl	gas	52	Tellurium	Te	solid	86	Radon	Rn	gas
18	Argon	Ar	gas	53	Iodine	I	solid	87	Francium	Fr	solid
19	Potassium	K	solid	54	Xenon	Xe	gas	88	Radium	Ra	solid
20	Calcium	Ca	solid	55	Caesium	Ca	solid	89	Actinium	Ac	solid
21	Scandium	Sc	solid	56	Barium	Ba	solid	90	Thorium	Th	solid
22	Titanium	Ti	solid	57	Lanthanum	La	solid	91	Protactinium	Pa	solid
23	Vanadium	V	solid	58	Cerium	Ce	solid	92	Uranium	U	solid
24	Chromium	Cr	solid	59	Praseodymium	Pr	solid	93	Neptunium	Np	solid
25	Manganese	Mn	solid	60	Neodymium	Nd	solid	94	Plutonium	Pu	solid
26	Iron	Fe	solid	61	Promethium	Pm	solid	95	Americium	Am	solid
27	Cobalt	Co	solid	62	Samarium	Sm	solid	96	Curium	Cm	solid
28	Nickel	Ni	solid	63	Europium	Eu	solid	97	Berkelium	Bk	solid
29	Copper	Cu	solid	64	Gadolimium	Gd	solid	98	Californium	Cf	solid
30	Zinc	Zn	solid	65	Terbium	Tb	solid	99	Einsteinium	Es	solid
31	Gallium	Ga	solid	66	Dysprosium	Du	solid	100	Fermium	Fm	solid
32	Germanium	Ge	solid	67	Holmium	Ho	solid	101	Mendelevium	Md	solid
33	Arsenic	As	solid	68	Erbium	Er	solid	102	Nobelium	No	solid
34	Selenium	Se	solid	69	Thulium	Tm	solid	103	Lawrencium	Lr	solid
35	Bromine	Br	liquid								

About a quarter of the elements are nonmetals. Some elements, like oxygen and hydrogen, are gases under normal conditions. However, at extremely low temperatures they may become liquid or even solid.

ALLOYS

Metals are not always very useful when pure. The layers of atoms can easily slide over each other (as in graphite), which makes the metal too soft. For better properties, other metals are often added. The mixture is called an alloy. For example, brass is an alloy of copper and zinc.

Above Table of elements. The numbers indicate the number of electrons in an atom of each element. Symbols for the elements are also given (for example H, He). Scientists use these when writing chemical formulae. The state given is that at room temperature and pressure.

Right Mercury is an element and a metal, but unlike other metals, it is liquid at room temperature. It does not wet most surfaces and clings together in smooth, shiny drops. It is very poisonous and should not be left uncovered as even its vapour is very toxic.

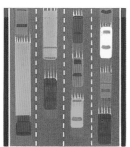

traffic moves freely

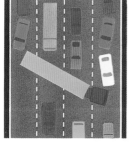

large truck causes jam

Above The smooth flow of traffic on a motorway can be upset by one large stationary lorry. Adding a few large atoms to a metal with small atoms has a similar effect. For example, pure aluminium can be bent and stretched easily as its atoms flow over each other. By adding copper atoms, to make duralumin alloy, the metal is given more strength.

Aluminium is a light metal. It can be made stronger by mixing in a little copper. The alloy produced is called duralumin. It is used to build aircraft. In duralumin, the larger copper atoms stop layers of aluminium atoms sliding over each other.

Steel is an alloy in which a little carbon (and sometimes other elements as well) have been added to iron. Steel is one of the strongest alloys known. It is commonly used to make the framework in large buildings.

SYNTHETIC MATERIALS

A material made by chemical processes in a factory is called a synthetic material. Plastics such as polythene and PVC (polyvinyl chloride) are synthetic. So are modern fibres such as nylon and polyester. Materials like this have one feature in common: they are made from lots of small molecules which link together in chains to form much larger molecules.

Materials made from chains of small molecules are called polymers ('poly-mer' is from two Greek words meaning 'many' and 'parts'). The name of a polymer often tells you how it is made. For example, when small molecules of ethene join, they make poly(ethene) – commonly known as 'polythene'. Different polymers have different types of small molecule in their chains. Not all polymers are synthetic. Wool, cotton, and silk are natural polymers.

Plastics like polythene and PVC are easy to mould and shape and are called thermoplastics. They melt at temperatures not much higher than that of boiling water. When solid, they can be re-melted and re-solidified any number of times.

Some plastics cannot be re-melted. There are cross-links between their chains which keep them in a strong structure. Plastics like this are called thermosets. Saucepan handles are often made of a thermoset plastic.

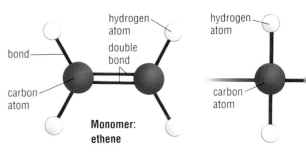

Above Models of ethene and polythene molecules. Polythene is a polymer, formed when the short molecules of ethene called the monomer join together to form a long chain.

FORMING A COMPOUND

When two or more elements combine, they form a compound. The combining can take place in various ways (see pages 99–100), but the atoms stick together.

Sodium is a metal that burns as soon as it comes into contact with air. Chlorine is a deadly poisonous gas; even tiny amounts affect your breathing. When sodium burns in chlorine, the result is a harmless compound called sodium chloride – common salt.

The explanation of this chemical change depends on the electron arrangement.

Atoms have a nucleus with a cloud of electrons around it. It is the number and arrangement of these electrons which decides what kind of an atom it is and how it will behave chemically.

Sodium has 11 electrons: 2 are fairly close to the nucleus; 8 are in a neat arrangement called a shell outside that; and the final one is out on its own.

Chlorine has 17 electrons. It has 2 close to the nucleus and 8 in a neat shell, like sodium. The last 7 are in a shell outside that. In other words, this outer shell has one electron missing from the neat arrangment of eight.

When chlorine and sodium join up, the odd sodium electrons behave as if they belong to the chlorine, and the chlorine behaves as though it has eight electrons in its outer shell. As long as the two substances stay together, they are unreactive – they cannot join up with anything else. It is as though the chlorine provides a sheath round the dangerous odd electron of the sodium.

CUPS, SAUCERS, AND GLASSES

Clay consists of tiny 'plates'. When mixed with water, these can slide over each other, so the clay becomes a smooth, mouldable material which can be formed into cups, saucers, and other shapes. When water is driven out by 'firing' in a furnace, the material goes hard. Unfortunately, it is also riddled with tiny pores, so it soaks up water. To make it waterproof, the fired clay is glazed. It is given a glass–like coating.

Glass is a strange material. Its atoms are in irregular arrangements like those in a liquid, but they are held together so firmly that they cannot change positions.

ORGANIC OR INORGANIC?

You will have heard certain foods described as 'organic' in the shops. This term is used to mean that they were grown without the use of chemicals. Scientifically this does not mean much because fertilizers like bone meal or dried blood are just as much chemicals as

Above A section through a china plate, magnified 130 times. The china at the bottom is porous. The glaze at the top makes the plate waterproof.

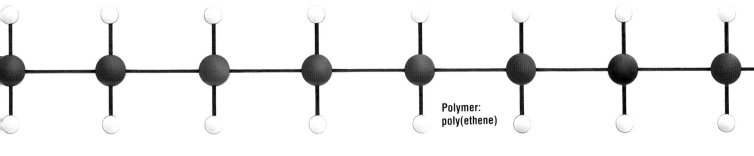

Polymer: poly(ethene)

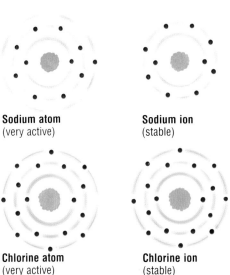

Sodium atom (very active)

Sodium ion (stable)

Chlorine atom (very active)

Chlorine ion (stable)

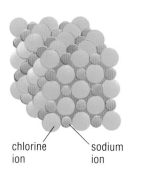

chlorine ion

sodium ion

Sodium chloride crystal

any artificial or synthetic fertilizer. Living organisms, such as us, are made from carbon compounds (see page 65). In science, it has become the custom to refer to *all* carbon compounds as organic compounds – whether made in living things or in a laboratory or factory. The study of these materials is called organic chemistry, while inorganic chemistry deals with all other materials. There are millions of different compounds in the world, but life depends on carbon.

Left Atoms which have gained or lost electrons are called ions. To end up with full electron shells, a sodium atom must lose an electron, and a chlorine atom must gain one. That is what happens when sodium chloride is formed.

GROWING AND CHANGING

Your body is made of tiny cells which are built from atoms. Cells are the basis of life. They make it possible for living things to grow, change, and produce copies of themselves. But to do all this, they must contain detailed instructions.

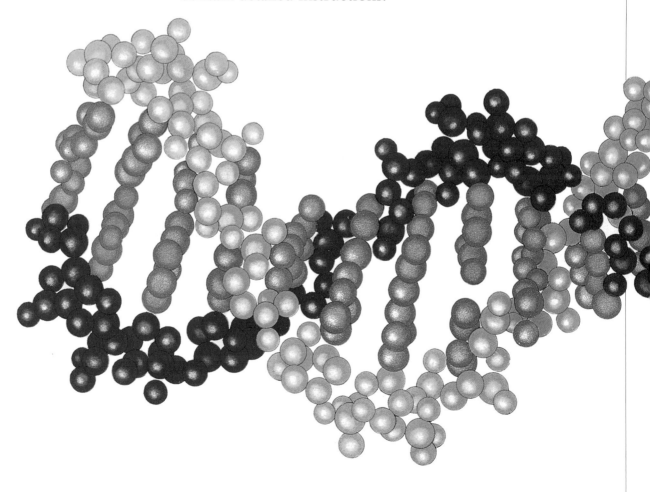

THE SECRET OF LIFE

*L*iving things are called organisms. They include animals, plants, and microscopic forms of life such as bacteria. Unlike the non-living things in the last chapter, organisms can grow and change in the most amazing way. For example, a hen's egg can become a chick and a tiny acorn may grow into a large oak tree. Also, living things can reproduce themselves. They contain a complicated chemical code which is used to make more organisms of the same kind.

Below The double-helix structure of a DNA molecule, shown as a computer-generated model. The structure was first suggested in 1953 after years of patient detective work by different scientists. It solved a variety of problems, including the difficult one of how cells carry genetic information.

The secret of life is found in the cells that make up all living things. Cells can be many different sizes. One of the biggest cells is an ostrich egg, which is about 10 centimetres across. The smallest cells are bacteria. A hundred of them would fit across this full stop.

All organisms are made of atoms. But even things as small as bacteria are much larger than atoms. A single bacterium could well contain over one million million atoms!

Right This scanning electron microscope photograph shows spores of the bacteria which cause the disease anthrax in farm animals. It is magnified about 5000 times. A computer has added colour to distinguish the spores from the background.

ANIMAL AND PLANT CELLS

Animals can look different and yet have certain things in common, such as legs, heads, and hearts. In the same way, cells can look different but have some things in common.

In a plant or animal, every cell has a 'control centre' called a nucleus. This contains a special chemical code which controls what features the plant or animal will have. For example, your skin, muscles, and brain are all made of cells. All these cells have a nucleus with a code for the colour of your eyes and hair, whether you are tall or short, the shape of your nose and ears, and hundreds of other characteristics as well.

In the nucleus, the substance that carries the chemical code is called DNA, which stands for deoxyribonucleic acid. No two people have exactly the same DNA, unless they are identical twins. Like your fingerprints, your DNA is unique to you. The DNA in, say, your skin cells is the same as in your blood and muscle cells. So cells in your toes contain information about the colour of your eyes!

Outside the nucleus of a cell is a jelly called the cytoplasm. This contains food and many other substances. It is a kind of chemical factory where the materials needed for living, growing, and changing are produced. The nucleus controls what goes on in the cytoplasm by sending chemical messengers to it.

In plant cells, the cytoplasm also contains little green blobs called chloroplasts. These have a green substance called chlorophyll in them which absorbs the energy in sunlight. Plant cells use this energy to make their food from incoming materials (see page 66).

The cytoplasm is surrounded by a thin bag called a membrane. Food and waste products can pass through the membrane. Outside the membrane, plant cells have a thick wall made of a tough material called cellulose. Animal cells do not have a cell wall.

Sometimes, cells can be invaded by viruses, which are small enough to pass through the membrane. Outside a cell, viruses are inactive, and more like large chemical molecules. But once inside, they disrupt and take over the cell in order to reproduce.

Right A cross-section through a typical animal cell, magnified about 2500 times. The nucleus is the control centre in which the DNA is stored. The vital chemical reactions of life take place in the cytoplasm. The membrane which surrounds the cell holds it together, but allows new materials to enter and waste materials to go out.

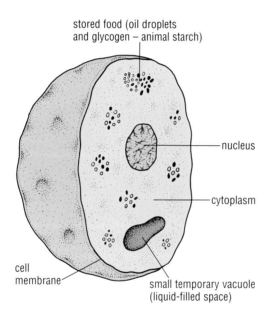

stored food (oil droplets and glycogen – animal starch)

nucleus

cytoplasm

cell membrane

small temporary vacuole (liquid-filled space)

Right A cross-section through a typical plant cell, magnified about 2500 times. Like an animal cell, it has a nucleus, cytoplasm, and outer membrane. But it also has green chloroplasts for absorbing energy from sunlight, a large vacuole containing sap, and a thick wall made of cellulose.

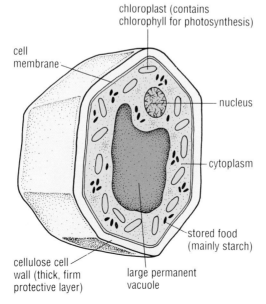

chloroplast (contains chlorophyll for photosynthesis)

cell membrane

nucleus

cytoplasm

stored food (mainly starch)

cellulose cell wall (thick, firm protective layer)

large permanent vacuole

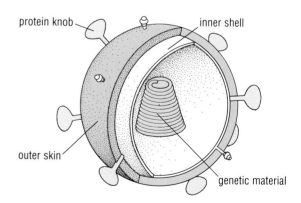

protein knob

inner shell

outer skin

genetic material

Above A virus magnified 1,000,000 times. Viruses invade the nucleus of cells, stop them working properly, and take over the chemicals to reproduce themselves, so spreading the infection. The virus shown here causes AIDS.

ONE CELL OR MANY?

Some organisms consist of just one cell. Organisms like this usually live in water, otherwise they would soon dry out. The amoeba is a single-celled organism that lives in pond water and other wet places. It looks like a tiny blob of jelly. It 'eats' by wrapping itself round its food.

Most organisms consist of many cells collected together. For example, algae may consist of just one cell, or they can be made up of strings of cells, or even millions of cells, as in the seaweeds.

As a newborn baby, you probably had about five million million cells in your body! By now, you are likely to have more than ten times that number.

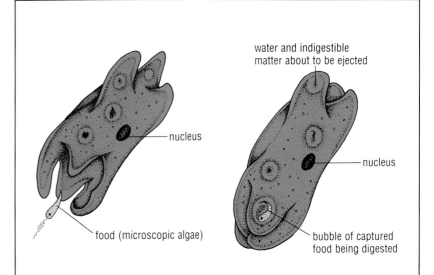

water and indigestible matter about to be ejected

nucleus

nucleus

food (microscopic algae)

bubble of captured food being digested

Above An amoeba is a single-celled organism about the size of a pinhead. It eats by surrounding its food and absorbing it.

HOLDING CELLS TOGETHER

Plants and animals are all built up of cells. As the more complex plants and animals have many millions of cells, they need some sort of framework to hold them together and prevent them drying out.

Plant cells are more rigid than animal cells. There are two reasons for this. First, unlike animals cells, plant cells have a thick cellulose wall. Second, in plant cells, the cytoplasm contains a big cavity, filled with a watery liquid called cell sap. You have probably seen the bouncy castles in leisure parks which hold themselves up by air pressure. In a similar way, cells are kept firm by pressure from their sap.

In some animals, the cells build an external case called an exoskeleton. The shell of a crab is one example. In other animals, the cells build an internal framework, such as the skeleton in your body. Both types of skeleton have large numbers of cells distributed through them, but the cells are embedded in strong, non-living materials. For example, bone consists of materials such as calcium phosphate, which make them hard, reinforced with tough protein fibres that give springiness. However, the cells that produced these strong materials are still there, spread through the bone.

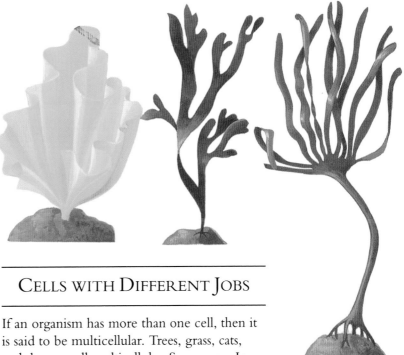

CELLS WITH DIFFERENT JOBS

If an organism has more than one cell, then it is said to be multicellular. Trees, grass, cats, and dogs are all multicellular. So are you. In plants and animals like this, the cells are specialized – different cells have different jobs to do. Even within a single part, like a leaf, cells are designed to do particular jobs – such as making food, or controlling the flow of air or water.

The structure and shape of a cell partly depends on the job it has to do. For example, cells near the surface of a leaf are long and thin so that light can pass through them easily. They also contains more chloroplasts for absorbing the energy in sunlight.

Above There are about 7000 different species of seaweed, most of which are algae. Algae are organisms that can be microscopic with just one cell, or enormous multicellular growths like the brown seaweeds. These can grow to 45 metres.

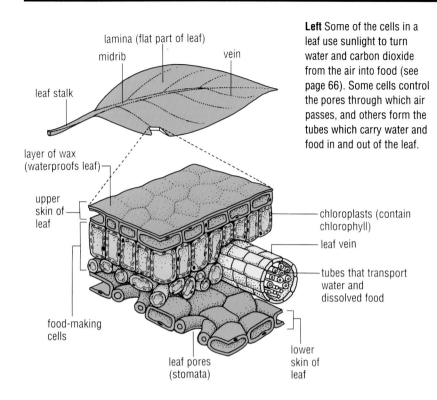

lamina (flat part of leaf)
midrib
vein
leaf stalk

layer of wax (waterproofs leaf)

upper skin of leaf

chloroplasts (contain chlorophyll)

leaf vein

tubes that transport water and dissolved food

food-making cells

leaf pores (stomata)

lower skin of leaf

Left Some of the cells in a leaf use sunlight to turn water and carbon dioxide from the air into food (see page 66). Some cells control the pores through which air passes, and others form the tubes which carry water and food in and out of the leaf.

In animals, the cells have an even greater variety of jobs to do than in plants. For a new human life to begin, a sperm cell from the father must combine with an ovum (egg cell) in the mother. In a sperm cell, the cytoplasm is drawn out into a long, thin tail. This allows the sperm cell to 'swim' so that it can reach the egg cell.

Your body contains millions of nerve cells. They carry messages in the form of electrical signals to and from the brain. In a nerve cell, the cytoplasm is drawn out into a long, thin nerve fibre. Nerve cells are the longest cells in the body. A single cell might run from your big toe to the base of your spine.

In animals muscle cells link together to form muscle fibres. These in turn form bundles which are the muscles. Nerve impulses make muscle cells shorten. That is what happens when a muscle contracts and your arm moves.

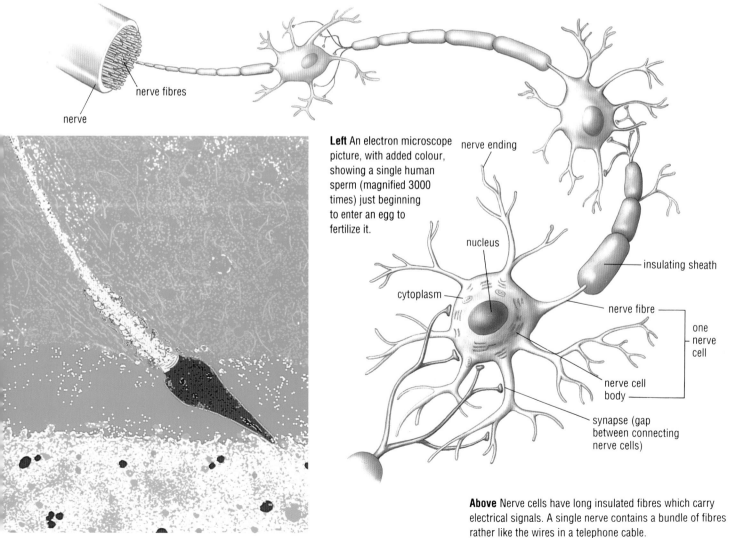

nerve fibres

nerve

Left An electron microscope picture, with added colour, showing a single human sperm (magnified 3000 times) just beginning to enter an egg to fertilize it.

nerve ending

nucleus

cytoplasm

insulating sheath

nerve fibre

one nerve cell

nerve cell body

synapse (gap between connecting nerve cells)

Above Nerve cells have long insulated fibres which carry electrical signals. A single nerve contains a bundle of fibres rather like the wires in a telephone cable.

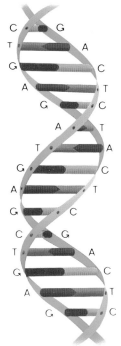

Above A drawing of part of a molecule of DNA. For simplicity, the groups of atoms which form the steps of the spiral ladder are shown as bars with different-shaped ends. There are four types, called bases. They are thymine (T), adenine (A), cytosine (C), and guanine (G). T can only link to A, and C can only link to G.

CARRYING THE CODE

You started life as a single cell, formed when a sperm cell combined with an egg cell. The new cell grew, then divided into two. These in turn grew and divided into two… and so on, in a process called cell division. Each new cell carried an exact copy of the DNA code from the original. At first, the new cells were all alike. Later, specialized cells formed to become the different parts of your body. But each cell still carried that same special code which is unique to you.

A molecule is a group of atoms. DNA is a substance whose molecules each contain many millions of atoms. The atoms are arranged in a shape rather like a spiral ladder. It is called a double helix.

In a DNA molecule, the sides of the ladder are made from atoms of hydrogen, oxygen, carbon, and phosphorus. The 'rungs' are pairs of substances called bases. The bases are known as adenine, cytosine, guanine, and thymine, usually called A, C, G, and T for short. They are made from atoms of hydrogen, oxygen, carbon, and nitrogen. In each base, there are between 13 and 16 atoms.

Remarkably, all the information needed to build a human being or other living thing can be stored as a code which uses just the four bases A, C, G, and T. The secret of the code lies in the order of the bases. Each 'word' of the code is a sequence of three base letters called a triplet (for example ATG).

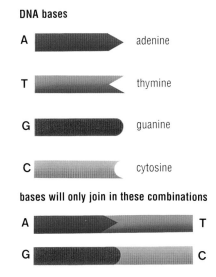

DNA bases

A — adenine
T — thymine
G — guanine
C — cytosine

bases will only join in these combinations

A ——— T
G ——— C

Above The four different bases in DNA, and how they can link. Pairs of bases form the bars in the picture of DNA on the left of this page. There are many millions of base pairs in a single molecule of DNA. It is the sequence of these base pairs which stores the genetic information.

On the back of this book there is a bar code. It stores information as a sequence of light and dark lines. DNA stores genetic information in a similar way. However, its code is the sequence of base pairs up the spiral ladder.

Different sections of the ladder are called genes. Each gene carries information about a different characteristic and might be about 1000 rungs of the ladder long. The genes are linked together into much longer, separate sections called chromosomes. Except for the sex cells a human cell contains 46 chromosomes in 23 pairs. Altogether, there are about 100,000 genes in a human cell.

Left Amber is formed from the resin which comes from the bark of a tree. These unfortunate flies stuck to the resin about 30 million years ago and were preserved when the resin hardened into amber. This is one of the few ways we have of finding out what creatures living in prehistoric times really looked like. However, extracting DNA from such remains is extremely difficult.

Below A DNA molecule copies itself by first unzipping the two strands of the helix. Then unattached bases connect up to the free ends, so that two complete and identical molecules are formed in place of the original one. Both carry the complete DNA code.

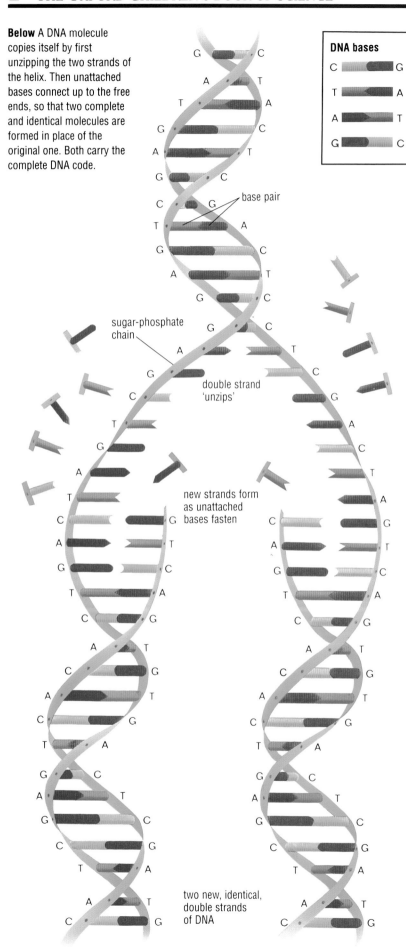

DNA bases

base pair

sugar-phosphate chain

double strand 'unzips'

new strands form as unattached bases fasten

two new, identical, double strands of DNA

A code is no good unless it can be decoded. The decoding of your DNA works like this. The different cells in your body are largely built from substances called proteins. The cells manufacture these proteins from incoming materials. Your DNA code stores information about what proteins must be made. 'Messenger' chemicals carry this information from sections of DNA into the 'factory' part of the cell. In this way, your cells make the proteins which give you black hair, brown skin, blue eyes, and so on.

COPYING THE CODE

The DNA can copy itself – provided there are plenty of unattached bases around. Think of the two halves of the double helix as the two sides of a zip fastener. It is a special kind of zip fastener because its teeth are different. They are the bases A, C, G, and T. Bases A and T can fasten only to each other. Bases C and G can fasten only to each other. So if the DNA molecule is unzipped, a loose A floating about will fasten to a T, a loose T will fasten to an A, and so on. In this way, the two halves of one molecule becomes two complete molecules, each identical to the original. That is how the genetic information is passed on to new cells.

REPRODUCING LIFE

In humans and most other animals and plants, the 'babies' inherit half their DNA from their mother and half from their father, so they can end up with some of the characteristics of each parent. Reproduction like this is called sexual reproduction. Of the 23 pairs of chromosomes in a human cell, one of each pair is provided by the mother and the other by the father. However, which one in each pair is a matter of chance. That is the main reason why individuals vary so much from one to another.

In some organisms, the new 'babies' are just like the old. For example, an amoeba reproduces by splitting in two. Each new cell has the same DNA as the 'parent'. This is called asexual reproduction (reproduction without sex).

Right The 23 pairs of human chromosomes, shown arranged in sequence under a microscope. Half the chromosomes (one in each pair) are provided by the mother, and half by the father. The two at the bottom right are the sex chromosomes. In this case, they are both X, so the person is a female. A male would have one X and one Y chromosome.

Below This scientist is carrying out a genetic engineering procedure to help cure a patient whose immune system is not working properly. The screen shows the view through the microscope. On it, you can see the tip of the needle which will inject a corrective gene into a white blood cell.

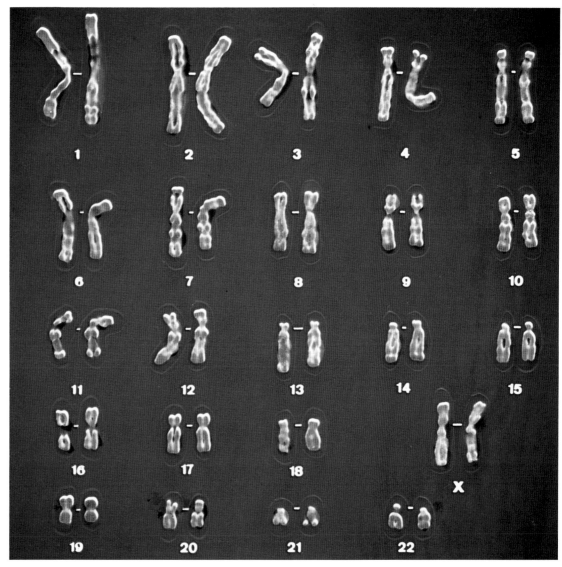

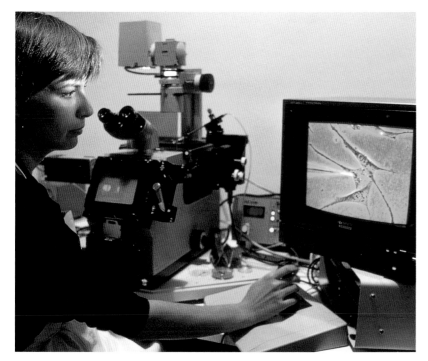

GENETIC ENGINEERING

Scientists have discovered ways of inserting new genes into DNA molecules. They call this genetic engineering.

Some dangerous and painful diseases are caused by faulty genes; cystic fibrosis and sickle-cell anaemia are two examples. Genetic engineering may offer a cure for these. Genetically engineered bacteria can make chemicals, such as the insulin which diabetics need. Also, sheep can be genetically engineered to produce milk suitable for human babies. However, many people are worried about the effects of genetic engineering. They do not like the idea that babies might one day be 'designed' so that they have specially chosen characteristics.

MADE WITH SUNSHINE

Without sunshine, there would be no plants or animals on Earth. The energy in sunlight drives a natural recycling system which takes atoms from the air and soil and uses them over and over again to build the bodies of living things.

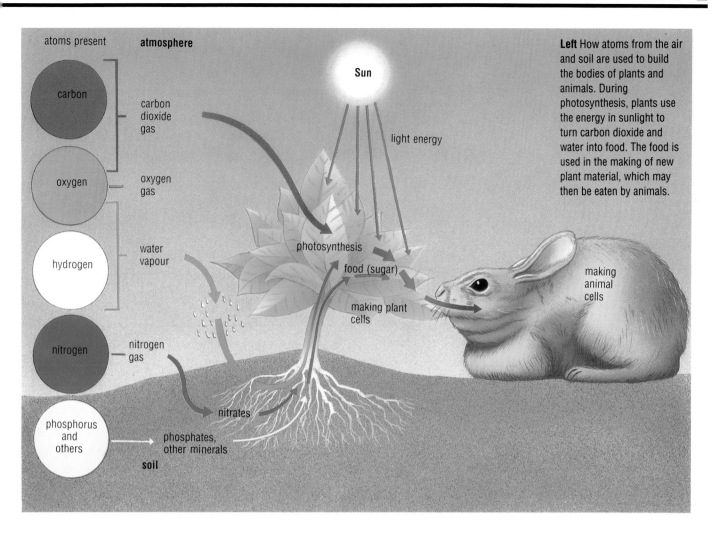

atoms present **atmosphere**

carbon

carbon dioxide gas

oxygen

oxygen gas

hydrogen

water vapour

nitrogen

nitrogen gas

phosphorus and others

phosphates, other minerals

soil

nitrates

Sun

light energy

photosynthesis

food (sugar)

making plant cells

making animal cells

Left How atoms from the air and soil are used to build the bodies of plants and animals. During photosynthesis, plants use the energy in sunlight to turn carbon dioxide and water into food. The food is used in the making of new plant material, which may then be eaten by animals.

*I*n California, USA, there is a giant redwood tree called General Sherman. Standing over 80 metres high, it weighs a massive 2500 tonnes and is the biggest tree on Earth. Yet its atoms have come almost entirely from the air! Those atoms will not stay in the tree forever. In time, they will form the bodies of other plants and animals, eventually returning to the air again. They are part of a remarkable recycling process which includes you and all plants and animals – a process driven by sunshine.

Like other living things, you are mainly made from atoms of carbon, hydrogen, oxygen, and nitrogen. All of these atoms are present in the atmosphere. Combined in one way, they form gases. Combined in other ways, they can form leaves and wood, or flesh and blood although small amounts of extra elements are needed as well. Turning one arrangement of atoms into another is part of the complicated chemical process of living and growing.

Left The trees in the forest are absorbing the Sun's energy through their leaves. They use this energy to turn carbon dioxide and water, plus minerals from the soil, into new growth. When the trees die, the materials in them will be returned to the soil and used again.

Elements in your body

oxygen 65%

carbon 18%

hydrogen 10%

nitrogen 3%

calcium 2%

phosphorus 1%

others 1%

Above The main elements used in the human body. Atoms of these elements are combined in various ways to form the different tissues and organs. About 60% of the body consists of water, which accounts for most of the hydrogen and oxygen present.

FOOD: MAKING IT OR TAKING IT

Living things need food to live and grow. It gives them energy. But it also supplies the raw materials for building new body tissue. In other words, it supplies the atoms which combine together to make the different parts of the body.

Unlike animals, plants cannot eat, so they have to make their own food using substances from the air and soil. They take in carbon dioxide gas through their leaves, and water through their roots. Then, using the energy in sunlight, they turn the carbon dioxide and water into a type of sugar called glucose. This is their food. The food-making process is called photosynthesis (photo means 'light'; synthesis means 'making new substances'). For photosynthesis to take place, plants need light energy from the Sun.

Plants have a substance called chlorophyll in their leaves to absorb the energy in sunlight. Chlorophyll is green, which is why leaves are green.

Glucose is not the only substance made by plants. Some glucose is turned into cellulose, the tough, fibrous material which forms the cell walls of plants (wood is mainly cellulose). Some is changed into starch or oil and stored in stems, roots, seeds, and fruits, some is used to make the proteins in cells. To make proteins, small amounts of extra elements are needed from the soil. The materials which contain these elements are often called minerals.

Plants have an elaborate network of tubes for carrying liquids from one part to another. You can see bundles of these tiny tubes if you carefully cut through the stem of a plant. Those that carry water (and dissolved minerals) from the roots to the leaves, where photosynthesis takes place are xylem tubes. Those that carry dissolved glucose and other substances made in the leaves to wherever they are needed are called phloem tubes.

Animals cannot make their own food. They have to eat plants or other animals. When you eat a potato, you are really feeding on the plant's own supply of stored starch. It was a big, fat, swollen stem in the soil, until someone dug it up.

Below A Venus fly-trap. When the damselfly touches the plant, it will close up, trap the fly, and dissolve its body. It does this to extract vital elements which it cannot get from the soil.

when **carbon** and **oxygen** atoms are arranged like this, they form molecules of **carbon dioxide** gas

when **hydrogen** and **oxygen** atoms are arranged like this, they form molecules of **water**

Right How atoms of carbon, oxygen, and hydrogen can join together in different combinations to form substances which are completely different.

when **carbon**, **hydrogen**, and **oxygen** atoms are arranged like this, they form long molecules of **cellulose**, the tough fibrous material in plants (only a small part of one molecule is shown)

ENERGY FROM FOOD

You get your energy by 'burning up' your food. Like ordinary burning, it is a chemical reaction which involves oxygen. But in the body, there are no flames. Instead, the energy is released in your cells by a much cooler reaction between dissolved food (in the form of glucose) and oxygen. This process is called respiration. People usually think that respiration means breathing. But breathing is just one way of getting oxygen so that respiration can take place.

Plants also respire, so they need oxygen. But plants can make their own oxygen. It is another product of photosynthesis.

OXYGEN IN BALANCE

Animals and plants get energy from their food by respiration. Glucose and oxygen are used up, and carbon dioxide and water are made. You can tell there is water vapour in your breath by huffing on a cold window and watching it steam up.

This equation describes what happens during respiration:

$$\text{glucose} + \text{oxygen} \rightarrow \text{carbon dioxide} + \text{water} + \textit{energy}$$

During photosynthesis, the opposite happens. Plants use light energy from the Sun to turn carbon dioxide and water into glucose and oxygen.

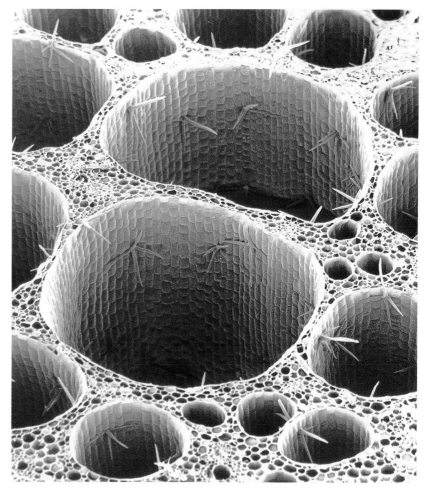

Above Section of the stalk of a waterlily magnified 25 times. The tiny tubes are xylem and phloem tubes for carrying water and dissolved substances. The larger tubes help get air to the roots, which are underwater.

This is how scientists summarize what happens during photosynthesis:

$$\text{carbon dioxide} + \text{water} + \textit{energy} \rightarrow \text{glucose} + \text{oxygen}$$

Gases must flow in and out of leaves for photosynthesis and respiration to take place. The gases pass through tiny holes called stomata, which are mainly on the underside of the leaves. Stomata are normally closed at night, but open during the day, when the movement of gases in and out of the leaf is at its greatest.

Like animals, plants need oxygen. During daytime, when there is plenty of light, plants make far more oxygen than they need. However, in total, plants give out more oxygen than they take in. Animals do the opposite. So the amount of oxygen in the atmosphere stays steady.

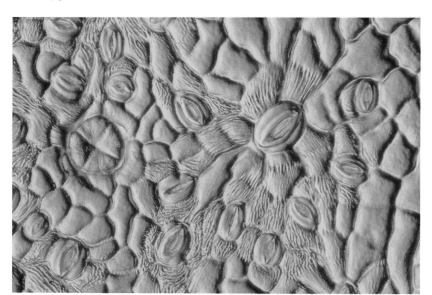

Left The surface of a leaf magnified 1400 times. Scattered over the surface are tiny boat-shaped holes called stomata, which allow gases to enter and leave the leaf. Cells on either side of these holes swell up when their size needs reducing.

RECYCLING CARBON

Carbon is one of the main elements in living things. There are carbon atoms in the tissues and organs which make up your body, there are carbon atoms in plants, and there are carbon atoms in the carbon dioxide gas which animals breathe out and plants take in. Plant and animal waste is decomposed by bacteria. Some of these bacteria give out carbon dioxide gas when they respire.

Oil and natural gas were formed from the remains of tiny sea creatures, and coal from plants which died many millions of years ago. They are known as fossil fuels and contain large amounts of carbon. When these fuels are burned, carbon atoms which were 'locked up' so long ago are released into the atmosphere in carbon dioxide gas.

Carbon atoms are used over and over again as they pass from the atmosphere into plants, sometimes into animals, and then back into the atmosphere again. This process is called the carbon cycle.

Nowadays, people like to recycle materials rather than waste them. The carbon cycle is an example of natural recycling.

UPSETTING THE BALANCE

Unfortunately, human activity is upsetting the balance of carbon dioxide in the atmosphere. Burning fossil fuels puts more carbon dioxide into the air than plants can remove. Carbon dioxide has a similar effect to glass in a greenhouse – it lets in sunlight but traps the heat. Without this effect, the Earth would be much colder than it is. But the extra carbon dioxide may be slowly warming the Earth and disturbing its weather systems. This is called global warming, or the greenhouse effect.

Forests cover about one-fifth of the Earth's land surface. People sometimes call forests the 'lungs of the Earth' because of the way they help to renew our atmosphere. However slowly but surely, the Earth's forests are being destroyed by human activity. Sometimes they are cut down for timber. Sometimes they are burnt down to clear space for development. Burning the forests is putting more than 7000 million tonnes of extra carbon dioxide into the atmosphere every year and adding to global warming. The destruction of the forests means that there are fewer plants to absorb carbon dioxide and make oxygen.

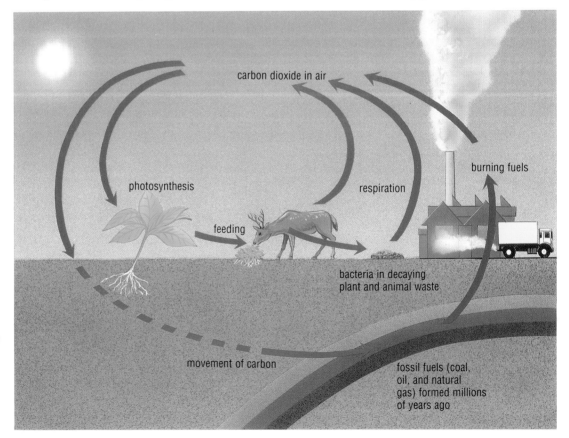

Right This diagram of the carbon cycle shows how carbon atoms can pass from the atmosphere to plants, animals, possibly the ground and fuels, and back into the atmosphere again. In fact, there are several cycles happening together.

RECYCLING NITROGEN

Living things need nitrogen. Four-fifths of the Earth's atmosphere is nitrogen, but plants cannot make direct use of this gas. Instead, the nitrogen atoms are used to make nitrates which can be absorbed by roots. Nitrates get into the soil in several ways. Lightning makes chemicals in the air which are washed into the soil, where they form nitrates. Some bacteria use nitrogen in the air to make nitrates. Others make nitrates from rotting plant and animal waste. However, some bacteria have the opposite effect, and put nitrogen back into the air. In this way, nitrogen atoms are used over and over again. Scientists call this the nitrogen cycle.

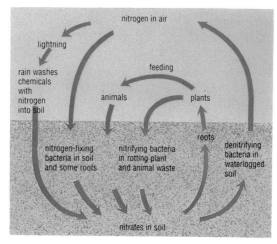

Above This chart of the nitrogen cycle shows how nitrogen atoms can pass from the atmosphere to the soil, plants, animals, soil again, then back into the atmosphere. As with the carbon cycle, there are really several cycles happening together.

Below Deforestation in Central America. Trees have been removed from this forest and the remnants burnt. In time, the exposed soil will be eroded by wind and rain. Around the world, destruction of tropical rainforests like this is happening on a vast scale and is adding to global warming.

Above One stage in a food chain: a chameleon shoots out its very long tongue to catch a grasshopper before eating it. The grasshopper is a plant-eater. So materials which originally came from plants will be reused in the body of the chameleon.

When plants die, their nitrogen is naturally returned to the soil. But with crops, this does not normally happen because plant material is taken away for people to eat or process. To replace the missing nitrogen, farmers add fertilizers to the soil. Usually these are chemical fertilizers, made in factories, but sometimes they are natural fertilizers like rotting compost or manure. Farming that uses only natural fertilizers is called 'organic'.

Right The roots of this broad-bean plant have nodules on them. The nodules contain bacteria which are nitrogen-fixing – they take in nitrogen gas from the air and make nitrates. When absorbed by the roots, the nitrates supply the plant with the nitrogen that it needs.

Enriching soil with fertilizers can mean bigger and better crops. But if too much fertilizer is used, surplus nitrates may be washed into streams and rivers and pollute the water.

CHAINS, WEBS, AND PYRAMIDS

Leaves grow on a plant, snails feed on the leaves, and blackbirds feed on the snails. In this way, materials in the plant are reused as they pass from one living thing to another. This process is called a food chain. The plant is known as the producer because it makes the food in the first place. The animals in the chain are called consumers.

With most living things, the feeding relationships are more complicated. This is because most animals and plants belong to several food chains.

In one area of countryside, horses, snails, grasshoppers, voles, rabbits, cows, and sheep all feed on grass. Snails are eaten by hedgehogs and thrushes. Kestrels eat thrushes and voles. Foxes eat voles and rabbits. And humans eat rabbits, cows, and sheep. If you can unravel this puzzle, the result is a food web: a complicated network of interlinked food chains.

Right A food web, showing the feeding relationships between some of the living things in one area of countryside. Each arrow runs from the organism which is eaten to the organism which eats it. In this example, grass is the producer, and the animals are all consumers.

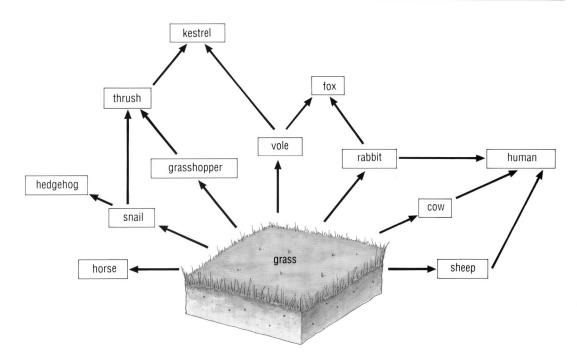

Below A food pyramid shows the amount of material being eaten at different stages in a food chain. Living things in each level are food for those in the level above. However, each organism needs food for its own life processes, so there is always less available for the next level up.

There are two important reasons why scientists study food chains and webs. First, they can predict the likely effects of pollution – for example, how pollution affecting grass might poison kestrels, even though the kestrels do not actually eat the grass. Second, it is possible to learn more about populations, and how these might be under threat.

For example, in a simple food chain it might take 4000 leaves to feed 400 snails, and 400 snails to feed four blackbirds. This idea is sometimes shown as a food pyramid. If only half the number of leaves were available, then the snail population and the blackbird population would both halve – unless alternative foods could be found.

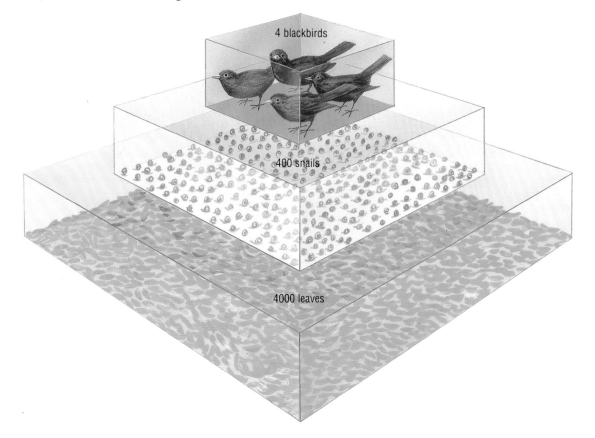

A LOT OF ROT

Once we have no further use for something, it becomes waste. Humans produce huge amounts of waste. Some rots away naturally, and some can be reused, but much is unnecessary. Many products can be made to last longer by slowing down the rate at which they rot.

Waste plant and animal matter is called organic waste. It includes unused food and most sewage. In time, organic waste is digested (broken down into simpler substances) by microscopic living things called microbes, which include bacteria and moulds. We say that the waste 'rots away', but it does not really disappear. During rotting, it is changed into a liquid. If this seeps into soil, its vital elements can be reused in new plants.

If waste rots away naturally, it is said to be biodegradable. But not all waste is like this. For example, glass and plastics do not rot; they are non-biodegradable. Non-biodegradable rubbish can be a considerable nuisance. If cans, bottles, and plastic cups are dropped in the streets, they stay as unsightly litter until someone clears them up.

PROBLEMS WITH PACKAGING

About a quarter of our household rubbish is packaging. We buy cakes in boxes, screws and door knobs in bubble packs, and potatoes pre-packed in plastic bags. Packaging makes goods look more attractive and tempting to buy. But many people feel that we could do with much less of it. Packaging adds to our rubbish problem. Also, the materials have to be manufactured, and that is an extra drain on the Earth's resources.

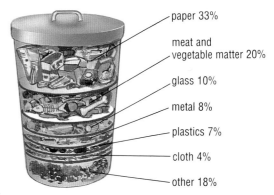

paper 33%
meat and vegetable matter 20%
glass 10%
metal 8%
plastics 7%
cloth 4%
other 18%

Above A typical family puts over 2 tonnes of rubbish into its wastebin every year. Here, you can see the percentages of different materials in household waste.

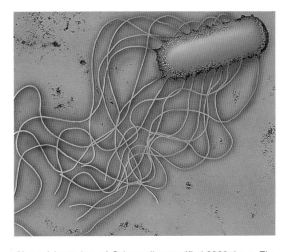

Above A bacterium of *Salmonella* magnified 2200 times. The wiggly strands are called flagellae. The bacterium uses them to move about. Bacteria like this live in raw meat and eggs, and are a major cause of food poisoning.

Left A waste landfill site. About 90 per cent of all household waste is dumped on sites like this. Before dumping starts, the site may be lined with clay to stop any harmful liquids soaking into the groundwater beneath. Deep in the rotting waste, bacteria produce methane gas.

Right Packaging is often necessary to protect goods while they are being stored or transported in large numbers. Unfortunately, the packaging materials end up as unwanted rubbish which must be disposed of.

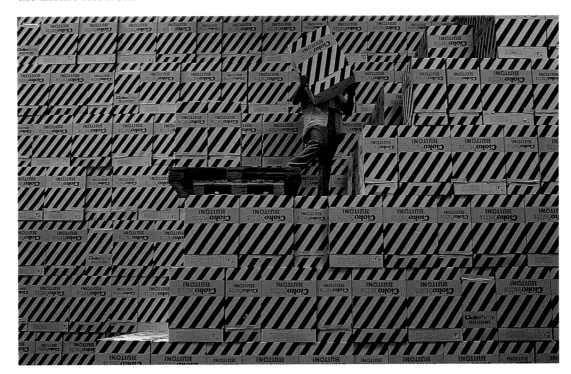

Packaging has its good points. It protects some goods from knocks and jolts when being transported – eggs and televisions, for example. And it helps improve food hygiene. In self-service stores, packaging guarantees that foods are not touched by shoppers with dirty hands, and it can protect delicate foods from bruising.

One problem with packaging materials is that many of them are non-biodegradable. That is because they are plastics. Fortunately, over a period of time, the ultraviolet radiation in sunlight makes some plastics crumble into a powder. The plastic is still there, but it takes up less space. Some shops use 'biodegradable' plastic bags. These crumble away more quickly than normal because starch has been mixed in with the plastic. The starch is biodegradable and when it is gone, there is nothing left to bind together the particles of plastic which remain.

ROTTING FOOD

Many of the foods you buy have 'use by', 'sell by', or 'best before' dates on them. This is because, even with the freshest foods, the rotting process is already under way. Substances called enzymes, naturally present in the food, are partly to blame. They speed up chemical changes so that the taste and texture of the food are altered. But rotting is mainly caused by microbes which digest the food by releasing more enzymes.

Not all microbes are harmful. Every day, we take in millions with our food which have no effect on us at all. Indeed, some microbes are actually useful. For example, it is the action of microbes which helps turn milk into cheese and yoghurt. However, there are plenty of microbes which make food rot.

Killing microbes

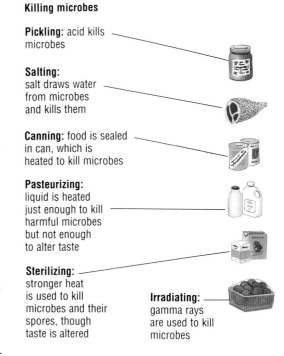

Pickling: acid kills microbes

Salting: salt draws water from microbes and kills them

Canning: food is sealed in can, which is heated to kill microbes

Pasteurizing: liquid is heated just enough to kill harmful microbes but not enough to alter taste

Sterilizing: stronger heat is used to kill microbes and their spores, though taste is altered

Irradiating: gamma rays are used to kill microbes

Stopping microbes from multiplying (or slowing the process)

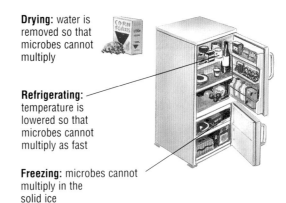

Drying: water is removed so that microbes cannot multiply

Refrigerating: temperature is lowered so that microbes cannot multiply as fast

Freezing: microbes cannot multiply in the solid ice

Above The main methods of preserving food. These all rely on depriving microbes of the conditions which they need to live or multiply.

Right This sequence of photographs shows an apple at different stages as it rots. The last photograph was taken about two months after the first. During rotting, chemicals called enzymes, some of which are released by bacteria, slowly break down the apple into a liquid which the bacteria can use as food.

Microbes are already present in some foods, though most are destroyed by cooking. However, there are microbes floating around in the air, and they can settle on food whether it is cooked or not. If the conditions are right, microbes reproduce and multiply very quickly, and a few soon become several million. Microbes like warm conditions, ideally about the same as the human body temperature (37°C). They also need watery surroundings in order to multiply.

PRESERVING FOOD

There are many ways of preserving food. Some are better than others at slowing the rotting process. However, they may change the taste, texture, and nutritional value of the food. All of these methods kill the microbes or try to stop them multiplying.

Drying was one of the first methods of preserving food. Then came salting. Salt draws out the water from food. It also takes water from the microbes, which kills them. Pickling kills microbes as well. They cannot survive in the acid of the vinegar.

Canning was first developed during the 19th century: food is sealed in its container and then heated so that microbes are killed. Pasteurizing is another form of heat treatment, used on milk and fruit juices.

Refrigerating slows the rate at which microbes multiply and enzymes act. Freezing stops microbes reproducing because their watery surroundings are now solid. However, refrigerating and freezing do not kill the microbes. Once the food has thawed and warmed up, the microbe activity starts again.

Above This ship's biscuit is over 200 years old. Before the days of fridges and freezers, storage of food was a problem on long voyages. Instead of bread, sailors often had to rely on very dry biscuits called 'hard tack' like the one above.

IRRADIATED FOOD

Foods can also be preserved by irradiating them with gamma rays. The radiation kills microbes and destroys some of the enzymes which encourage rotting. The method appears to work well with fresh fruit and vegetables. Strawberries which are three weeks old look as fresh as on the day they were picked! However, there have been fierce arguments over this use of radiation, and it is illegal in many countries. Irradiated food has a longer shelf life, which means less wastage and lower costs. However, many scientists are concerned that the radiation might cause chemical changes in the food whose effects we just cannot predict.

MORE PRESERVATION

Food is not the only organic material which needs preserving. More than 4000 years ago, the Ancient Egyptians were concerned with preserving the body after death. They believed that the body was needed by the soul in the next world. Preservation was helped by the dry heat in the tomb.

Louis Pasteur was a French chemist who, in 1861, showed that airborne microbes were a cause of food decay. In one of his experiments, he partly filled two glass flasks with broth (meat soup), boiled the broth, and then left the flasks to cool. One of the flasks was sealed, the other was partly open to the air. Several days later, the broth in the sealed flask had not changed, but the broth in the unsealed flask had gone bad. Pasteur realized that the cause of the decay must have come in with the air. He also realized that heat treatment could kill off whatever tiny organisms might cause the food to decay.

The process of pasteurization is named after Pasteur. One method of pasteurizing milk is to heat it to about 70°C for 15 seconds and then cool it quickly. This rapid heat treatment kills off the harmful microbes without altering the taste of the milk. However, it does not kill off their spores – cells which can develop into more microbes.

Sterilization is a process which uses a higher temperature for longer. It kills the harmful microbes and their spores, though it does alter the taste of the milk. Long life UHT (ultra heat treated) milk is prepared like this.

Above The *Mary Rose*, King Henry VIII's favourite ship, sank in 1545. In 1982, this section of it was recovered from sediments in the Solent, near Portsmouth. To stop the exposed timbers rotting in the air, the water in them is gradually being replaced with a special resin.

The Egyptians also developed techniques of mummification. Organs such as the heart, liver, and lungs were removed. The body was dried by treating it with a type of salt, before being wrapped in bandages and sealed in a coffin.

Today, archaeologists are often faced with the task of preserving old timbers which have been found in the ground or under the sea. Once exposed to the air, deterioration can be very quick. So archaeologists inject special resins into the timber to protect it.

PASTEUR'S DISCOVERY

If food is left to rot, mould and maggots can soon appear on it. At one time, people thought that the food actually changed into mould and maggots. Today, we know that the maggots come from eggs laid by flies which land on the food. We also know that the decay is caused by microbes.

Above Louis Pasteur at work in his laboratory. In front of him, you can see some of the flasks in which broth and other liquids were either sealed or left exposed to the air.

DEALING WITH SEWAGE

Sewage is a mixture of water, human urine, and excrement, as well as unused food, grease, soap, and dirt. It contains microbes which are harmful to humans and cause disease. Disease-causing microbes like this are sometimes called 'germs'.

Two hundred years ago, people living in towns and villages often threw their sewage straight into the streets. Gutters became a breeding ground for germs which caused cholera and other dangerous diseases. In big cities, sewers emptied into rivers which were also a source of drinking water. For example, Londoners got their drinking water from the River Thames and also put their sewage into it. In 1858, the smell of the Thames was so bad that it became known as 'the Great Stink'. Bad sanitation affected the rich as well as the poor. In 1861, Queen Victoria's consort Prince Albert died of typhoid, caught from the drains in Windsor Castle.

Today, many cities have treatment plants to deal with sewage, though in some places untreated sewage is still put into the sea. In a treatment plant, sewage is filtered, sludge is allowed to settle, and microbes feed on the harmful substances in the liquid and sludge. The process produces clean water which can be discharged into a river or the sea. There is a harmless solid waste which can be used as fertilizer, and some of the microbes produce methane gas. Methane is the same as natural gas and can be collected and used as a fuel.

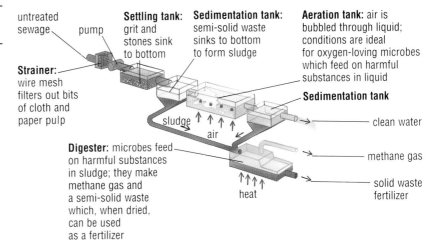

untreated sewage — pump

Strainer: wire mesh filters out bits of cloth and paper pulp

Settling tank: grit and stones sink to bottom

Sedimentation tank: semi-solid waste sinks to bottom to form sludge

Aeration tank: air is bubbled through liquid; conditions are ideal for oxygen-loving microbes which feed on harmful substances in liquid

Sedimentation tank

sludge — air

Digester: microbes feed on harmful substances in sludge; they make methane gas and a semi-solid waste which, when dried, can be used as a fertilizer

heat

clean water

methane gas

solid waste fertilizer

Recycling seems like a good idea because it cuts down waste and means that fewer new materials have to be used. But there are problems. Recycling materials takes energy (gas or electricity for example) and it can be costly. Also, some materials are more suitable for recycling than others.

Aluminium is an expensive metal to extract and produce in the first place, so it is well worth recycling. Paper is more difficult because it has to be de-inked. In recycled form, it may not have the same quality as the original. And cutting down trees to make new paper can be cheaper than reprocessing old paper, even though it seems to be a waste of timber. Recycling glass is not always economic either. The basic raw material for making glass is sand – one of the most abundant materials on Earth. Without careful management, the energy used in transporting old glass bottles and jars can easily wipe out all the savings made by recycling them.

Above A sewage treatment plant. The raw sewage is separated into liquid and semi-solid sludge. Then microbes feed on the harmful substances in the liquid and the sludge. The result is clean water, methane gas, and solid waste which can be used as a fertilizer.

Below Rubbish being piled up inside an incinerator plant. The plant is also a power station. When the rubbish is burnt, the heat is used to make steam. This turns turbines which drive generators.

RECYCLING

Household rubbish contains many materials that can be recycled. Sorting these materials can be difficult after they have been dumped, so many householders do some of the sorting themselves before throwing away their rubbish. In many towns, there are schemes for collecting aluminium waste (cans, milk-bottle tops, and kitchen foil), wastepaper (newspapers and magazines), and glass (bottles and jars). Some plastics can be recycled. So can the steel and other metals from cars which are no longer fit for the road.

Much of our unrecycled household rubbish ends up in landfill sites, but that can be a waste of perfectly good rubbish! When microbes feed on organic waste in the airless conditions deep in a landfill site, they produce methane gas. This can be collected by a network of pipes and used as a fuel.

Some household rubbish is burnt in giant incinerators. The rubbish is reduced to a much smaller pile of ash and, at some plants, the heat is used to generate electricity. However, like other fuel-burning systems, incinerators add to global warming because they give out carbon dioxide gas. Incinerators have filters to remove pollutants from their waste gases. Particles of smoke and ash are removed by electrically charged plates which attract smoke and ash in the same way as the front of a television screen attracts dust (see pages 164–5).

Below Water pollution along the shoreline in Cumbria, England. The foam is caused by detergents which get into the sea water from sewage outlets. It is harmful to marine life because it stops vital oxygen getting into the water.

HAZARDOUS WASTE

Some waste is far too hazardous to dump at ordinary landfill sites. Waste from chemical factories needs special treatment plants or incinerators – though some is still dumped into rivers or the sea. However, there is one type of waste which is more hazardous than any other, and which no incinerator can deal with – nuclear waste.

Nuclear waste is a mixture of radioactive solids, liquids, and gases. It comes from the fuel cans, which nuclear power stations have to replace at regular intervals. It gives off highly dangerous radiation but, sealed in a steel and concrete container, this is not a problem because the radiation is absorbed. The real danger arises when any leakages occur – for example, if there is an accident at a nuclear power station. If a small amount of radioactive gas is breathed in, it can cause cell damage deep in the body, which may lead to cancer. Similar dangers arise from radioactive dust. If it falls on grass, it can enter food chains or the water supply and so into our bodies.

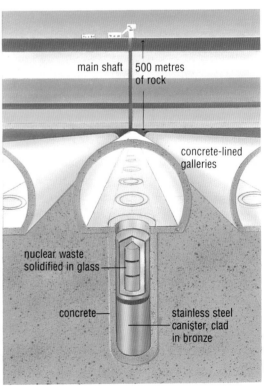

main shaft | 500 metres of rock

concrete-lined galleries

nuclear waste solidified in glass

concrete

stainless steel canister, clad in bronze

Above A nuclear waste repository. The radioactive waste, in strong, sealed, corrosion-proof containers, is stored in concrete-lined pits beneath galleries deep underground. The repository must be in ground which will remain geologically stable for thousands of years.

In time, the radiation from radioactive material weakens. Scientists talk about the half-life of a material, this being the time it takes for the strength of the radiation to halve. For example, radioactive radon gas has a half-life of 3.8 days. This means that its radiation takes 3.8 days to halve in strength, though it never completely vanishes. Some of the materials in nuclear waste have half-lives of thousands of years, and it will be a very long time before their radiation has fallen to a reasonably safe level.

Nuclear waste is not particularly bulky. Britain's entire output of high-level (highly radioactive) waste over the last 30 years would fill no more than two average houses. But the waste will need extremely safe storage for many centuries, deep underground or under the sea. Before it can be stored, there are several major problems to solve. Containers must be designed so that they are guaranteed not to crack or corrode over hundreds of years. Areas of rock must be found which are absolutely free from any geological movement. And a safe method of transport must be set up so that there is no risk of a leak if the truck or train which carries the waste crashes.

CORROSION

Few cars last longer than about 15 years. People who own old cars often complain about the problems of rotting bodywork. Cars do not really rot, but the steel in them (which is mainly iron) does corrode. A slow chemical change takes place in which iron atoms combine with oxygen atoms from the air to form a brown, flaky material called rust (iron oxide).

Corrosion is not always a bad thing. Aluminium corrodes, but when it does, the aluminium oxide which builds up is not flaky like rust. Instead, it forms a thin, even layer which seals the surface and protects the metal from further corrosion. When aluminium is anodized, an electric current is used to give its surface an even thicker protective coating of aluminium oxide. When polished, the coating gives an attractive finish. In many houses, the window frames and outside doors are made of anodized aluminium.

Left This Viking sword is more than 900 years old. Some of the iron in the blade has rusted away. Where air and water are present, iron chemically combines with oxygen to form rust. That is why the blade has deteriorated so badly. But the gold on the hilt looks as new as on the day the sword was made. The silver too has not corroded.

RUST TEST

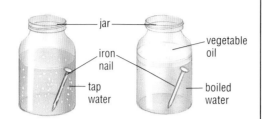

The experiment above shows that water alone cannot make iron rust. Air must be present as well.

One iron nail is left in tap water. This water contains dissolved air, and also tiny air bubbles. The other iron nail is left in boiled water. This water is free of air, and there is a layer of vegetable oil floating on it to stop any air getting in. The boiled water must be allowed to cool before it is poured into the jar. Also, it must be poured very slowly, so as not to create any air bubbles.

After a few days, the nail in the tap water goes rusty, but the nail in the boiled water does not.

Below Sydney Harbour Bridge, Australia, has a span of over 500 metres. It carries eight traffic lanes, two rail tracks, and a footpath. Its steel structure is protected from corrosion by a coating of paint. But this is continually being damaged by wind, rain, and sea spray, so repainting the bridge is a never-ending job.

Some metals do not corrode at all. Chemically, they do not react with air or water. Gold has always been highly valued, because of its rarity, its beautiful colour, and its resistance to corrosion. Golden objects, buried in the ground for centuries, still look as bright and gleaming as on the day they were made.

STOPPING THE CORROSION

Steel is our most commonly used metal, because it is very hard and strong and relatively easy to produce. But being mainly iron, it has one major disadvantage – it rusts. Stainless steel contains chromium and nickel which stop it rusting, but it is far too expensive to use for big items like girders, cars, ships, and bridges.

For iron and steel to rust, both air and water must be present. Without water, the iron and oxygen atoms are unable to combine. There are several methods of stopping, or at least slowing, rusting. The simplest is to coat the metal with a protective layer of paint or plastic so that air and water are kept out. But this only works until the coating chips, cracks, or wears away. A more effective method is galvanizing: the iron or steel is given a coating of zinc which keeps air and water out. It also has a chemical effect which means that the zinc corrodes in preference to the iron. When zinc corrodes, it forms an even layer of zinc oxide. This acts in a similar way to the oxide layer on aluminium. It forms a protective layer which stops further corrosion.

Left and above Zinc bars can be attached to the steel hull and propeller casing of a ship to reduce corrosion. Known as anodes, the bars have a chemical effect: they corrode rather than the iron, which is the main element in the steel.

Corrosion is a problem on the steel hulls of ships because the salt in sea water speeds up rusting. However, pieces of zinc or magnesium can help solve the problem.

Like zinc, magnesium is a sacrificial metal – it corrodes in preference to iron. A ship's hull has zinc or magnesium bars attached to it. These corrode instead of the hull.

Processed foods are often sold in steel cans. To stop the cans corroding, they are given a thin coating of tin. In fact, we usually call cans 'tins', even though this is not the main material in them. Tin is especially suitable for food cans because it is non-toxic.

Corrosion can be a nuisance, and it can be expensive to deal with. But sometimes, tackling corrosion is, literally, a matter of life or death. Older road vehicles have annual safety checks to make sure that corrosion has not damaged brake pipes or weakened the structure of the body. Aircraft are mainly made from non-rusting metals like aluminium and titanium. But they must still be inspected regularly for other forms of corrosion.

CUSTARD, GLUE, AND CONCRETE

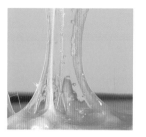

*L*iquids which are not quite liquids, materials which set solid – there is a great deal of chemistry going on around the house. Scrambled eggs and detergents depend on the way in which atoms and molecules stick together. So do custard, glue, and concrete.

It also sticks handl

Far right When a light beam is passed through pure water, you cannot see it. But if it passes through a substance like white of egg, which has large molecules, the light bounces off the molecules and becomes visible.

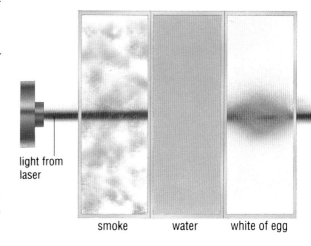

light from laser

smoke   water   white of egg

WHEN IS A LIQUID NOT A LIQUID?

*I*f you mix sand, salt, and water, the sand settles to the bottom and the salt dissolves in the water. The mixture of salt and water is called a solution. In this case, the solution is a clear liquid which looks like plain water.

Raw egg white is a mixture of water and a substance called albumen. Albumen is a type of protein. Proteins are an important part of all body cells, and one feature of them is that they have large molecules.

Raw egg white may contain water, but it seems very different from an ordinary liquid. So how is it different? You can find a clue to the answer if you pass a beam of light through water and also through some raw egg white. If the water is really pure and clean, the beam is almost impossible to see because there is nothing to reflect the light into your eyes. But if you pass the beam through the raw egg white, the beam becomes visible – in the same way as a sunbeam becomes visible in a room full of dust.

In the egg white, the large protein molecules scatter light. The molecules are big enough to do this, but too small to settle like sand and too small to be visible themselves. Mixtures like this, with particles too small to see and too small to settle, are called colloids.

In raw egg white, the protein molecules are themselves made up of chemicals called amino acids, linked together in long chains. The chains become rolled up into tiny balls. It is these which scatter the light.

Below Modern adhesives are so powerful that they can even stick a car to an advertising hoarding!

to teapots.

Above A piece of sponge cake magnified about 50 times, showing the porous texture.

Below Metals have microscopic pits and cracks on their surface. This photograph shows a section of carbon mild steel plate magnified about 200 times. The photograph was taken using polarized light, which produced the different colours of the tiny crystals.

WHISKING AND WINDING

If you place some raw egg white in a cup and whisk it, it will become cloudy. This is because bubbles of air become trapped in it. If you whisk the egg white for a long time, it will becomes stiff – which is how meringues are made. But if you stop before it becomes stiff, the egg white behaves quite differently from how it did before whisking. For example, it is much easier to pour from one cup to another.

No matter how long whisked egg white is left, it will never go back to the way it started. It has become denatured. If you fit a pencil (the six sided type) into the chuck of a drill and turn it rapidly with the end in the container, the denatured egg will climb up the pencil.

Albumen is a long-chain protein with the chains rolled into balls. When you whisk the egg white, the chains become unwound. Twirling the pencil is rather like twirling a fork in spaghetti: the chains wind themselves round and begin to climb.

There are many liquids that have long-chain molecules and behave like denatured egg white. Liquids like this are called non-Newtonian liquids. They do not behave like ordinary liquids, whose properties were first described by Sir Isaac Newton.

BAKING CHANGES

Whisking changes egg white. One way to make an even bigger change is to cook the egg white. The effect this produces is called coagulation. The material is thick and no longer like a liquid. It is quite impossible to change it back to plain egg white again. Coagulation is used when making cakes and pancakes.

When you bake a cake, the egg and flour make a stiff skeleton which holds the cake up. Before baking, the mixture is sometimes beaten to put air bubbles into it. These expand and produce the holes which make the cake light. Often, baking powder is also used. This is a mixture of sodium hydrogencarbonate ('bicarb') and citric acid. When the mixture becomes wet and warm, bubbles of carbon dioxide are produced.

GLUES AND HOW THEY WORK

Gelatin is a protein. It is extracted from dead animals by boiling skins or bones. In cookery, it is used to make jelly (although vegetarian jellies contain an alternative which does not come from animals). Until the 1930s, gelatin was used by joiners and carpenters as glue to stick wood together. However, it was not waterproof.

Nowadays, the art of making glues has become very specialized. Scientists can make glues that will stick things together so firmly that the joint is stronger than the pieces being joined.

Sometimes glues are used to join new pieces together, sometimes they are used to join pieces which have broken. To understand how a glue works, you must start by thinking about what happens when a material breaks.

A material like, say, hard toffee is made of molecules. There are forces between the molecules which hold them together (see page 100). Normally, these forces are strong enough to keep the toffee in one solid slab. But if you start to bend the toffee, the molecules on the outside of the bend will be pulled apart and the toffee will break. The forces between molecules are only strong when the molecules are very close together.

To mend the toffee, you would have to fit the two pieces together so accurately that the molecules are close enough to join up again. But, before the break, the molecules were only a few ten millionths of a millimetre apart. So the chance of joining them all up is very remote. However, if you wet the two surfaces, some of the toffee will dissolve in the water. (In other words, the water is a solvent for the sugar in the toffee.) The water gives the molecules a chance to move around and find places where they can join up. When the water evaporates, the toffee forms one hard, solid slab again.

Polystyrene cement, the glue used on plastic models, works rather like water on toffee. It contains a solvent which dissolves some of the plastic so that molecules are free to move. When the solvent evaporates, the joint sets hard.

Materials like wood and metal are not dissolved by glue, but they do have microscopic pits and cracks on their surface. If the glue can get into these, it can anchor itself to the parts being joined. That is why it helps to roughen surfaces before glueing.

If you dip a piece of glass in water and lift it out slowly, most of the water run offs. The water molecules are not attracted strongly enough to the glass to stick to it. But if you put some washing-up liquid in the water, the liquid sticks to the glass – it wets the glass.

this end is attracted to grease but not water

detergent molecule

this end is attracted to water but not grease

grease

grease particle surrounded by detergent molecules which will stick to water

Left Detergent molecules have one end that likes grease and the other end that likes water. When they surround a grease particle, they effectively glue it to the water.

Modern adhesives make use of the wetting effect. The glue must wet both surfaces and then turn solid to make the joint permanent. That explains why you need different glues for different materials. A glue that will wet glass might not wet polythene.

GLUEING GREASE TO WATER

Grease and water do not mix on their own. So, to wash away grease, you have to add soap or detergent (such as washing-up liquid) to the water. In a way, soaps and detergents are like glue. They are attracted to water and to grease. They fasten the grease molecules to the water molecules and make a solution.

Rub a little butter on your hands. In plain cold water, it will not wash off. Now put a little washing-up liquid in the water. This time, you can remove the butter easily because the detergent glues it to the water.

Below Detergents were used to deal with the oil pollution on the coast of Alaska after the oil tanker *Exxon Valdez* went aground in 1989. Eleven thousand people took part in the cleaning-up operations.

WHITER THAN WHITE

White fabrics tend to turn yellow with age, so modern soap powders contain chemicals to make your white fabrics look whiter and brighter. They work like this. Daylight contains visible light which you can see and invisible ultraviolet light which you cannot. The chemicals absorb the ultraviolet and use its energy to give off extra blue light. This counteracts the yellow (see page 22 for how blue plus yellow makes white). It also means that there is more visible light coming from the fabric than is falling on it. So the fabric seems to look 'whiter than white'.

ENZYMES AT WORK

The problem with soap and some detergents is that, although they work well on grease, they will not work on coagulated proteins such as dried blood or cooked egg. 'Bio' detergents have been developed to overcome this problem. They contain chemicals called enzymes which 'digest' the proteins.

There are many natural enzymes in your body. Their job is to speed up vital chemical processes. For example, when you eat, digestive enzymes break down your food into simpler substances which will dissolve in water. The enzymes in soap powders work in a similar way. They turn the proteins into substances which will dissolve in water.

Below Another use for concrete. In Hollywood there is a tradition that famous film stars make and sign impressions of their hands in wet concrete on the sidewalk outside Grauman's Chinese Theatre. Here, Marilyn Monroe and Jane Russell are making their hand prints.

CEMENT AND CONCRETE

Any glue can be called a cement; but most people think of cement as the material used in concrete and mortar. You buy it as a grey powder, made from limestone and clay which have been burnt and pounded. When it is mixed with water, crystals start to grow. Water molecules become trapped inside the crystal structure, so the water disappears and the whole mixture becomes hard. If there are stone chippings and sand in the mixture, they become glued together to form the material we call concrete.

Above Blue crystals of copper sulphate. If heated, water molecules in the crystals are driven off and a white powder is left. However, a few drops of water restores the colour.

It may seem odd that something can be made harder by adding water. But there is an experiment which shows this. Copper sulphate is a chemical which, in water, grows into large blue crystals. If these are heated, they become a white powder. This weighs less than the crystals because water has been forced out. If water is added, the blue colour comes back and blue crystals can be grown again.

When making up a cement mix, the precise recipe is important. If there is not enough water, or too much sand, then the material will crumble when it hardens.

Concrete can support heavy weights. But if you clamp a concrete beam at one end and hang a weight on the other it will soon break – rather like the slab of toffee. The concrete withstands compression well, but not stretching. Steel rods, on the other hand, are good at withstanding stretching. Reinforced concrete contains steel rods. It combines the compressional strength of concrete and the tensile strength of steel.

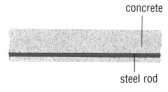

concrete

steel rod

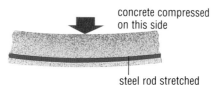

concrete compressed
on this side

steel rod stretched

Above and left When a beam is bent, one side is compressed and the other is stretched. Concrete can stand compression but not stretching. If the stretched side of the beam is reinforced with a steel rod, this can take the strain. The photograph shows the enormous number of steel rods used to reinforce the concrete jacket on a Norwegian oil platform.

MORE HOUSEHOLD CHEMICALS

Acids are corrosive. They eat into some metals, fabrics, and skin. There are plenty of acids in the home. But they are usually in a dilute (watered down) form. Lemon juice contains citric acid, which gives it its sour taste. There is also citric acid in other citrus fruits such as oranges and grapefruit. Vinegar contains ethanoic acid. There is lactic acid in milk, and tannic acid in tea.

Alkalis are the chemical opposites of acids. Like acids, they are corrosive. But mixed with an acid, they can neutralize (cancel out) the acid effect. Alkalis, such as ammonia, are used in many household cleaners. Oven cleaners contain sodium hydroxide (caustic soda) which is strong enough to attack burnt grease – and also extremely dangerous. Indigestion tablets contain bicarb to cancel out the effect of an 'acid stomach'.

Scientists use the pH scale to measure how strong an acid or alkali is. They can use specially treated paper which turns a different colour, depending on the pH. The pH scale goes from 0 to 14. The strongest acid is 0, 14 is the strongest alkali, and 7 is neutral (neither acid nor alkali). Pure water has a pH of 7. Gardeners often test the pH of their soil because they know that some plants will not grow if the pH is wrong.

APPROXIMATE pH VALUES	
Concentrated hydrochloric acid	0.1
Contents of human stomach	1.0 – 3.0
Soft drinks	2.0 – 4.0
Lemon juice	2.2 – 2.4
Vinegar	2.4 – 3.4
Cider	2.9 – 3.3
Cows' milk	6.3 – 6.6
Drinking water	6.5 – 8.0
Eggs	7.0 – 8.0
Washing soda (sodium carbonate)	11.0 – 12.0
Quicklime	12.4
Caustic soda (sodium hydroxide)	14.0

Left The pH values of some common materials found in the home. A pH of 7 is neutral. The higher the number, the more alkaline the material is. The lower the number, the more acid the material is.

A MATTER OF CHANCE

*M*ention luck or chance to most people and they
will probably think about games or gambling.
But chance plays an enormous part in our lives.
Right at the beginning of life, it determines
which characteristics we inherit. And all
scientific laws involve chance.

Right Although there are only two ways in which a single tossed coin can come down, there are eight possible ways in which three coins tossed at the same time, or one coin tossed three times can come down.

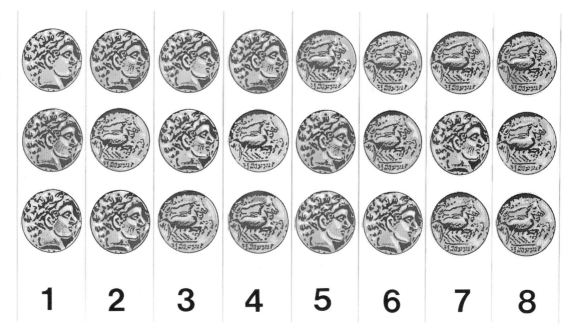

1 2 3 4 5 6 7 8

Left This image was constructed by a computer using a process called fractal geometry, in which shapes are repeated on a smaller and smaller scale. Millions of such designs are possible. Pure chance determines how any one of them starts off. In the pattern shown, the swirl at the centre is repeated many times in different sizes.

MEASURING CHANCE

During a weather forecast, the forecaster may say that there is a 50 per cent chance of rain today, or that there is only a 1 in 10 chance of rain during an open air concert tomorrow. To understand these statements, there are several ideas which need to be sorted out.

First, the percentage. This is a way of writing 'out of 100', so 50% means 50 out of a 100 (as a fraction, 50/100, or 1/2). Next, the 50% chance of rain today. This means that, if you could find out what happened on 100 different days when atmospheric conditions were the same as today, then it would have rained on 50 of them. Finally, the 1 in 10 chance of rain tomorrow. This means that if you could find out what happened on the day following each of 10 days when atmospheric conditions were the same as today, then it would have rained on only one of them.

The word 'probability' is sometimes used when talking about chance. If the probability or rain is 1 in 2 then there is a 50% chance of rain. In other words, it is likely to rain on about half the days when atmospheric conditions are the same. The word 'about' is extremely important here. The rules of probability do not tell you what will actually happen. They only tell you what is likely to happen on average.

CERTAINTY

If something is absolutely certain to happen it has a probability of 1 in 1 (or 100%). For example, if you throw a stone straight up into the air in a completely open field, the probability of it coming down to the ground again is 1 in 1.

If something is absolutely certain not to happen it has a probability of 0. For example, the probability that, by flapping your arms, you could fly like a bird is 0! But the majority of chance happenings have a probability that is somewhere between 0 and 1.

TOSSING A COIN

In many games, the referee tosses a coin to decide which team will have the choice of starting first or second, or in which direction they will play. One of the captains has to choose head or tails. It seems to be a very fair way of deciding – provided the coin is genuine and is not the same on both sides!

The probability of the coin coming down heads is 1 in 2 (50%). Yet sometimes, if you keep on tossing a coin, it will come down with the same side up many times in succession. It is surprising how many people believe that if you go on tossing the coin your luck will change. But no matter how many times you toss the coin, the probability of it being heads next time is still 1 in 2 (50%).

Imagine that you toss a coin and get 20 heads in succession. Surely there must be a very high chance of the next toss being a tail? The answer is no! In reality, there is still a 1 in 2 (50%) probability of the next toss producing a head. If this seems a little odd, just think what it would mean if the probability did change the more times you tossed the coin. For this to happen, the coin would need a memory. It would have to remember exactly how many times it had been tossed before!

Now imagine that you are playing a game in which you try to predict the result of tossing three coins. Here, the probability of all three being heads is only 1 in 8 (12.5%). That result is arrived at by thinking about what happens as you toss each coin. The first coin could be heads or tails. The second coin could also be heads or tails, so there are four possible results so far. In other words, the probability of two heads is 1 in 4 (25%). The third coin could also be heads or tails. So the probability of all three coins being heads is 1 in 8 (12.5%).

Probability comes into play when you throw a dice. This has six numbers on it. So the probability of throwing, say, a six is 1 in 6 (16.6%). With a pair of dice, the probability of throwing a double six is 1 in 36 (2.7%). Of course, this all depends on there being no cheating! Probability is soon upset if the dice are 'loaded' – in other words, if they are weighted on one side. But even loaded dice cannot guarantee particular numbers.

CHANCE AND LIFE

When making decisions, people do not always take a realistic view of probability. For instance, the probability of being killed in a car accident is very much greater than that of being killed in an plane crash. Yet there are many people who will happily travel in a car, but refuse to fly because they think that it is too dangerous.

In real life, it is rare to find things that are 100% certain, with a probability of 1 in 1, but many people believe that you can.

Left It is often said that lightning cannot strike the same place twice, but this is not true. In fact, the conditions that led to the first strike, like this one in Arizona, are more likely to occur again.

Someone may ask a doctor if an operation will be successful, but this is not really a fair question. An operation may have worked perfectly 500 times before, but there is no absolute guarantee of a complete success on the 501st. However, there is a very high probability that it will be!

SCIENTIFIC LAWS

Chance affects the laws of science. Earlier, you read that if a stone is thrown up into the air, the probability of it coming down again is 1 in 1. In reality, this is not quite true! Everyone would be surprised if the stone did not come down because, they might argue, the law of gravity tells you that it must. But it is important to remember that scientific laws are only statements about what is most likely to happen. They cannot tell you that something will definitely happen.

OBEYING THE LAW?

Here is a story which illustrates what a scientific law is. A baby is sitting in a pram with a teddy bear. The baby drops the teddy bear over the side and a passer-by picks it up. The baby is pleased and repeats the experiment several times. Then the baby is given a biscuit. After a while, the baby decides to try the experiment again and drops the biscuit over the side, but it falls into a puddle, so no one picks it up.

The baby has performed two different experiments with the following results:

Hold a teddy bear out and let go, and it goes down and then comes back.

Hold a biscuit out and let go, and it goes down and does not come back.

If the baby had been a scientist he or she might have said:

'The common pattern in these two things is that if you hold something out and let go, it goes down.' A non-scientist might say that this is because of the law of gravity. But a scientist might also add the following:

'In all my experiments so far, something has moved in a particular way. So it is very likely that it will always move in that way. But I cannot prove that it will.'

PROBABILITY OF ...		
pigs flying	0	(0%)
a girl being colour blind	1 in 200	(0.5%)
choosing the winning number on a roulette wheel	1 in 37	(2.7%)
a boy being colour blind	1 in 12	(8.3%)
throwing a particular number on a dice	1 in 6	(16.7%)
throwing heads when tossing a coin	1 in 2	(50%)
losing your money if you buy one of 200 raffle tickets	199 in 200	(99.5%)
a ball coming down when thrown	1 in 1	(100%)

Left Chart showing the probabilities of various events, with the least probable at the top and the most probable at the bottom.

Matter is made up of atoms and molecules (groups of atoms). These are constantly on the move. In air for example, the molecules rush about at high speed in every possible direction. They bump into anything that is in the air.

Think of a stone which is just starting to fall through the air. It is being hit by air molecules on all sides, but if billions more molecules hit it underneath than on top, it might move upwards. However, the chances of it happening are minute. They are much less than the chances of someone having a big win on every fruit machine in the world!

Left Ranks of fruit machines in a Las Vegas casino. Although a few individual gamblers may win large sums, it is the owners of the machines who make a steady income.

Above This crowd scene has some regularity because the people are sitting in rows. But the distribution of those in red, or wearing hats, or shading their eyes, is random.

regular arrangement

irregular arrangement

Above If 20 beads are thrown onto a table, both these arrangements are equally probable. Because the lower one is irregular we tend to think that it is more probable.

Someone once calculated the probability of a brick jumping off a table because more molecules were hitting it underneath than above. It is 1 in 10 with 10,000,000,000 noughts after it! However bricks are large. Microscopic things are much more likely to be affected by the motion of molecules around them. When, in 1827, botanist Robert Brown used a microscope to study pollen grains in a liquid, he noticed that the grains were wriggling about as if alive. The motion, now called Brownian motion, was due to the bombardment by molecules in the liquid.

WHY SCIENTIFIC LAWS WORK

Scientific laws tend to work most of the time because of the vast numbers of atoms or molecules involved. This example may give you some idea of how big the numbers are. If you emptied a glassful of water into the sea, it would, in a few years, become completely mixed up with all the Earth's water. However, if you then took a glass of water from any river, lake, sea, or tap in the world, it would contain about 1 000 of the original molecules.

RANDOM FALL

If you throw a handful of beads on to a table and they end up arranged in regular rows and columns, your friends will assume that some kind of trick was involved – the probability of it happening is so small.

You would normally expect that, if you threw a handful of beads onto the table, they would land in a random, irregular arrangement. Surprisingly, the probability of any particular irregular arrangement is exactly the same as that of the regular arrangement! You can see why this is if you think as follows.

Suppose you marked the positions of all the beads in the irregular arrangement and then threw again. If all the beads went into exactly the same places as before, you would be just as surprised as with the regular pattern. The reason we think that the regular arrangement is less probable than the irregular one is that it is very much easier to recognize the regular pattern, so we tend to lump all the irregular ones together as the same. Strictly speaking, all the arrangements are random including the first! 'Random' simply means that the pattern has been left entirely to chance. Of course, when you throw the beads, you are much more likely to get an irregular arrangement than a regular one. That is because there are billions of times more irregular arrangements than regular ones.

PROBABILITY AND TIME

If the film of an old chimney being blown up is run backwards, the chimney appears to grow out of a pile of rubble. This seems to be against the natural course of events. If a pile of rubble is blown up it is much more probable that it will end up as another irregular pile of rubble rather than a regular, complete chimney. Watching the highly improbable take place, we conclude that time must be running backwards.

Sometimes, on films, a wave advances and retreats across a sandy shore, and writing is mysteriously left on the sand. This too is highly improbable because waves are more likely to wash away writing than create it! As with the growing chimney, the trick is produced by running the film backwards.

The growing chimney and the appearing writing seem wrong because our instinct is that things do not become more regular on their own. It is this which may give time its direction. As time advances, things naturally tend to a state of confusion (see page 183).

HEREDITY AND CHANCE

Chance plays an important part in the way life develops. You inherit some characteristics from your mother, some from your father, and some which are passed down from earlier generations. However, which characteristics is a matter of chance. It depends on which particular sperm out of millions fertilizes which particular ovum (egg).

It is possible to work out the chances of different characteristics being handed down, though only probabilities can be predicted, not certainties. Racehorse breeders select horses for mating so that they have the best chance of producing a foal with the special characteristics needed for racing. But there is no guarantee that two champion racehorses will produce another champion.

GAMES AND GAMBLING

Games of chance seem to be as old as recorded history. However, there is an important difference between games that depend entirely on chance and those that only partly depend on it. For example, tossing a

coin is a game of pure chance. So is throwing dice and gambling on the results. But a game like Monopoly, in which dice are thrown and moves are made on a board, also involves some skill because you have to decide what to buy and what to sell. Nearly all games involve some element of chance. Even in the Olympic Games, athletes need a little luck as well as a lot of skill.

Roulette is a game that depends purely on chance. The roulette wheel has 37 small compartments round its rim, numbered 0 to 36. The operator spins the wheel and then throws in a tiny ball. This travels round the rim in the opposite direction to the spin of the wheel. Eventually, the ball ends up in one of the compartments. To play the game, people bet on different numbers.

Each time the wheel is spun, the probability of the ball falling in any one compartment is only 1 in 37. But it is surprising how many people believe that they are on a 'winning streak' and expect to be more lucky than others.

It is well worth remembering that anybody who operates a gambling game is doing it to make money. So, on average, it will be the players who lose, not the person who runs the game. Overall, more money will be lost than will be won. Of course one player may win a lot of money. It is that hope that keeps gamblers playing.

Above The chance of the ball falling into any one of the 37 compartments round the edge of the roulette wheel is exactly the same, provided that the wheel is properly balanced. So the probability of a particular number being called is 1 in 37.

Far left Items from the gaming rooms in a casino: gambling chips representing different amounts of money, dice used in many games involving pure chance (or mainly chance), and a hand of cards in which skill and experience play a part as well as chance.

HOLDING THE WORLD TOGETHER

Magnets attract iron, gravity pulls you downwards, and electric forces keep your body in one piece! But where do all these forces come from? The search for an answer has taken scientists right to the heart of the atom and back to the beginning of time.

Y ou have probably felt the force between two magnets. The force of gravity is pulling on you at this very moment. Without electric and nuclear forces, nothing in the world could exist. This chapter looks at the different types of force, the particles of matter which produce them, and some of the mysteries that surround them.

MYSTERIOUS MAGNETISM

Bring the ends of two magnets towards each other, and you can feel a force between them. It may be a force of attraction, or a force of repulsion, depending on which ends are close together. The forces seem to come from points near the ends of each magnet – called the north pole and the south pole of the magnet. Two north poles will repel each other, so will two south poles. But a north pole and a south pole will attract.

Magnets have another strange feature. If you hang them up by a thread, they turn so that they lie in a north–south direction. The effect is used in a compass.

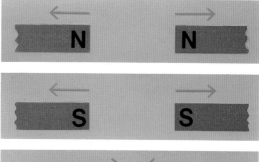

Above How the magnetic poles at the ends of two magnets push or pull on each other. Like poles repel; unlike poles attract.

The compass effect explains how the poles of a magnet were named. When people realized that one end of a magnet tried to point north, they started to call that end the 'north pole'.

Today, we know why magnets try to lie north–south. The Earth itself behaves like a giant, weak magnet whose poles pull on the poles of other magnets. However, that still leaves another puzzle to solve.

Left The aurora borealis, or northern lights. Shimmering displays like this are produced when electrically charged atomic particles streaming from the Sun are pulled towards the polar regions by the Earth's magnetic field. As the particles hit atoms and molecules in the Earth's upper atmosphere, light is given off.

Right The 2 km diameter ring of the particle accelerator at Fermilab, near Chicago, USA. The track of a car's headlights mark out the service road above the tunnel in which the accelerator is housed. Giant machines like this are needed to probe deep into atoms and find out more about the forces that hold their particles together.

Left The launch of the first human expedition to the Moon's surface in 1969. Overcoming the pull of the Earth's gravity was a major problem for the project planners. A huge three-stage rocket, with engines developing up to 3400 tonnes of thrust, was needed to lift the tiny three-person Apollo 11 spacecraft into space with enough speed to reach the Moon.

Below A tower block in East London about to be destroyed by gravity. The structure is weakened by controlled explosions on some of the 21 floors of the building. Gravity does the rest.

North poles are attracted to south poles, so a magnet's north pole ought to point south! The reason it does not is that the Earth's magnetic north pole is not really a north pole at all! Despite its name, it is the same type of pole as the south pole of an ordinary magnet.

Magnetic materials are those which are attracted to magnets and can be magnetized (made into magnets). The only strongly magnetic materials are the metals iron, nickel, and cobalt, and certain alloys (mixtures) containing them. For example, steel is mainly iron, and most steels are strongly magnetic.

We now know that magnetism comes from atoms, which can themselves behave like tiny magnets. In most materials, the magnetic effects almost cancel out so that they are too small to notice. However, in a few materials the magnetic effects combine to give a stronger result.

Magnetism is a mysterious force. Two magnets may be separated by an empty space. Yet, somehow, each can 'tell' the other that it must move! People sometimes say that each magnet produces a magnetic field which influences the other. This describes the effect, but it does not explain it.

MYSTERIOUS GRAVITY

Here is a chance to watch another effect, just as mysterious as magnetism. Hold a pencil out in front of you. Then let it go. It starts moving towards the ground all by itself! People say that 'it is pulled by gravity'. But this does not explain how the Earth manages to 'tell' the pencil that it has to start moving downwards.

Scientists understand many of the effects of gravity, even if they cannot fully explain them. Gravity is always a force of attraction. And there is a gravitational attraction between all masses – even between you and the person next to you, although that force is far too small to notice. The more mass things have, and the closer they are, the stronger is the gravitational pull between them. The force of gravity between you and the Earth is strong enough to keep you on the ground. However, the force of gravity between you and someone nearby is extremely weak – less than one billionth of your weight!

Gravity holds us to the Earth. It holds the Moon in orbit around the Earth, and the Earth and other planets in orbit around the Sun. It pulls over long distances and is the major force in the formation of stars and galaxies. Yet compared with magnetism, it is relatively weak. The Earth is huge. But its gravitational pull on, say, an iron nail can easily be beaten by the magnetic pull from a tiny magnet.

ELECTRIC FORCES

When some materials are rubbed, they become charged with static electricity. The charge produces forces. For example, a charged comb will attract tiny pieces of paper.

There are two types of charge. Scientists call them positive (+) and negative (–) because they seem to be opposite in kind. Charges of opposite types attract each other, but charges of the same type repel.

All atoms have tiny charges in them. That is where charges come from. But the amounts of negative and positive charge are normally equal. So, overall, materials are neutral (uncharged). Rubbing two materials together can transfer charge from one to the other. One ends up with more positive charge, the other with more negative.

Opposite charges are needed to produce an attraction. So it may seem strange that a charged comb can attract something uncharged like a piece of paper. However, the 'uncharged' paper has equal amounts of positive and negative charge scattered through it. One type is attracted to the comb, the other type is repelled. But because of the positions of the charges, the attractions win.

Above This photograph of the Earth was taken from the Apollo 11 spacecraft when it was close to the Moon. Gravity keeps the Moon in orbit around the Earth. Without it, the two would quickly move apart.

In the paper, the attracted charges are pulled slightly closer to the comb. The repelled charges are pushed slightly further away. This means that the attractions are slightly stronger than the repulsions. That is why the paper is pulled towards the charged comb.

Experiments with a comb show the effects of electric forces, but electric forces have a much more important part to play in the world than this. They are the forces which hold atoms together to form the materials around us – and in us.

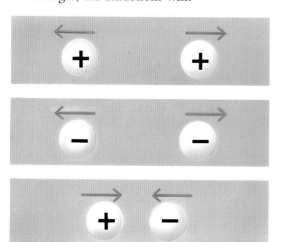

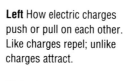

Left How electric charges push or pull on each other. Like charges repel; unlike charges attract.

Right This girl has become charged up by touching a van der Graaff generator. Her hairs and head have like charges on them. This means that the hairs repel each other and try to stand out from her head.

INSIDE ATOMS

Atoms are far too small to see; no picture can really show what they are like. However, from the results of their experiments, scientists have created descriptions – called models – to help them think about atoms. No one claims that any model is the complete truth. It is just a tool for handling difficult ideas.

The following is one model of the atom. At the centre, there is a nucleus made up of particles called protons and neutrons. Protons have a positive (+) charge. Neutrons are uncharged. Much lighter particles called electrons move round the nucleus at high speed. They carry a negative (-) charge, which is equal but opposite to the charge on the proton. An atom has the same number of electrons as protons, so, overall, it is neutral (uncharged). Atoms of different elements have different numbers of protons, and therefore different numbers of electrons (see page 53).

Atoms of any one element can exist in several different versions, called isotopes. These all have the same number of protons (and electrons), but different numbers of neutrons. Usually, one isotope is much more common than the others. For example, nearly 99 per cent of carbon atoms have 6 protons and 6 neutrons in the nucleus. However, some carbon atoms have 6 protons and 8 neutrons. This rare isotope is called carbon-14 because the total number of particles in its nucleus is 14. The common isotope is called carbon-12.

UNSTABLE NUCLEI

Some types of atom have unstable nuclei. In time, each nucleus breaks up by shooting out a tiny particle or burst of wave energy, or both. If atoms have unstable nuclei, scientists say that the material is radioactive. The break-up of the nuclei is called radioactive decay, and the particles or waves that are shot out are known as nuclear radiation. There are three main types of nuclear radiation: alpha particles, beta particles, and gamma rays.

Below Atoms of any one element have the same number of protons and electrons, but they may have different numbers of neutrons. These different versions of an element are called isotopes. In an atom, the electrons behave like smeared-out clouds of charge, as shown here. But to compare electron arrangements, diagrams often show electrons in simple circular orbits.

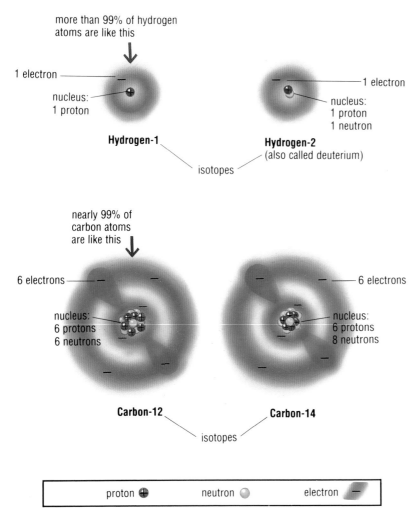

more than 99% of hydrogen atoms are like this

1 electron

nucleus: 1 proton

Hydrogen-1

1 electron

nucleus: 1 proton 1 neutron

Hydrogen-2 (also called deuterium)

isotopes

nearly 99% of carbon atoms are like this

6 electrons

nucleus: 6 protons 6 neutrons

6 electrons

nucleus: 6 protons 8 neutrons

Carbon-12

Carbon-14

isotopes

proton ⊕   neutron ◯   electron ▬

Above Some radioactive materials are so hazardous that robot arms must be used to handle them. The operator is behind protective shielding. Here, a radioactive liquid is being poured from a beaker into a flask.

Alpha particles are each made up of 2 protons and 2 neutrons, so they are positively charged. Beta particles are electrons, so they are negatively charged. It may seem strange that electrons can come from the nucleus. However, when some nuclei decay, a neutron is changed into a proton, an electron, and a tiny, almost undetectable particle called a neutrino.

Gamma rays are bursts of wave energy. They are a member of the electromagnetic family (see page 172) and are like X-rays.

While some isotopes (different versions of atoms) are stable, others are not. For example, carbon-14 has unstable nuclei and is radioactive, while carbon-12 has stable nuclei, so is not radioactive. The break-up of unstable nuclei takes place at random, but in some materials it happens more quickly than in others. In a sample of carbon-14, it takes 5700 years for half the atoms to decay. It takes another 5700 years for half of the remaining atoms to decay, and so on. Scientists say that carbon-14 has a half-life of 5700 years. Uranium-235 has a much longer half-life: 710 million years. Iodine-128 has a half-life of only 25 minutes.

HOW CAN THEY TELL?

Atoms are far too small to see with a microscope, but in 1911 a team of scientists at Cambridge, led by Ernest Rutherford, carried out an experiment which first gave an idea of what atoms are like inside.

In the experiment, gold foil was bombarded with alpha particles from a radioactive material. Alpha particles have a positive charge and are much smaller than atoms. A specially treated screen detected the alpha particles. It gave off a pin-prick of light whenever it was hit by one.

The researchers found that nearly all of the alpha particles went straight through the foil. However a few were repelled so strongly that they bounced almost straight back. Rutherford's explanation was that the atoms must be largely empty space. The atoms must also contain concentrated bits of matter which repelled the few alpha particles that met them head on. Here then was evidence of a positively charged nucleus.

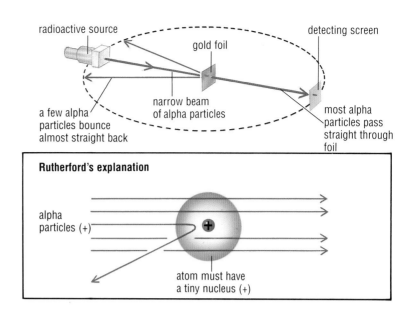

Rutherford's explanation

alpha particles (+)

atom must have a tiny nucleus (+)

Above If a beam of alpha particles (+) is directed at some thin gold foil, most of the particles pass straight through, but a few bounce almost straight back. Rutherford's explanation for this was that each atom must be largely empty space with a tiny positive (+) nucleus at its centre.

MORE ELECTRIC FORCES

Electrons (-) are attracted to protons (+). So electric forces help hold the atom together. Electric forces also hold atoms to each other. This can happen in several ways.

For example: common salt (sodium chloride) is made from sodium and chlorine atoms. However, some electrons have passed from one to the other (see page 55), leaving the sodium with a positive (+) charge and the chlorine with a negative (-) charge. Charged atoms like this are called ions. In salt, the negative (-) chlorine ions and positive (+) sodium ions attract each other strongly. They stick together to form a hard, solid crystal.

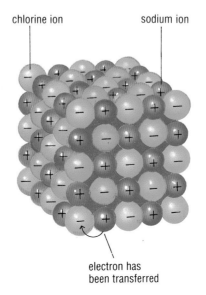

chlorine ion   sodium ion

electron has been transferred

Left A crystal of common salt (sodium chloride) is held together by electric forces. Sodium atoms have each lost an electron to become sodium ions (+). Chlorine atoms have each gained an electron to become chlorine ions (-). Each ion is attracted strongly to the ions next to it, because these have an opposite charge.

Right Electric forces make water molecules stick to each other. The forces arise because water molecules have slightly positive and negative parts which attract opposite charges on molecules nearby. However, the forces between the molecules are relatively weak, which is why solid water (ice) melts so easily.

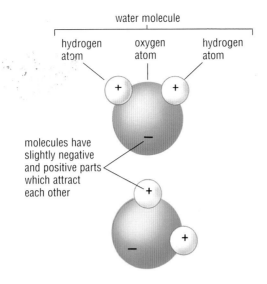

water molecule

hydrogen atom   oxygen atom   hydrogen atom

molecules have slightly negative and positive parts which attract each other

Below A pond skater on the surface of water. The electric forces holding water molecules together are strong enough to stop very light things, like an insect, pushing through the surface. The effect is called surface tension. It can make the water look as though there is a skin on it.

The smallest 'bit' of water you can have is a water molecule. It is made up of two hydrogen atoms and one oxygen atom. Electric forces hold the atoms together. The atoms share some of their electrons. By attracting the positive charges in the atoms, these shared electrons act like a 'glue'.

Water molecules also stick to each other because of the way their electrons are distributed. In a water molecule, the oxygen part is slightly negative, while the hydrogen parts are slightly positive. So a negative part of one molecule tends to stick to a positive part of another. In frozen water, these attractions hold the molecules firmly together. In liquid water, the attractions keep breaking, so the molecules are free to move past each other.

You can see the electric 'stickiness' of water for yourself. Water forms drips because its molecules cling to each other. Water molecules are also attracted to some other types of molecule, which is why things are wet when you lift them out of water – they still have water molecules sticking to them.

In different ways, all materials are held together by electric forces. When a chemical change takes place – during burning for example – electrons become rearranged. So the forces produced by muscles, engines, or explosions are all the result of lots of tiny electric forces in action.

Right Burning is a chemical reaction in which the substance acting as the fuel combines with oxygen. Large amounts of energy can be released as the atoms join together in new arrangements. Usually some heat is needed to set off the reaction.

STRONG AND WEAK

When scientists started to study the nucleus, they realized that they had a puzzle on their hands. Positively charged protons were concentrated in this tiny space, and the repulsion between them must be huge. So why did the nucleus not fly apart? There had to be some other, immensely strong force of attraction binding the protons and the neutrons together. Scientists now call this the strong nuclear force – a different type of force from those found before. It only pulls over very short distances, which is why the nucleus is so small.

Radioactive decay seems to be caused by a different, much weaker force. Scientists call this the weak nuclear force.

FISSION AND FUSION

The strong nuclear force is the source of the immense power released in nuclear reactors, in nuclear explosions, and – on a much larger scale – the Sun.

The fuel cans in a nuclear reactor contain atoms of uranium-235, an isotope whose nuclei are easily disrupted by slow-moving neutrons. To start up a reactor, a beam of neutrons is fired into its core. If a neutron hits a uranium-235 nucleus and is absorbed, it makes the nucleus unstable. The nucleus quickly decays by splitting into two smaller, more stable nuclei, and two or three more neutrons as well. The splitting process is called fission. These neutrons may cause further fission and release more neutrons – and so on in a chain reaction. But special materials are placed in the core to slow down and control the reaction.

During fission, the strong nuclear force pulls neutrons and protons into more stable arrangements. This releases energy which makes the reactor heat up. In a nuclear power station, heat from a reactor is used to make steam. The steam turns the turbines which drive the generators.

Below Nuclear fission (splitting). A neutron hits a nucleus of uranium-235, making an unstable nucleus which splits into two smaller parts, along with some neutrons. The process releases energy. The neutrons may hit more uranium-235 nuclei, causing more fission in a chain reaction.

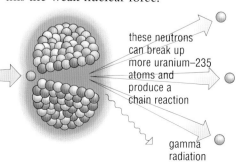

neutron splits
uranium–235 nucleus

these neutrons can break up more uranium–235 atoms and produce a chain reaction

gamma radiation

The Sun also gets its energy from the strong nuclear force, but not by fission. Deep in the Sun, hydrogen nuclei collide and join to form bigger, more stable nuclei. There are several stages to the process, but the end result is that helium nuclei are formed. The joining of nuclei in this way is called fusion. Once again, it is the strong nuclear force which pulls neutrons and protons into more stable arrangements, releasing huge amounts of energy in the process.

THE QUANTUM WORLD

The behaviour of atoms and their particles can seem very different from that of the large, everyday objects around us. For example, electrons can sometimes behave like particles and sometimes like waves. Also, particles in the atom are restricted in the amounts of energy they can have. An electron cannot speed around the nucleus in any orbit; it has to keep to certain levels. It can change levels, but only in sudden jumps.

To explain these various features of the atom, scientists have developed the quantum theory. One important idea in this theory is that energy cannot be divided into smaller and smaller bits. It is only available in tiny 'packets', called quanta. Obtaining energy is rather like buying sugar in a supermarket. You cannot have any amount – you can only buy an exact number of packets. One of the early successes of the quantum theory was that it explained how atoms give out light – just like when you switch on a lamp, or burn something.

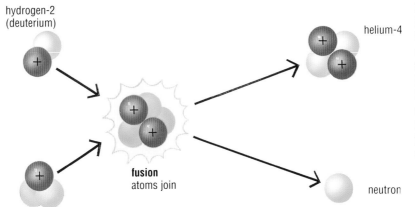

Above Mushroom cloud from a nuclear bomb test. Explosions like this are the result of uncontrolled chain reactions in which there is very rapid fission of almost pure uranium-235 or plutonium-239. Apart from the devastation they cause, nuclear weapons release radioactive gas and dust into the atmosphere which can be a long-term health hazard for people round the world.

hydrogen-2
(deuterium)

fusion
atoms join

hydrogen-3
(tritium)

helium-4

neutron

Left Nuclear fusion (joining). Fast-moving nuclei of hydrogen-2 and hydrogen-3 collide and join before forming a nucleus of helium-4 and a neutron. Energy is released as a result. The Sun is powered by a more complicated fusion process that starts with hydrogen-1.

Right A quantum display: Las Vegas, USA. Light is given off when electrons fall to a lower energy level in their atoms. But first, the electrons have to be lifted to a higher level. An electric current is a very convenient way of making that happen.

Below How an atom gives out light, according to the quantum theory. Some outside energy source raises an electron to a higher level in the atom. When the electron falls back to a lower level, it loses energy. This is emitted as a burst of wave energy called a photon. Light is made up of photons.

According to the quantum theory, heat or electricity, or some other effect, may give electrons enough energy to jump to higher levels in an atom, but eventually they fall back again. Each time an electron falls to a lower level, a quantum of energy is lost. This is given off in in the form of particle called a photon. A beam of light is really a collection of photons. Photons are particles, yet scientists often talk about 'light waves'. There is no contradiction here. In the quantum world, waves can behave like particles and particles can behave like waves (see page 177).

The quantum theory is highly mathematical. Its great strength is that its predictions match the experimental evidence. For example, using the quantum theory, scientists can accurately predict the colours of the light which different atoms give out.

All things are made of atoms, so the quantum theory applies to large objects as well as atoms. However, quanta are so small that their individual effects cannot be noticed until one is down to the scale of atoms.

FUNDAMENTAL FORCES

So far, five different types of force have been mentioned: magnetic, gravitational, electric, strong nuclear, and weak nuclear. One major question which interests scientists is whether these forces are linked in any way.

During the last century, scientists began to realise that electricity and magnetism are linked. An electric current produces magnetism – this happens in an electromagnet. Also, a wire moving through a magnetic field can produce an electric current – this effect is used in a generator (dynamo).

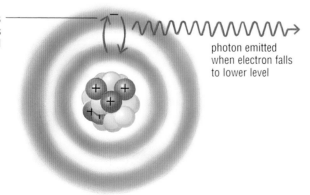

if electron gains energy, it jumps to a higher level

photon emitted when electron falls to lower level

Right A possible family tree of forces. Most scientists think that the Universe started with the Big Bang, around 15 billion years ago, when huge amounts of energy and then matter started to expand. At that time, the four fundamental forces may have been different varieties of one type of force.

Below One of the detectors at the HERA particle accelerator, Hamburg, Germany. In the centre, protons will collide with electrons at extremely high speeds. Particles created in these collisions will enter the ring of detector chambers round the outside. The experiments should provide more information about quarks and the gluons that bind them together.

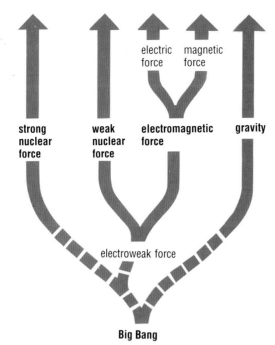

strong nuclear force

weak nuclear force

electric force   magnetic force

electromagnetic force

gravity

electroweak force

Big Bang

When more was known about the atom, the link between magnetism and electricity became clearer. A current is really a flow of electrons. Atoms contain moving electrons. So atoms will have a magnetic effect.

Scientists now group electric and magnetic forces together, and call them electromagnetic forces. In the world around us, there seem to be four fundamental forces: electromagnetic, gravitational, strong nuclear, and weak nuclear. But that is not the end of the story. The search is on for further links between these different types of force.

Scientists have already found the connection between the electromagnetic force and the weak nuclear force. In high-energy experiments, these merge into one – called the electroweak force. At much higher energies, all four forces may merge. These were the conditions which scientists think existed 15 billion years ago, just after the Universe had been created in a giant explosion called the Big Bang.

Mathematically, it may be possible to link the four fundamental forces by treating particles, not as points, but as tiny lines called strings. Ideas like these may sound rather strange, but they are needed so that extremely complicated mathematical equations can give sensible answers.

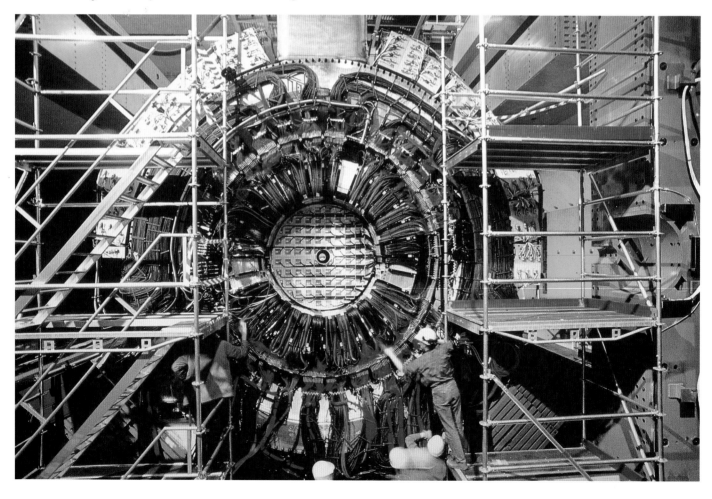

Below Protons and neutrons are each made up of three quarks. These carry a fraction of a + or - charge and come in two 'flavours' (up and down) and three 'colours' (red, green, and blue). In ordinary matter like this, quarks always combine in threes, so there is one of each 'colour'. Together, they produce a charge of +1 or 0: Single quarks are never found.

FUNDAMENTAL PARTICLES

Researchers use giant machines called particle accelerators to investigate atoms and their particles. Beams of particles are speeded up before being smashed into stationary atoms or each other. Computers, linked to detectors, show the tracks of the 'fragments' from each collision. By studying the tracks, researchers can find out information about the particles involved in the collision.

Atoms are made up of electrons, protons, and neutrons. However, results from particle-accelerator experiments suggest that neutrons and protons are themselves made up of smaller particles called quarks. High-energy accelerators can produce all sorts of weird and wonderful matter. But, in ordinary matter, there are two 'flavours' of quark, called up and down, each in three 'colours', called red, green, and blue. Quarks do not really have a flavour or colour of course. The names are just for convenience, and the people who thought them up liked ice cream!

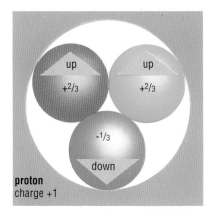

proton
charge +1

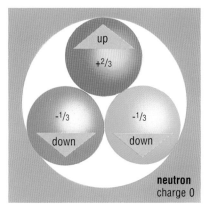

neutron
charge 0

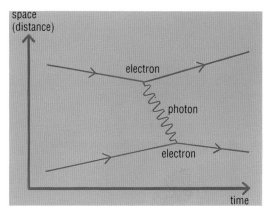

Above Physicist Richard Feynmann devised diagrams like this to show how particles behave. Here, two approaching electrons repel each other by exchanging a photon. The diagram is a graph which shows how the separation of the particles changes with time.

From their experiments, physicists have developed a picture of matter which they call the standard model; this says that matter is made up of two groups of particles: quarks and leptons. Quarks combine to make neutrons and protons. Leptons include electrons and neutrinos.

Particles exert forces on each other by exchanging 'messenger' particles called gauge bosons. Photons are the gauge bosons which carry the electromagnetic force. For example, two electrons will push on each other by exchanging a photon. Similarly, gluons are the gauge bosons which carry the strong nuclear force. So gluons are responsible for holding the nucleus together.

Physicists have found the gauge bosons which carry the weak nuclear force. But, at the time of writing, a gauge boson for gravity has not yet been discovered. The standard model is a useful tool, but it is not the last word on the subject.

Right According to the standard model, ordinary matter is made up of the quarks and leptons shown in the top box. When these matter particles exert forces on each other, they do so by exchanging other particles called gauge bosons (bottom box). For example, an electron repels another electron by exchanging a photon.

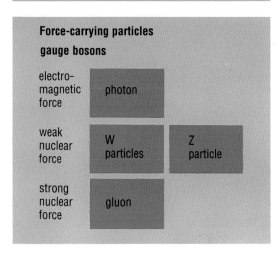

THRILLS AND SPILLS WITH g

*P*ulled by the Earth's gravity, with nothing to slow them, falling things have an acceleration which scientists call *g*. Few powerful cars can match it. But ride in a rollercoaster or a jet, and you can experience 3*g* or more, or the weightlessness of zero *g*.

The Earth's gravity tries to make all things accelerate downwards. When skydivers plummet towards the ground, the force of air resistance limits their speed, but without it they would go on getting faster and faster, and would pass the speed of Concorde in just under a minute!

Air resistance affects some things more than others. For example, in air, a feather falls much more slowly than a hammer. But with no air, both would gain speed at the same rate. Astronaut Alan Shepherd demonstrated this when he held a feather and a hammer side by side above the airless surface of the Moon and dropped them. Both hit the ground together.

ACCELERATING AT *g*

Scientists often measure speed in metres per second (m/s). On Earth, if something starts falling and there is no air resistance to oppose its movement, its speed increases like this: 10 m/s after 1 second, 20 m/s after 2 seconds, 30 m/s after 3 seconds, and so on.

So, during the fall, the speed increases by 10 m/s every second: in other words, the acceleration is 10 m/s per second (written as 10 m/s^2). This is called the acceleration of free fall, or *g* for short. It is the same for all objects falling near the Earth, no matter how light or heavy they are.

In fact, 10 m/s^2 is only an approximate value for *g*. More careful measurements give a value of 9.81 m/s^2, though this varies very slightly from one part of the Earth to another.

Moving away from the Earth, the acceleration of free fall decreases because the Earth's gravity becomes weaker. The Moon's gravity is much less than the Earth's. On the Moon, the acceleration of free fall is only 1.6 m/s^2.

A PUSH IN THE BACK

Imagine that you are sitting in a racing car. The car accelerates forward. Its speed is 10 m/s after one second, 20 m/s after two seconds, 30 m/s after three seconds – in other words, the car's acceleration is the same as the acceleration of free fall, *g*. As the car accelerates forward, the driver's seat gives you a firm push in the back. The push you feel is equal to your weight and you experience an acceleration of 1*g*.

For a car, 1*g* is a very high acceleration. Under normal circumstances, a typical family car produces a maximum forward acceleration of only about 0.2*g*. However, in a shunt-type collision where one car goes into the back of another, the car at the front might easily be pushed forward with an acceleration of 5*g* or more, even in a low-speed crash. This is why head restraints are so important for passengers. Without them, the head tends to stay where it is when the body is pushed forward by the seat. The strain on the neck can produce dangerous whiplash injuries.

SLOWING DOWN

If something loses speed instead of gaining it, it is decelerating. Car collisions can produce very high decelerations. The problem here is that the car slows down, while the passengers tend to keep going. Modern cars are designed to keep the deceleration as low as possible during a collision. This is done by building the passenger compartment as a rigid safety cage, and making the bonnet and boot into crumple zones which collapse steadily in a collision. In the safety cage, passengers wear safety belts which stop them colliding with solid parts of the car that might cause injury.

One way of helping the body to withstand the high deceleration produced in a crash is to cushion it evenly in the direction of travel.

Left Ninety-three skydivers link together in a mass fall at a downward speed of about 50 metres per second (180 km/hour). Joining like this is extremely difficult. To adjust and match their vertical speeds, the skydivers have to alter the air resistance on them by changing their arm, leg, and body angles.

Right How the speed of a falling object (on Earth) increases if there is no air resistance to slow it. The speed goes up by approximately 10 metres per second every second. This acceleration is the same for all objects, whatever their mass.

Time		Speed
start of fall		0 m/s
after 1 second		10 m/s
after 2 seconds		20 m/s
after 3 seconds		30 m/s
... and so on		

In one of the rides the simulator becomes a racing car. As the car accelerates to overtake another one, you see it happen on the screen and feel a push in the back at the same time. As the view changes to a right-hand bend, you lean to stop yourself sliding to the left. When the brakes go on, you brace yourself as you start to slide forward in your seat.

How is all this achieved? Simply by tilting the simulator backwards, forwards and sideways. If your view of the outside world is cut off, your body has no way of telling whether a push from your seat is the result of gravity or acceleration. The simulator can make you think that you are accelerating forwards by tilting you backwards.

Above Cars are designed to have a crumple zone at the front. It saves lives by collapsing evenly so that the deceleration in a crash is lessened.

That is why some cars have inflatable air-bags. It is also the reason why many military transport aircraft have rear-facing passenger seats. Passengers can withstand much higher decelerations in rear-facing seats. However, airlines are reluctant to fit them because they do not think that the paying public will accept the idea of flying facing backwards.

ALL ABOARD THE SIMULATOR

You can feel the effects of acceleration and deceleration without having any speed at all. Just try riding in a simulator at a fairground or leisure park. A typical simulator is a windowless capsule which holds about 20 people. They sit in rows and watch a screen at the front.

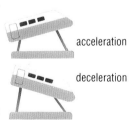

Right A fairground simulator tilts passengers backwards to give them the effect of acceleration, and forwards for deceleration. Sealed inside a capsule like this, there is no way of telling that the effects are not being caused by speed changes.

acceleration

deceleration

Right Fairground and leisure-park rides like this can give accelerations of up to 3*g*. In the ride shown, this is achieved by moving quickly in a circle.

Deceleration is achieved by tilting you forward. For tight turns, you are tilted to the left or right.

Exciting though they are, simulators like this can never exceed about 0.5*g*. To experience higher *g* values, you have to choose more dramatic rides, such as those provided by rollercoasters and aerobatics.

ROLLERCOASTER RIDES AND MORE

Imagine that you are sitting in a rollercoaster car. The restraining bar comes down over your shoulders. Ahead is the steep ramp which will take you to a height of 20 metres or more. This is probably the worst moment of the ride – it is now too late to change your mind! Once at the top, the car starts to roll downhill, gaining speed as it does so. Hurtling through the bottom of the first dip, the car rises again but your body is still trying to go downhill. You are pressed into your seat with a force which is three times your normal weight. You are now feeling the effects of a 3*g* acceleration. However, the 3*g* effect is produced not by speeding up or slowing down, but by movement in a curve. The extra push on your body comes not from the back of the seat, but from the part of the seat beneath you.

Many leisure-park rides use tight curves to produce *g* values of up to about 3*g*. Accelerations like this cause no trouble for normally fit and healthy people. However, jet-fighter pilots and astronauts may have to tolerate much higher *g* values during a flight. To prepare themselves, they train in a huge machine called a centrifuge. This has a long, rotating arm with a tilting cabin at the far end. As the arm moves round, the cabin banks, rather like a motorcycle going round a corner. Seated in the cabin, the pilot or astronaut feels increasing *g* values as the arm gathers speed.

When you hurtle through a dip on a rollercoaster ride, blood tends to drain from your head towards your feet. At an acceleration of 3*g*, this does not normally cause any problem.

At higher *g* values, the loss of blood from the brain would cause a temporary blackout. Pilots of highly manoeuvrable jets often 'pull' 5*g* when they fly round tight curves or loops. Blacking out under these circumstances would mean losing control of the aircraft. To overcome the problem, pilots wears a *g*-suit. The suit partly inflates during tight turns so that the legs, arms and stomach area are squeezed. This restricts the flow of blood from the head and prevents a blackout.

Above Riders in this rollercoaster are experiencing nearly zero *g* as they go through the top of the loop. At the bottom, however, their acceleration will rise to 3*g*.

Right The pilot in the first picture is about to be whirled round on the end of a giant arm. In the second picture, you can see the effect of a 7*g* acceleration on his face.

ZERO *g*

Astronauts orbiting the Earth float around in their spacecraft feeling weightless. They experience zero *g*.

You do not have to go into space to feel weightless. Imagine that you are in a lift and standing on some bathroom scales. Suddenly the cable snaps and the lift starts to fall. (There are safety devices on real lifts to stop this happening.) As the lift accelerates, you accelerate as well. Your body no longer presses on the scales because the scales fall away from you as fast as you fall towards them. The zero reading on the scales tells you that you are weightless. You feel weightless as well because your body has none of the forces up through it which you would experience when standing on firm ground.

Give a small downward push with your feet and you will 'float' up to the ceiling of the lift. You are not really floating of course; you are still falling, but inside a box which is also falling. With no windows to show you what is happening outside, your feeling of weightlessness might be due to a lack of gravity. You have no way of telling whether it is or not.

Below These NASA astronauts are experiencing weightlessness. However, they are not in space. They are aboard a large Boeing jet aircraft which, for a few minutes, is flying along a special trajectory like that of a thrown ball. In effect, the astronauts are falling, and the aircraft's cabin is falling along exactly the same path. So the astronauts can 'float' freely inside it.

THE 20+*g* CLUB

Some animals have evolved features that increase their chances of survival by allowing them to withstand high *g* values.

Right A housefly can achieve an acceleration of 20*g*. This is more than the human hand can produce, which is one reason why flies are so difficult to swat.

Left The click beetle can out-accelerate any other creature. It makes its escape by jackknifing into the air with a peak acceleration of over 400*g*.

Above *Pachycephalosaurus* was a dinosaur which used its head like a battering ram. During a collision, the deceleration of its head would have been over 20*g*.

Above Squirrels have specially adapted front legs to absorb the shock of landing from great heights. Their deceleration can be 20*g* or more.

There is one rather strange consequence of free fall. In free fall, you cannot feel the effect of gravity. You accelerate downwards, yet experience the sensation of zero *g*!

Some leisure parks have rides that allow you to experience zero *g*. One of these is rather like a falling lift. You sit in a cage which is hauled to the top of a tall tower and then dropped. The cage falls down a track which levels out smoothly at the bottom. Another ride that can almost reach zero *g* is a giant galleon which swings backwards and forwards. The closer you are to the vertical during the swing, the closer you are to zero *g*.

Astronauts need to train for zero *g*, but rides of the type found at leisure parks can only achieve zero *g* for a second at most. For longer spells of weightlessness, astronauts fly in a special aircraft with an empty but padded passenger compartment. Having built up enough speed, the aircraft climbs, then dives, following the same sort of trajectory as a ball does when thrown a long way. Inside the aircraft, passengers can 'float' for several minutes before the aircraft has to pull out of its dive.

INTO ORBIT

In a space shuttle orbiting the Earth, astronauts can experience zero *g* for days on end. Deep in space, the weightlessness might be due to lack of gravity, but the space shuttle is not deep in space. Its orbit is only about 300 km from the Earth's surface, and gravity at that height is almost as strong as it is down on the ground.

So zero *g* in an orbiting spacecraft is not due to lack of gravity. It results from the way the spacecraft moves. Like a lift with a snapped cable, an orbiting spacecraft is falling freely, but it has so much forward speed that the curve of its fall exactly follows the curve of the Earth. As a result, the craft falls without getting any closer to the ground. Astronauts inside the spacecraft follow exactly the same path as the craft itself. They too are falling freely and experiencing the sensation of zero *g*.

From pictures on television, living in a spacecraft looks like fun. Pens and toothbrushes float around, and you can perform somersaults in mid-air. In reality, zero *g* causes problems. You cannot drink from an open cup because the liquid would float away, you cannot eat some foods because the crumbs would float away, and you cannot sleep in a normal bed because you would float away. Worse still, long-term exposure to zero *g* may weaken bones and affect blood circulation.

Right Stone A is dropped from the top of an imaginary tower, hundreds of kilometres high. It falls freely, straight to the ground. Bullet B is shot from the barrel of a gun. It too falls freely, but it has forward speed as well. Spacecraft C also falls freely, but it has so much forward speed that the curve of its fall never brings it any closer to the ground. It stays in a circular orbit.

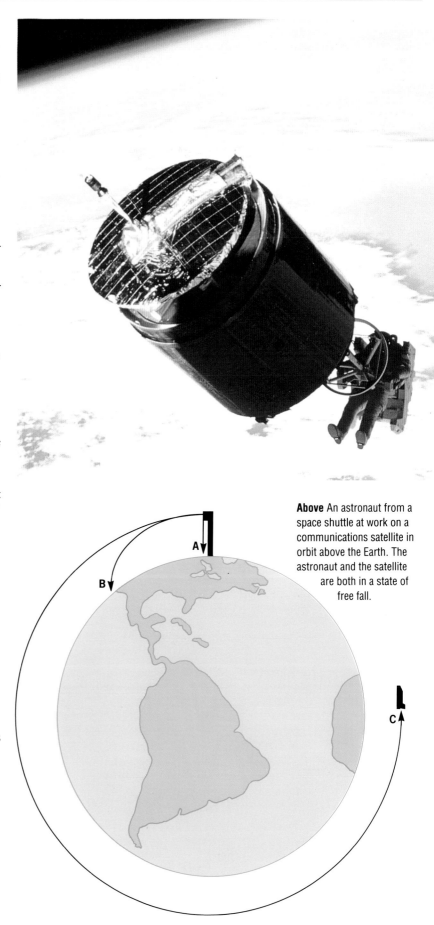

Above An astronaut from a space shuttle at work on a communications satellite in orbit above the Earth. The astronaut and the satellite are both in a state of free fall.

FLIGHT AND FLOW

*W*e live at the bottom of a deep ocean of air. We cannot see the air, but we can see the effects of the forces it can produce. These can uproot trees and hold aircraft and birds in the sky. You also use them when you play table tennis or drink through a straw.

The atmosphere stretches for hundreds of kilometres into space, but the bulk of the air lies within 10 km of the Earth's surface. Down at sea level, the weight of all this air produces a very high pressure – equivalent to the weight of 10 tonnes pressing on every square metre. The pressure has a squashing effect that pushes inwards on everything, but amazingly, we do not get crushed. This is partly because we have developed bodies which are strong enough to cope with the pressure, and partly because there is air trapped inside us pushing out.

DRINKING UNDER PRESSURE

When you use a drinking straw, you are relying on the pressure of the air in the atmosphere. By expanding your lungs, you remove air from the straw. This lowers the pressure inside. So the air outside presses on your drink and forces it up the straw.

If the atmosphere cannot press on your drink, a straw will not work. Try the effect for yourself. Put a straw into a small glass bottle, nearly full of drinking water. Seal the gap between the bottle and the straw with Blu-Tack or Plasticine. Then see how much water you can suck up!

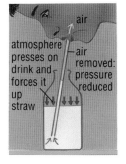

Above When you use a drinking straw, atmospheric pressure pushes the liquid up the straw.

Left A tornado rips across farmland in the USA. Tornadoes, also known as 'twisters', can be from about 50-500 m across. In them, violent winds can whirl round at more than 350 km/h.

Right This hovercraft is pushed along by propellers and supported by a cushion of higher-pressure air underneath. Horizontal fans draw in air to maintain the pressure. A large rubber skirt reduces leakage of air from the sides.

PRESSURE TRICK

Here is a trick that uses atmospheric pressure to support the weight of some water. Make sure you do it over a sink!
Fill a beaker with water. Place a piece of stiff, flat card over the top of the beaker. Hold it there while you turn the beaker upside-down. Then let go of the card!

BLOWERS AND SUCKERS

Hovercraft use air pressure. They have powerful fans to increase the pressure of the air underneath them. This produces enough upward force to support their weight. Air leaks away under the sides of the hovercraft, but the fans keep pushing in air to replace it.

Vacuum cleaners make use of atmospheric pressure. They have a fan which pushes out air. This lowers the pressure inside, so the atmosphere pushes more air into the cleaner, carrying the dirt and dust with it. Most cleaners have a paper bag in them, which has lots of tiny holes that act as a filter. This lets the air pass through but traps the dirt and dust.

A vacuum is really a space with no air in it at all. But the cleaner is still called a 'vacuum' even though the fan does not remove all of the air in the sucking part.

The first vacuum cleaner was invented by Herbert Booth in 1901. In his early experiments, he drew air through a tube, put a handkerchief over the end of the tube, and noticed that the handkerchief trapped dirt and dust. He had discovered the principle of the vacuum cleaner.

Booth's first vacuum cleaner was not very portable. It had an air pump driven by a petrol engine and was towed by a team of horses! If you wanted your house cleaned, the cleaner would be parked outside while Booth's workers pulled long tubes through your windows and into the rooms. Later, Booth tried making smaller cleaners. But the first really successful domestic machines were made by William Hoover, who started production in 1908. Essentially, they were the same as today's machines.

Above and right The wing action of a robin. The outermost feathers provide most of the forward force, while the innermost feathers supply the lift.

SUPPORTED BY WINGS

Aircraft are kept up in the sky by air pressure. But the process is quite different from that used in drinking straws and hovercraft. With an aircraft, the flow of air across the wings produces an upward force. It is of course the wings which move, rather than the air. But the result is the same, and it is easier to think about the effects of airflow.

A wing works because of one simple principle: if air is speeded up, its pressure drops. An aircraft has a wing section called an aerofoil which is specially shaped to speed up the flow of air across the top of the wing and reduce the pressure there.

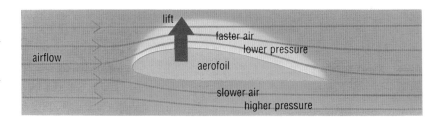

As the pressure under an aircraft's wing is greater than the pressure above, an upward force is produced. This force is called lift.

Birds' wings also have an aerofoil section to produce lift. But birds get additional lift and forward movement by beating their wings. The feathers themselves move rather like the slats on a venetian blind. On the upbeat, the feathers open so that air passes easily between them. On the downbeat, they close to form the aerofoil.

Above Air travels faster over the top of a wing than the bottom. As the air speeds up, its pressure is reduced. The higher-pressure air underneath pushes the wing upwards.

Right Some sports parachutes are designed to behave like aerofoils. They move through the air like hang-gliders, rather than coming straight down. The parachutist controls the flight by pulling on cords which make the parachute flex.

Left An aircraft's wing is specially shaped to produce lift as it moves through the air. Increasing the wing area gives greater lift and a lower landing speed, but it also produces more drag (air resistance). Designers have to make a compromise between the two.

Insects also fly by beating their wings, but in most cases the beat is much faster than that of a bird. For example, certain midges beat their wings over 1000 times a second! Insects' wings are thin membranes supported by tough veins. Some wings are so small that scientists puzzle over how the insects manage to fly at all. Someone once said that it was scientifically impossible for bees to fly, but no one had ever told the bees so they kept on flying!

Bats are the only mammals capable of true flight. They probably evolved from tiny shrew-like creatures which gradually developed the ability to glide. Their wings are two flaps of skin which stretch from the tips of their very long fingers to their ankles.

AIRFLOW IN ACTION

Here are two experiments which use the idea that speeding up air reduces its pressure and produces a force. The first one shows the wing effect.

Hold a piece of paper at one end so that the top is level with your mouth and the other end is curving downwards. Now gently blow across the top of the paper. The paper should lift. Blowing across the paper makes the air go faster and reduces the pressure on that side. So the paper is pushed upwards by the higher-pressure air underneath.

Hold a piece of card very close to one end of a cotton-reel. Blow hard through the other end and let go of the card. (To keep the card lined up with the cotton-reel, push a pin through the card so that it projects into the hole.) You won't be able to blow the card away! As the air flows through the narrow space between the card and the cotton-reel, it speeds up and its pressure drops. Higher-pressure air on the other side pushes the card towards the cotton-reel.

Left This racing yacht has raised an additional, large sail at the front called a spinnaker. It provides extra forward force when the yacht is travelling with the wind behind it. To balance out the forces on the yacht, the spinnaker is put out on the opposite side to the mainsail – the nearest of the sails in this photograph.

Above A yacht's sail acts as an aerofoil. The airflow across it produces a sideways force. By setting the sail at a suitable angle, the boat can be moved in any direction within the blue zone. The yacht also needs a centreboard or a keel sticking down into the water. Without it, the wind would push the yacht sideways instead of straight ahead.

Right A yacht cannot sail directly into the wind. To move upwind, it has to follow a zig-zag course. Changing direction is called tacking. During each tack, the sail must be set on the other side of the boat. At the same time, the crew move over to the opposite side. Their weight helps balance the sideways force on the sail so that the boat is not blown over.

CLOSE TO THE WIND

Sailing yachts and dinghies use the force of the wind to move them along. But they do not need the wind behind them. The big triangular sail can be used as an aerofoil, so that there is a sideways push on it. Using this force, the person at the helm can make a yacht move in almost any direction – apart from straight into the wind and about 30 degrees either side.

By following a zig-zag course, it is possible for a yacht to move upwind (against the wind direction). Changing direction like this is called tacking.

The sideways push on a sail causes a problem. It means that the hull of the boat will also be pushed sideways unless something is done to stop it. This is one reason why yachts and dinghies have a keel or centreboard sticking down into the water – it resists sideways movement.

IN A SPIN

When a ball moves through the air, air resistance slows it and gravity pulls it down. But if the ball is spinning, there is a sideways force on it as well. If you play table tennis, you will know that spin can make a ball swerve very strongly in one direction. Spin is also used in several other ball sports. Tennis players may spin the ball when serving to make it dip downwards. A spinning cricket ball will 'swing' – though air acting on the seam can also push it sideways. If a golf ball is sliced, it spins. But this is sometimes a nuisance, because the ball ends up where the golfer does not want it!

The sideways force on a moving, spinning ball is caused by a pressure difference. When a ball moves through the air, some of the air 'sticks' to its surface. This air is carried round by the ball as it spins. As a result, the airflow is faster on one side of the ball than on the other. This produces a pressure difference which causes the sideways force on the ball.

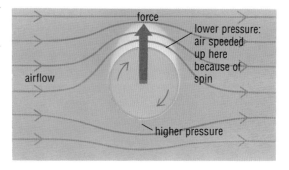

force

lower pressure: air speeded up here because of spin

airflow

higher pressure

Above and left Footballers can give the ball spin to make it swerve. When a moving ball spins, it drags air round with it, making the airflow faster on one side than on the other. This means that the air pressure is lower on one side than the other, so there is a sideways force on the ball.

HOVERING BALL

If you put a light ball into an upward jet of air, the pressure changes can make it hover! You can try this yourself with a vacuum cleaner, provided the tube can be connected for blowing instead of sucking. You will also need a table-tennis ball or inflatable ball.

Hold the nozzle of the tube so that the airflow is upwards. Then hold the ball about 25 cm above the nozzle and release it. You may need to experiment to get the best hover. For example, you could put a funnel over the nozzle to speed up the airflow. If the airflow is too strong, you may be able to open an airhole on the nozzle to reduce it.

FLOATING AND SINKING

A stone sinks in water yet a ship weighing thousands of tonnes can float. A submarine can do both, and a balloon with over a tonne of helium in it can even float in air. There are several factors which decide whether something will float or sink, and being light or heavy is only one of them.

Far right Humpback whales swimming off the Australian coast. Humpbacks can be 12 m long and weigh 65 tonnes, yet with full lungs they have enough buoyancy to float. The upthrust from the surrounding water is strong enough to support their weight.

Below Hot-air balloons taking off during the annual Albuquerque International Balloon Festival in the United States. In the same way as ships are buoyant in water, hot air balloons are buoyant in cooler air around them. Although they can weigh 3000 kg or more – most of which is the hot air inside – they are still a little lighter than the air they displace.

*I*f something floats, people say that it is buoyant, but the difference between floating and sinking can be very small. Fish and whales can do both, as can submarines and human divers. Many animals, including humans, have discovered how to change their buoyancy.

WHY THINGS FLOAT

Here is an experiment to try in the garden, or somewhere else where you can slop water around. Fill a bucket to the brim with water. Take an empty plastic lemonade bottle with a screwtop, and hold it upright by the neck. Now try pushing the bottle under the water. You will feel an upward force on the bottle. This is called an upthrust. The further you push the bottle into the water, the stronger the upthrust will be. Pushing the bottle into the water has one other effect as well. Water overflows from the bucket and makes a mess on the ground! This is because the bottle has displaced (pushed out) some of the water.

The upthrust on the bottle is produced by water pressure. The water in the bucket is heavy and tries to squash the bottle from all sides. It pushes inwards on the sides and upwards on the bottom. Overall, the result is an upward push. If the bottle is completely under the water, the water pushes down on the top as well. But the upward push on the bottom is still stronger because the water there is deeper and at greater pressure.

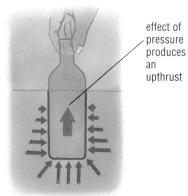

effect of pressure produces an upthrust

pressure is greatest where water is deepest

Above When a bottle is held in water like this, the pressure pushes in on the sides and on the bottom. However, the upward push is strongest. That is why there is an upthrust on the bottle.

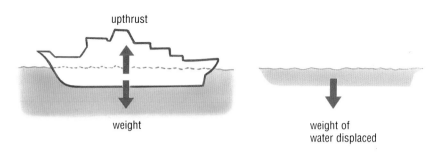

upthrust

weight

weight of
water displaced

Above When a boat floats in water, some water is displaced. Archimedes' principle says that the upthrust is equal to the weight of water displaced. The law of flotation says that the upthrust must equal the weight of the boat – or the boat will sink. So, the weight of the boat, the upthrust, and the weight of water displaced are equal.

LOOKING INTO LAWS

Scientists have found a law which can predict the size of an upthrust. It is called Archimedes' principle, after the Greek scientist who investigated the effects of water displacement, in about 250 BC. The law applies to objects in any liquid or gas, though it is described here for water: the upthrust on something is equal to the weight of water displaced.

Think back to the experiment with the lemonade bottle. If the bottle displaces one kilogram of water, then the upthrust is equal to the weight of one kilogram. The more water is displaced, the stronger the upthrust.

Weight, the force of gravity, is always trying to pull things downwards. For example, if you are in a swimming pool, your weight will try to pull you to the bottom. Of course it might not succeed and you may float – it all depends on the size of the upthrust. If the upthrust is strong enough to support your weight, you will float. If the upthrust is less than your weight, you will sink.

If you are floating, the upthrust balances your weight. In other words, the upthrust is equal to your weight. But Archimedes'

principle says that the upthrust is also equal to the weight of water displaced. Put these two ideas together and you end up with another law, the law of flotation. It applies to things floating in any liquid or gas, but is described here for water: if something is floating, its weight must be equal to the weight of water displaced.

So, if you weigh 40 kilograms, and are floating, then your body has displaced 40 kg of water. If a ship weighs, say, 10,000 tonnes, the builders talk about it having a 'displacement' of 10,000 tonnes.

MASS AND WEIGHT

Mass is the amount of matter in something. It is measured in kilograms (kg).

Weight is the force of gravity. Like other forces, scientists measure it in newtons. On Earth a mass of 1 kg weighs about 10 newtons. However, in everyday language, people are more likely to say that 'it weighs one kilogram'. For easy reading, this book uses the words 'weigh' and 'weight' in their everyday sense, but, strictly speaking, this is not scientifically correct.

Understanding the difference between mass and weight is important if you go into space! On Earth, a mass of 1 kg weighs about 10 newtons. On the Moon, where gravity is much less, it would weigh under 2 newtons. But the amount of matter has not changed. The mass is still 1 kg.

FLOATING IN AIR

There is over 50 km of atmosphere above us. The air may be invisible, but it is very heavy. For example, the air in your bedroom probably weighs as much as you do! Your body displaces some of this air, which means that there is a small upthrust on you. According to Archimedes' principle, the upthrust is equal to the weight of air displaced. Typically, that might be about 5 grammes – about the same as the weight of a sugar cube. It is not very much, but it does mean that the weight shown on your bathroom scales is about 5 grammes less than your true weight.

Right A balloon will float provided its total weight is no more than the weight of air it displaces. This balloon contains 2500 kg of hot air. It displaces 3000 kg of cold air. So the fabric, basket, burners, gas bottles, and crew can weigh up to 500 kg before the balloon is too heavy to float.

Balloon and contents

hot air 2500 kg

fabric and load (basket, burners, crew) 500 kg

total 3000 kg

Air displaced by balloon

cold air 3000 kg

total 3000 kg

Right This airship is filled with helium, a gas which is lighter than air, and also cannot burn. Engines drive ducted fans on either side of the passenger cabin. The fans propel the airship. They can also be swivelled up and down for low-level manoeuvering. To climb, dive, or turn, the pilot alters the angles of the fins at the back of the airship.

If your body was made of a material so light that you weighed less than 5 grammes, then you would float upwards! It sounds impossible. Yet it is exactly this idea which is used in airships and balloons.

A large, fully inflated hot-air balloon displaces about 3000 kg of air. So if the weight of the complete balloon, including the load, fabric, and air inside, could be kept to less than 3000 kg, then the balloon would float upwards. But there is a problem. Inflating the balloon with cold air puts almost 3000 kg of air inside it! So virtually all the weight allowance has been used up – just on air! Heating the air with a gas burner solves the problem. The heat makes the air inside the balloon expand, so that some is pushed out of the hole at the bottom. If, say, half a tonne (500 kg) of air is pushed out, then the hot air inside the balloon now weighs only 2500 kg. Provided the load and fabric weigh no more than half a tonne, the balloon will rise.

Some balloons are filled with helium rather than hot air, but the basic idea is still the same. Like hot air, helium is lighter than the cold air it displaces, so the 'missing' weight can be made up by the balloon material and any load that has to be lifted.

FLOATING HIGH OR LOW

The more a ship is loaded, the lower it floats in the water. Scientifically speaking, this is because it has to displace more water in order to produce the stronger upthrust needed to support the greater weight. However, there is a safe limit to how far a ship can be loaded, and it comes long before the water is about to cover the deck.

A ship which floats too low in the water is unstable. If a wave starts to make it roll, it may capsize completely.

Until the 1870s, some greedy ship owners would deliberately overload their ships, insure the cargo for more than its value, wait for the ship to sink in a storm, and then pocket the insurance money. Ships like this became known as 'coffin ships' and they cost the lives of many seamen. Appalled by the waste of life, a British politician, Samuel Plimsoll, campaigned for safe loading lines to be a legal requirement on ships, and this became effective in 1876. Today, by international agreement, all large vessels are marked with safe loading lines. These are often called Plimsoll lines.

Below A severe storm might always drive a sailing ship onto the rocks. But until legislation was passed in the 19th century, many ships were also lost because of overloading. Too great a load makes a ship unstable so that it turns over easily.

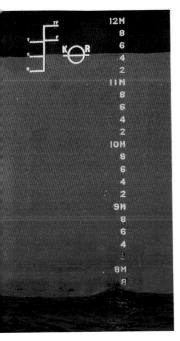

Above This cargo ship has Plimsoll lines on the side to show safe loading levels for different types of water:
TF - tropical freshwater
F - freshwater
T - tropical salt water
S - summer, salt water
W - winter, salt water.
'KR' is a code for the registering authority. The scale indicates the draught of the vessel (depth below the water-line) in metres.

If you look at the side of a ship, you will see that it has several safe loading lines marked on it at different levels. This is to allow for the fact that the ship will float lower in some types of water than in others. It all depends on the temperature of the water and the amount of salt. A ship weighing 10,000 tonnes will always displace 10,000 tonnes of water when afloat. But warm fresh water takes up slightly more space than the same weight of cold, salty sea water. So the ship must float lower in the warm fresh water in order to displace 10,000 tonnes.

Another way of looking at this is to use the idea of density. Warm, fresh water has a slightly lower density than cold, salty sea water – it has slightly less mass in every cubic metre. The lower the density, the lower in the water the ship will float.

The different loading lines are needed so that a ship which is loaded while in cold, salty water will not become unstable if it sails into warm fresh water.

HYDROMETERS AT WORK

A hydrometer is a small float with a scale on it. It is used for comparing the densities of liquids. The lower the density of the liquid, the lower the hydrometer floats. To take the reading, you see how far up the scale the liquid level comes.

Brewers use hydrometers to check the strength of their beer. Beer is mainly water, but it also contains alcohol and other ingredients to produce the taste. Strong beer has more alcohol in it than weak beer – alcohol is less dense than water. So a hydrometer will float lower in strong beer than weak beer. Dairies also use hydrometers for checking milk. Fat and cream are less dense than water, so the more watery the milk, the higher the hydrometer will float.

MAKING ADJUSTMENTS

Submarines need to sink as well as float. For this, they have ballast tanks in their hull. To dive, valves are opened so that the tanks are flooded with sea water. This provides extra weight. To surface, compressed air is pumped into the tanks so that the water is pushed out into the sea again.

When travelling underwater, a submarine uses tiny, moveable 'wings' called hydroplanes to help it descend or climb. These can be angled up or down so that the force of the water flow lifts the nose or pushes it down.

Fish have to cope with density changes in the water. So they need to adjust their buoyancy. To make buoyancy changes, most fish have their own 'inflatable lifejacket' built in to their bodies! Called a swim-bladder, it is a long, air-filled space beneath the spine.

ballast tanks filled with water; submarine sinks

air pumped into ballast tanks; submarine rises

Above A submarine can sink or rise by making itself heavier or lighter. It does this by flooding its ballast tanks with sea water or forcing the water out with compressed air.

Right Once this submarine dives, it can stay submerged for months. Its engines get their power from a nuclear reactor. They do not burn fuel, so they do not need an air supply and produce no exhaust gases.

Right When a shark is swimming forwards, it descends or climbs like a submerged submarine, by altering the angle of the two horizontal fins at the front. However, without any forward motion it naturally tends to sink. And, unlike a submarine, it cannot adjust its buoyancy by taking in or removing air from its body.

If a fish needs more buoyancy, its swim-bladder takes in extra air and gets bigger. For less buoyancy, the air is removed so that the swim bladder becomes smaller. Some fish change the size of their swim-bladder by gulping or releasing air through their mouths. Others rely on air being brought in or removed by the bloodstream.

Sharks do not have swim-bladders. In sea water, a shark naturally tends to sink. To stop this happening it has to keep swimming, using its front fins rather like the hydroplanes on a submarine. Sometimes, sharks swallow all manner of strange things – stones, tin cans, and even old hub caps. This may be to reduce their buoyancy even more so that they can stay near the seabed.

The pilot of a hot-air balloon has to spend most of the flight adjusting the buoyancy. As the air in the balloon cools, it contracts (takes up less space), so more air is drawn in from the outside. This weighs the balloon down and makes it less buoyant. To overcome this, the pilot gives frequent blasts on the gas burners to keep the air in the balloon hot. The hotter the air, the more buoyant the balloon becomes. Of course balloonists have another way of changing buoyancy. They reduce their loads. If the balloon sinks, the pilot can start throwing surplus weight over the side – gas bottles, sandwiches, flasks, and then the passengers!

Left The pilot of a hot-air balloon takes off by giving a blast on the gas burners. The giant flames heat the air inside the balloon. As a result, the air expands, and many kilograms of air are pushed out of the hole at the bottom. This makes the balloon lighter, so it starts to float upwards.

MAKING A MODEL DIVER

Take a piece of drinking straw about 5 cm long. Seal one end with a tiny piece of Blu-Tack (push well in so that none sticks out of the end).

Now wrap a small strip of Blu-Tack round the other end of the straw. This will weigh down the straw when it floats but still leave a hole in the bottom. You have now made your diver, but adjustments will be needed.

Put your diver in some water. It should just float, but with no more than 2 mm of straw above the water. Adjust the amount of Blu-Tack until this is right. Fill a large plastic bottle almost to the top with water. Float your diver in the water. Then put the cap on the bottle and tighten it. See what happens when you squeeze the bottle.

DEEPER AND DEEPER

The average human body is buoyant in water, so diving deep below the surface can be a problem because of the natural tendency to float upwards. In the Indian Ocean, pearl divers weigh themselves down by tying a heavy stone to one ankle with a rope. Once on the seabed, they collect their oysters, cut the rope, and then rise to the surface. On some dives, they reach depths of 20 metres or more, but they use no breathing equipment and may have to hold their breath for several minutes. Deep, breath-held diving like this is extremely dangerous. It usually leads to heart disease and early death.

Most divers carry breathing equipment. This is usually in the form of compressed air cylinders, with valves and breathing tubes attached. The equipment is called an aqualung or scuba (standing for 'self-contained underwater breathing apparatus'). The cylinders give divers extra buoyancy which they do not want, so they have to put weights on their belts to stop themselves rising to the surface. The number of weights can be adjusted to suit the person.

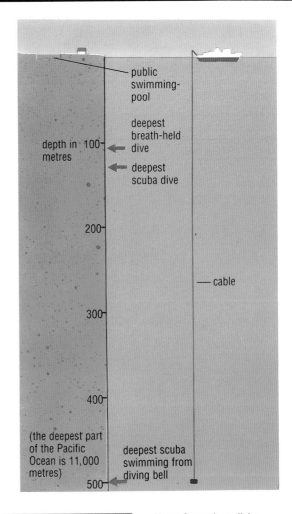

Above Some deep-diving records. The deepest breath-held dive was equivalent to diving the length of a football pitch. Scuba divers have swum from a diving bell at nearly five times that depth. The pressure on them was about 50 times the normal air pressure at the surface.

Left Scuba divers carry compressed-air cylinders on their backs. A valve on the cylinder fills the diver's breathing tube with air at the same pressure as the water outside. A valve in the mouthpiece lets in air from the breathing tube when the diver sucks on it. Another valve releases used air into the water when the diver breathes out.

As divers go deeper, one problem they have to contend with is the increasing pressure of the water around them. For example, at a depth of 10 metres the pressure is equivalent to the weight of more than 50 tonnes pressing in on the diver's body. To withstand this crushing pressure, the diver's lungs must be filled with air at an equally high pressure. The valves on the aqualung automatically adjust the pressure so that it matches that of the surrounding water. This automatic adjustment is vital. Without it, divers would either be crushed or their lungs would burst.

PRESSURE PROBLEMS

Breathing high-pressure air brings its own problems. The air you normally breath is 21 per cent oxygen and 78 per cent nitrogen. In your lungs, oxygen passes into the blood and is carried to the parts of the body that need it. But if you breathe in air at a high pressure, too much oxygen can enter your blood and cause oxygen poisoning. To begin with, this produces a similar effect to drunkeness, but eventually it can kill. To avoid oxygen poisoning, deep-sea divers need a reduced proportion of oxygen in their cylinders.

Nitrogen also causes difficulties for divers. Normally, nitrogen has little effect on our bodies. We breathe it in and straight out again, although a small amount is dissolved in our blood. But when a diver breathes high-pressure air, more nitrogen is dissolved. If the diver rises to the surface too quickly, the fall in pressure makes nitrogen bubbles form in the blood, rather as 'fizz' bubbles form in lemonade when you loosen the top. Divers call this condition the 'bends'. It is extremely painful and can be fatal.

To avoid the bends, divers must surface slowly, pausing every few metres for dissolved nitrogen to pass out of the blood and into the lungs. If they rise quickly, they may have to spend several hours in a decompression chamber on the surface. The pressure of the compressed air in the chamber is lowered very slowly to give time for the body to adjust.

Some divers have to work at depths of 50 metres or more. For this, they use a breathing mixture consistency of 10 per cent oxygen and 90 per cent helium.

Unlike nitrogen, helium does not dissolve in the blood, so problems with the bends are avoided. But breathing helium has a strange side effect: it alters the quality of your voice and makes you sound like Donald Duck!

To reduce the time divers have to spend descending and surfacing, they often work from a diving bell. This is rather like a heavy, upturned bucket with air trapped inside it. It is lowered into the water on the end of a long cable and acts as a temporary base for the divers. They enter and leave it through the hole in the bottom.

You can try the principle of the diving bell for yourself. Wedge a paper tissue in the bottom of a dry beaker. Next, turn the beaker upside-down, checking that the tissue does not fall out. Now push the beaker down into a sinkful of water so that it is completely submerged. Lift the beaker out again. The tissue should still be dry because it was trapped in a pocket of air.

Above It looks like a diving suit. Really, it is more like a miniature submarine. This equipment is designed to withstand the crushing pressure of the water at great depths. This means that the diver inside can breathe air at more normal pressures, so it is not necessary to ascend slowly or use a decompression chamber after the dive.

MOVING MACHINES

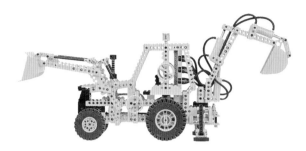

Machines can be as simple as a spanner or as complicated as a computer. Some have solid moving parts, others contain liquid or air. Some are hand-driven, others are powered by electricity. But all have one thing in common – they make work easier.

Some machines are so simple that you may not even recognize them as machines at all. Bottle-openers are machines, so are scissors and screwdrivers. And machines were around long before humans started making them. Like other animals, we have some machines built into our bodies – for example, our arms, legs, and fingers.

There are thousands of different machines for moving things: pliers, crowbar, car jack, vice, hand-whisk, nail clippers are just some examples. These, and other moving machines can be classified into two main types: force magnifiers and movement magnifiers.

Force magnifiers give out more force than you put in; in other words, the output force is more than the input force. Pliers are like this. When you squeeze the handle, the force produced at the jaws is much stronger than your grip. However, there is a price to pay for the increased force. To close up the jaws by a small distance, you have to move the handles through a larger distance.

Movement magnifiers give out more movement than you put in. A hand whisk is like this. Wind the handle quite slowly and the beaters spin round fast. But there is also a price to pay for this increased speed. The force from the beaters is less than the force on the handle; in other words, the output force is less than the input force. That it is why it is difficult to use a hand whisk on a stiff cake-mix.

Left A computer-controlled robot arm at work in a compact disc factory. Arms like this are fast and accurate, and are ideal for situations where human handling might otherwise contaminate the products with dust and grease.

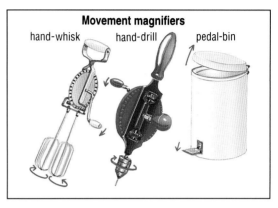

Force magnifiers
nail clippers ↓ bottle-opener ↑ pliers ↓
trolley jack

Movement magnifiers
hand-whisk   hand-drill   pedal-bin

Above Machines can be force magnifiers or movement magnifiers. With force magnifiers, you get out more force than you put in but the movement is reduced. With movement magnifiers, you get out more movement than you put in but the force is reduced.

Machines have many different mechanisms for applying a force and producing movement, but those that use solid parts to transmit the force rely on just five basic principles: the lever, linked wheels, the pulley, the ramp, and the screw.

Right Nature's own robot arms. A crab's claws give pincer-like grip and a high degree of movement. They too are computer-controlled, though the computer in this case is the crab's brain.

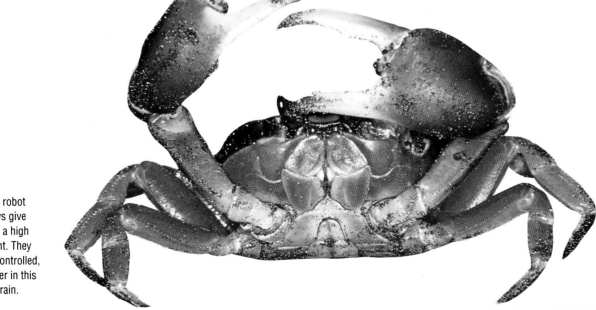

LEVERS

With a lever, there is one place where a force is put in, and another where a force is put out. The lever turns about a point called a pivot. The position of the pivot determines whether the lever will be a force magnifier or a movement magnifier. Nail clippers, pliers, and lever-type bottle-openers are all force magnifiers. In each case, the pivot is close to the output force and a long way from the input force. Machines like this give a high leverage.

If the pivot is closer to the input force than to the output force, the lever will be a movement magnifier. A pedal-bin mechanism is like this. The lid is moved by a rod which is connected very close to the hinge. You only need to move your foot down a little way to open the lid fully.

Right The main features of a lever: an input force, an output force, and a pivot. The position of the pivot can vary, depending on the type of lever. For a high output force, the load needs to be close to the pivot and the hand a long way from it.

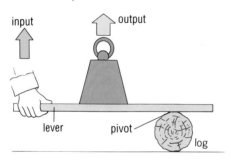

ANIMAL LEVERS

The principle of the lever is used in many animals – including you and me. Usually, the levers are movement magnifiers. They are arranged so that small muscle movements give large and rapid body movements.

The human arm is a movement magnifier (see also page 137). The elbow is the pivot. The muscles in the upper arm pull close to the pivot, raising or lowering the lower arm as they do so. Only small movements of the muscles are needed to produce large arm movements, which is why you can move your hands so quickly.

Kangaroos, frogs, and grasshoppers all use their legs as movement-magnifying levers to produce their dramatic leaps.

Right A leopard frog leaping from a shallow pond. The frog's legs are movement magnifiers. A small muscle movement produces a large leg movement – and a huge jump.

LINKED WHEELS

In many machines, wheels are used for transmitting forces. The wheels may be touching, or they may be linked by a belt or chain. Often the wheels have teeth. If so, they are called gearwheels.

Imagine two gearwheels in contact. If the input wheel is bigger than the output wheel, then the arrangement will be a movement magnifier. A hand-drill is like this. When you turn the handle, a large gearwheel drives a smaller gearwheel so that the drill-bit turns faster than your hand.

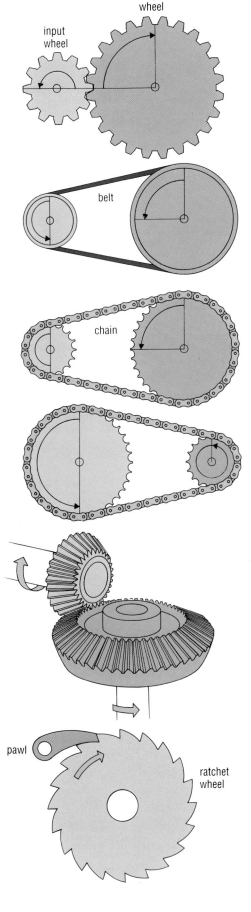

The small gearwheel turns the larger gearwheel slowly, but with increased force.

The effect is the same if the wheels are connected by a belt or chain. But now both wheels turn the same way.

A large wheel makes a small wheel turn faster, but with reduced output force. The chain wheels on a bicycle are like this.

Gearwheels like these can be used to transmit power in a different direction.

No linked wheels here. However, the pawl lets the ratchet wheel turn forward but not backward. The freewheel on a bicycle works like this.

Left Some of the ways in which wheels can be used in machines. Where wheels are linked, relative size affects the output speed and turning force.

In some machines, the wheels are arranged the other way round. A small input wheel drives a larger output wheel, giving a magnified turning force but reduced speed. The gearwheels in a car's gearbox are like this. By moving the gearstick, different combinations of gearwheels can be connected. Bottom gear gives the highest turning force but the lowest output speed. Higher gears are faster, but the gain in turning force is less.

PULLEYS

Pulleys also use wheels, but for lifting things rather than turning them. Their wheels are often in two blocks, linked by a long length of rope, chain, or cable. Pulleys are usually force magnifiers. In general, the more wheels they have, the more the force is magnified. The principle of a pulley is simple. You pull a rope downwards. Because of the way the rope is wound, several sections of the rope pull upwards together. The result is an increased lifting force.

Pulleys are very useful for lifting heavy loads. But, as always, there is a price to pay for the gain in force. When you pull on the rope, you have to move it downwards much further than the load is lifted upwards. Take the case of the pulley in the diagram below. If the load is to be raised by one metre, each section of rope between the two pulley wheels has to shorten by one metre. But both sections are part of the same rope, so you have to pull this down by two metres.

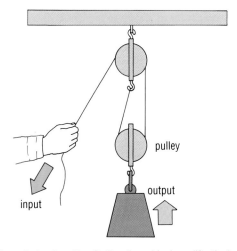

Above A simple pulley. Pulling the cable down lifts the load up. In this example, the output force is almost twice the input force, but the hand has to move twice as far as the load.

RAMPS

Ramps are the simplest of all machines. In fact, they do not really look like machines at all because there are no moving parts. However, they do act as force magnifiers. If you try to lift a loaded supermarket trolley straight up a kerb, the weight makes it very difficult. However, if you push the trolley up a ramp, you are still raising the trolley, but with much less force. So the ramp is a machine! As with any other force magnifier, there is a price to pay. When using a ramp, you have to push the load further.

Right A ramp is a machine because you can use it to raise a load with less force than by lifting it straight up. However, compared with a vertical lift, you do have to move the load further.

ramp

SCREWS

Imagine that you are putting a screw into some wood with a screwdriver. Every time you turn the handle, the screw goes a little further into the wood – perhaps less than a millimetre for each full turn. The screw is acting as a machine. It gives enough extra force to make a hole in the wood. But in return, your hand has to move much further than the screw.

Nuts and bolts also work using the screw principle; so do some car jacks. A screw is really a special type of ramp, but instead of rising in a straight line, it winds round and round. The spiral part of the screw is sometimes called the thread.

input force

output force

Above A screw is really a kind of ramp, except that it winds round and round. You have to turn the screwdriver a long way to move the screw in just a little. But there is a hugely increased force that pulls the screw into the wood.

MACHINES WITHIN MACHINES

Some machines contain other machines. The bicycle is one example. Levers are used to operate the brakes, to change gear, and to tighten or loosen the saddle and handlebars when adjusting their height. When you pedal, you move cranks, which are levers.

Above A mountain bike has broader tyres and lower gearing than a road bike. These features enable it to be ridden over much rougher and steeper ground.

Pedalling produces a turning effect which is carried to a gearwheel at the back by a chain. The gearwheel turns the back wheel. Overall, the pedals, cranks, gearwheels, and back wheel act together as a movement magnifier. In top gear, the bike moves more than 5 centimetres along the road for every centimetre you push the pedals. In lower gears, different-size gearwheels are connected to the chain. You do not travel so far for each turn of the pedals, but the pedals are easier to push.

A wheelchair is also a machine with other machines on it. The brakes are operated by levers. You make the chair travel along by moving the push-rims with your hands. The push-rims are smaller than the wheels and linked directly to them. This means that the wheelchair is a movement magnifier. If the push-rims are made even smaller, this puts the chair in a 'higher gear'. The chair can go faster, but it is harder to turn the push-rims.

Public buildings are often fitted with ramps so that less force is needed to raise a wheelchair from one level to another.

HYDRAULICS AND PNEUMATICS

In some machines, the forces are transmitted, not by levers or cables, but by a trapped liquid. They are called hydraulic machines. Examples include car brakes, trolley jacks, and the shovels on big diggers.

The principle of a hydraulic machine is simple. Two cylinders, filled with a liquid (usually oil), are linked by a connecting pipe.

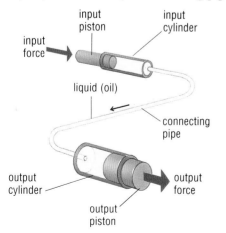

Above A hydraulic machine uses a liquid, such as oil, to transmit force from one place to another. When one piston is moved, liquid is pushed through the pipe so that the other piston moves.

In each cylinder, there is a movable piston. When one piston is pushed in, oil is forced along the connecting pipe so that the other piston is pushed out.

Hydraulic machines have one big advantage over machines with solid moving parts. The connecting pipe can be bent round corners, so that the input and output cylinders can be placed in almost any position or at any angle. In a car, for example, connecting pipes carry the braking force from the foot pedal, under the bodywork, to all four wheels. Designing a system of levers to do the same job would be very difficult.

Hydraulic machines can be force magnifiers or movement magnifiers. It all depends on the sizes of the input and output pistons. If the output piston has a bigger diameter than the input piston, then the machine is a force magnifier.

Pneumatic machines also have cylinders and connecting pipes, but these are filled with air rather than liquid. They tend to weigh less than hydraulic machines, though the forces transmitted are not usually so strong. They are often used in places where electric motors might be dangerous because of sparks.

Above A hydraulic platform being used to load cargo onto an aircraft. The shiny, silvery part is a piston. When oil is pumped into the red cylinder beneath it, the piston is pushed up and the platform rises.

Above This windmill in Thailand is used to pump water from a canal into a cultivated field nearby. Its frame is made of wood, and its sails from a reed-like material. For centuries, non-polluting, wind-powered machines have been used in various parts of the world to pump water, grind corn, and saw wood. Nowadays, they can also drive electrical generators.

POWERED MACHINES

Most simple machines work using human effort; someone has to move a handle, pedal, or rope. However, many machines have some other source of power – such as electricity.

Electrically powered machines used in the home include vacuum cleaners, drills, and even toothbrushes. In factories, most machinery is electrically powered. However, before electricity became widely available in the 20th century, factory machinery was turned by belts or ropes, driven by steam engines or water wheels. The linking mechanisms could be very complicated.

For fixed machinery, mains electricity is the most convenient source of power because it comes through a cable that can be hidden in the floor, walls, or ceiling. For portable equipment, like drills and hedgecutters, mains electricity is more of a problem.

The cable may not be long enough, it can get in the way or trip people up, and it may be cut or damaged by the equipment. One solution is to use batteries, but this is not ideal. Batteries that are light enough to be portable cannot deliver enough power for heavy-duty work. That is why many hedgecutters, lawnmowers, and chainsaws are powered by petrol engines.

UNDER CONTROL

All machines need something to control them. Usually, the controller is a human being. For example, to use a food processor, someone has to put all the ingredients into it and operate the switches at the right time.

To control a machine, you have to know exactly where it is and what it is doing. For this sensors are needed. Your eyes are sensors, and so are instruments that measure things like pressure, temperature, and speed.

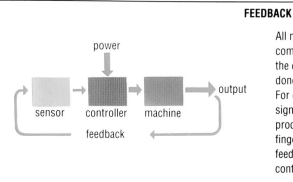

FEEDBACK

power → controller → machine → output

sensor

feedback

All machines, whether controlled by humans or computers, rely on feedback. As the machine does its job, the controller must assess its position and what has been done, and feed back suitable instructions to the machine. For example, if you use an electric drill, your eyes pick up signals about the depth of the hole, and your brain processes this information and decides when to tell your fingers to switch off the drill. This is an example of a feedback loop. Your eyes are the sensor, the brain is the controller, and the output is the work being done.

Below Industrial robots at work on a car assembly line. These robots are huge, computer-controlled arms with welding equipment at the end. They are welding separate steel sections together to form rigid car bodies.

Some machines do not need a human operator. They carry out their jobs automatically, usually because they are controlled by electronics. People sometimes say that they are computer-controlled, though the computer may be no more than a small box containing microchips.

The machines on a modern production line are often computer-controlled. Unlike human operators, computers do not get tired or bored and they do not need breaks – apart from for occasional maintenance. They can repeat the same task over and over again with great accuracy, and they can make decisions faster than people. They can also be built to work in conditions which might be too uncomfortable or dangerous for humans.

Computer-controlled machines in factories are sometimes called industrial robots, though they rarely have arms, legs, and faces like the robots in science-fiction films. Often, they are bolted to the floor, and have one great big arm which moves about. The part that does the job is fixed to the end of the arm. It could be a drill, a screwdriver, a paint spray, or welding equipment.

Industrial robots have two things in common with human operators. They need some method of sensing where they are, and instructions to tell them what to do. You use your eyes, ears, and fingers as sensors. Industrial robots usually rely on pressure-sensitive pads to tell them when they have touched something, though they may also use light sensors or video cameras. An industrial robot's instructions are called its program. The program has to be written by a human being, though some computers can now learn from what they have done and modify their program as they gain experience.

THE HUMAN MACHINE

*T*he human body is an incredible machine, with more parts than the most complex computer. It has climbed mountains, travelled to the Moon, and painted masterpieces. Today, it exists in over three billion versions, each one slightly different from all the rest. And you are one of them!

The human machine has taken over 3000 million years to evolve. It has a tough framework to support it, 'engines' to turn food energy into movement, and a sophisticated computer system to control its actions, its use of energy, and its balance.

Looked after properly, the human machine can give reliable service for many years. It can even repair itself!

THE SKELETON

Machines need a framework to carry their different parts. For humans, the framework is the skeleton. It has more than 200 bones in it, ranging in size from over 40 cm – the thigh bone – down to a few millimetres – the small bones in the ear.

Right The skeleton supports other parts of the body and protects vital organs from damage. Attached to the skeleton are hundreds of muscles which make the body move.

Left Gymnast Wang Xiuyun of China demonstrates the balance, control, flexibility, and strength which can be achieved by the human machine.

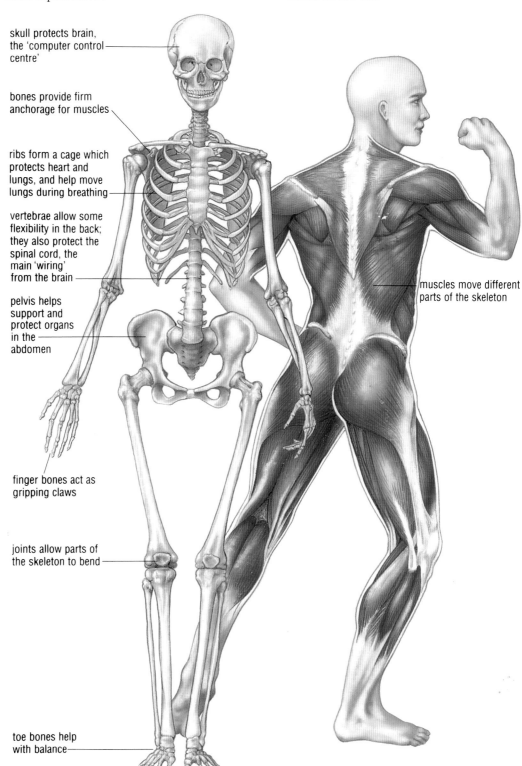

skull protects brain, the 'computer control centre'

bones provide firm anchorage for muscles

ribs form a cage which protects heart and lungs, and help move lungs during breathing

vertebrae allow some flexibility in the back; they also protect the spinal cord, the main 'wiring' from the brain

pelvis helps support and protect organs in the abdomen

finger bones act as gripping claws

joints allow parts of the skeleton to bend

toe bones help with balance

muscles move different parts of the skeleton

The bones are joined so that some parts of the skeleton are rigid, while others can bend.

Bone itself is a remarkable material. It contains living cells that are surrounded by hard, non-living mineral substances mainly made from calcium. The mineral part of bone is brittle, but it is reinforced by tough fibres made of a substance called collagen. The result is a material that is almost as strong as mild steel, and much lighter. And it has one special feature which mild steel does not – when broken it can mend itself. The living cells grow and release minerals to make new bone.

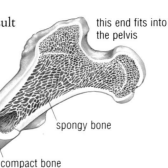

marrow
shaft
spongy bone
compact bone
this end fits into the pelvis

this end forms part of the knee joint

Above The femur (thigh bone) is the biggest bone in the body. Like other large bones, it has spongy bone in each head (end) and a hollow shaft. This makes it light, with little loss of strength. The shaft is filled with jelly-like bone marrow. Blood cells are made here. Bone itself consists of living cells surrounded by hard minerals, with tough fibres for reinforcement.

Right This gymnast is so flexible that she seems to be 'double-jointed'. However, she does not really have twice as many joints as everyone else. It is simply that some of her joints can bend much further than normal.

Right There are two main types of bendy joint. The swivel joint (also called the ball-and-socket joint) can bend in all directions. The hinge joint can only bend in one direction.

JOINTS AND MUSCLES

In the skeleton, joints are the places where two or more bones touch. Your body has over 70 bendy joints in it. There are two main types: the swivel joint and the hinge joint.

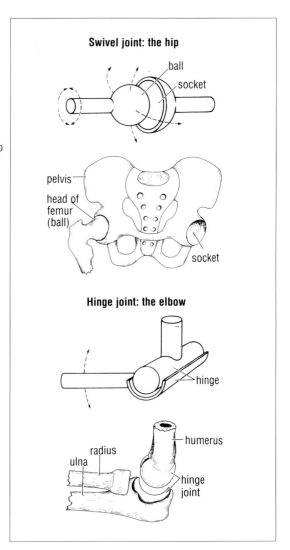

Swivel joint: the hip

ball
socket
pelvis
head of femur (ball)
socket

Hinge joint: the elbow

hinge
humerus
radius
ulna
hinge joint

Swivel joints can bend in any direction: backwards, forwards, or sideways. The hip is a swivel joint. It is sometimes called a ball-and-socket joint because the top end of the thigh bone is shaped like a ball, and it fits into a cup-shaped socket in the pelvis.

Hinge joints can only bend backwards and forwards, like the hinge on a door. The knee is a hinge joint. So is your elbow and any one of your knuckles.

Joints are moved by muscles. These are firmly anchored to the bones by strong fibres called tendons. The muscles are controlled by electrical signals called nerve impulses, which come from the brain or spinal cord and travel to the muscle along nerves. When they arrive, they make the muscle contract (get shorter). This moves the joint.

Muscles can only contract. To get back to their original shape, they have to be pulled. For this reason, they must work in pairs.

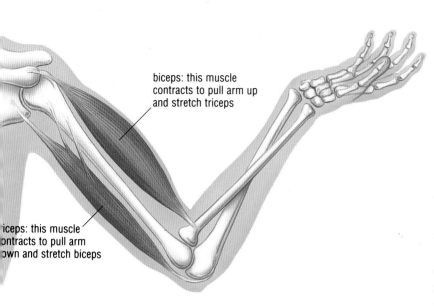

biceps: this muscle contracts to pull arm up and stretch triceps

triceps: this muscle contracts to pull arm down and stretch biceps

Fortunately, the muscles can work for short periods without oxygen. They can still release some energy from glucose, but the chemical reactions are incomplete, and the glucose is turned into lactic acid. This type of respiration is called anaerobic respiration ('anaerobic' means 'without oxygen'). In humans the muscles work without oxygen only for a minute or so, because the build-up of lactic acid soon stops them moving.

RACING ENGINES

In sprint races, athletes quickly use up their available oxygen and have to rely on anaerobic respiration. This means that, by the end of the race, they have built up an oxygen debt which must be repaid. They must breathe in extra oxygen to change the lactic acid into glucose, carbon dioxide, and water.

Marathon runners can sometimes get engine problems towards the end of a race. Their muscles are short of oxygen, so respiration becomes anaerobic and lactic acid starts to build up.

When one muscle contracts, it bends your arm. When a second muscle – its partner – contracts, it straightens your arm and pulls back the first muscle. A pair of muscles working like this is called an antagonistic pair. 'Antagonistic' means 'opposing'.

YOUR SIX HUNDRED ENGINES

Muscles are your engines. There are more than 600 of them in your body. Their fuel is a type of sugar called glucose, carried in by the blood supply. Like other engines, muscles need a supply of oxygen. This, too, is brought in by the blood.

Muscles can produce large forces and rapid movements. But to do this, they must release energy from their fuel. Many complicated chemical reactions are involved, but the net result is that glucose and oxygen are used up, while carbon dioxide and water are made. Scientist call this process respiration. The following equation summarizes what happens:

$$glucose + oxygen \rightarrow carbon\ dioxide + water + energy$$

The full name for this process is aerobic respiration ('aerobic' means 'with oxygen'). The unwanted waste products, carbon dioxide and water, must be removed from the muscles, so they are carried away by the blood.

During vigorous exercise, the lungs, heart, and blood system cannot always deliver oxygen fast enough for aerobic respiration.

Above Antagonistic (opposing) muscles in the arm. One muscle pulls the arm up, the other pulls it down again. Muscles have to be arranged in pairs like this because the nerve impulses which control them can only make them contract (shorten). They have to be pulled back to their original length again.

Right Exhaustion at the finish of an Olympic marathon. The problem is not just tiredness, but a build-up of lactic acid in the muscles which stops them working properly, and causes the legs to go wobbly. Lactic acid is produced whenever the muscles' demand for oxygen is more than the athlete's blood can supply.

THE FUEL FACTORY

Most engines run on only one type of fuel. It is usually petrol or diesel oil. The human engine can run on a wide variety of fuels – bread, potatoes, pizzas, spaghetti, eggs, rice, chocolate biscuits – whatever food you happen to fancy.

Most of the foods you eat cannot be directly used by the body as fuel. First, they must be processed by the body's 'fuel factory'. They must be changed into substances like glucose which will dissolve and can be carried by the blood. Changing food into a dissolved form is called digestion.

Digestion starts in your mouth when food is chewed and mixed with saliva. But it mainly takes place in the stomach and small intestine. These are part of the alimentary canal, or gut – a long tube which runs right through your body from mouth to anus. Parts of the gut are coiled up, but if it were stretched out it would be over 7 metres long.

As food passes along the gut, chemicals called enzymes get to work on it and change it into a dissolved form. Liquid substances, like glucose, then pass through the wall of the gut and into the bloodstream. This process is called absorption. It mainly takes place in the small intestine.

Some of the materials in food are not digested: the fibre in vegetables and fruits, for example. These, mixed with some unwanted water, pass out of the anus when you use the toilet. Fibre may be wasted by the body, but it is still an important part of a healthy diet. It provides bulk which helps to keep food moving along the gut and prevents constipation.

Right The alimentary canal, or gut, runs from the mouth to the anus. In the stomach and small intestine, food is digested – it is broken down into a form which will dissolve. In the small intestine, dissolved food is absorbed by the blood. In the large intestine, much of the remaining water is absorbed. This leaves a semi-solid waste containing undigested food.

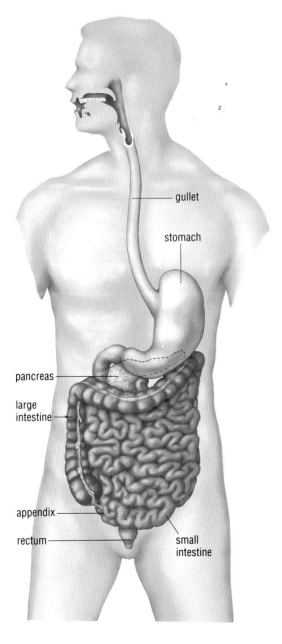

gullet

stomach

pancreas

large intestine

appendix

rectum

small intestine

CHEWING CHANGES

Bread contains starch, which does not dissolve in water. When you chew a piece of bread, it is mixed with saliva. This contains an enzyme that changes starch into glucose sugar – which does dissolve in water. Changing starch into glucose in your mouth is the first stage of digestion.

Try chewing a piece of bread very slowly for about five minutes. The taste should get sweeter as more and more starch is changed into glucose.

FUEL IN STORE

When you eat a meal, your digestive system gets to work on the food and produces plenty of glucose – the body's main fuel. This fuel ends up in the blood, but you cannot normally use all of it straight away. Much of it must be put into storage.

Storing fuel is one of the jobs done by the liver. It takes unwanted glucose from the blood and changes it into a substance called glycogen, which it can store. Later, if you need extra fuel, the liver changes glycogen back into glucose. Muscles also store glycogen, which can readily be changed into glucose as and when required.

There is limit to how much glycogen the body can hold, but fortunately the body has another way of storing surplus food. It can change it into fat. Later, if more fuel is required and all the body's glycogen has been used up, fat can be converted back into glucose. Fat is a useful reserve of stored energy. It means that humans can live for weeks without taking in food. It may be unhealthy to have too much fat, but it is important to have some.

THE FUEL LEAGUE

Food provides us with our fuel, and therefore our energy. Energy is measured in joules (J). A joule is about as much energy as you would need to lift this book upwards about 10 centimetres. A larger unit of energy is the kilojoule (kJ). 1 kilojoule is 1000 joules.

Some foods are a more concentrated source of energy than others. To compare different foods, their energy values are often given in kilojoules per 100 grams. You have probably seen this information printed on cans and packets. The table below the chart on the right gives some recommended average daily energy intakes, but actual requirements depend on how active people are.

Above The body can use a whole variety of foods as its fuel, but many of them have to be cooked first. Cooking kills microbes that might otherwise be harmful to the body. It also makes some foods more digestible.

Energy per 100 g in kJ	Types of food
600 to 1200	Mostly protein with a lot of fat and oil. Many vitamins, especially in fish oil.
300 to 3000	Mostly fat, especially butter and cheese. Eggs have a lot of protein and many vitamins.
1000 to 1600	Mostly starchy carbohydrate with a little protein. Some vitamins in wholemeal bread.
40 to 350	Contain a lot of water, some carbohydrate and protein. Very little fat. Very rich in vitamins.
100 to 300	Contain a lot of water with some carbohydrate and a little protein. Rich in vitamin C.
1000 to 2300	Mostly carbohydrate, especially sugar, with some fat and a little protein. No vitamins.

meat and fish
dairy produce
cereals
vegetables
fruit
sweets and cakes

Recommended daily energy intake		
Age	Boy	Girl
7–8	8250 kJ	8000 kJ
9–11	9500 kJ	8500 kJ
12–14	11,000 kJ	9000 kJ
15–17	12,000 kJ	9000 kJ

Above This chart shows a range of common foods and what they contain. It also gives in kilojoules typical amounts of energy obtained from each 100 grams of these foods. Fats are the most concentrated source of energy.

There are five main types of food: carbohydrates, fats, proteins, minerals, and vitamins.

Carbohydrates include sugary foods like sweet fruits and jam. They also include starchy foods such as bread, potatoes, rice, flour, cereals, and spaghetti. Carbohydrates are our main source of fuel. Overall, they provide us with about 50 per cent of our energy.

Fats include butter and cheese. They provide about 40 per cent of our energy. However, they are a very concentrated energy source, so we do not need to eat much of them.

Proteins are found in eggs, cheese, meat, and fish. They are used mainly for the growth and repair of body tissues. However, any spare protein can be turned into fuel.

Minerals are present in small quantities in many foods. They have no energy value, but are needed, in tiny amounts, for many of the body's functions. Minerals that we require include sodium, calcium, and iron. However, they must be taken in sparingly. For example, sodium comes from common salt, but a salty diet is very unhealthy.

Vitamins are another group of chemicals needed by the body in small quantities. They too have no energy value, but they are necessary so that vital chemical reactions in the body can work properly.

Most of the things we eat contain a mixture of the five types of food, although there may be more of one type than another. For example, we think of bread as a carbohydrate, yet it also contains some protein. In fact, a good proportion of our daily protein can come from bread because we eat so much of it.

Left This weightlifter is lifting over 150 kg. To produce a performance like this, a special diet is needed, as well as many hours of training. The diet must provide lots of energy, but also plenty of protein to build up muscles.

Right The strongest weightlifters of all are the super-heavyweights. Here you can see a typical daily menu for just one of them. It would be very unhealthy for most people.

WEIGHTLIFTER'S DAILY MENU

1 grapefruit	1 bowl cornflakes
7 pints milk	
8 steaks	12 eggs
30 slices of bread	1 kg cheese
	1 kg butter
4 tins pilchards	2 tins baked beans
1 rice pudding	1 pot honey

BODY CONTROL

Like any complex machine, the body needs a control system. This must sense what is happening in the outside world, and also monitor what is happening inside the body. People often say that we have five senses: sight, hearing, touch, taste, and smell. But parts of our body can sense things that we are not always aware of, like blood temperature and the amount of glucose. For the body to work properly, there are many factors which have to be monitored and controlled.

Minute-to-minute control of the body is carried out by the central nervous system. This has two main parts: the brain and the spinal cord. These are linked to the different areas of the body by nerves.

Some nerves have tiny sensors at the ends. They respond to changes by sending out electrical signals called nerve impulses. For example, there are sensors in your skin for detecting pressure, temperature, touch, and pain. And there are sensors in your ears which respond to sound.

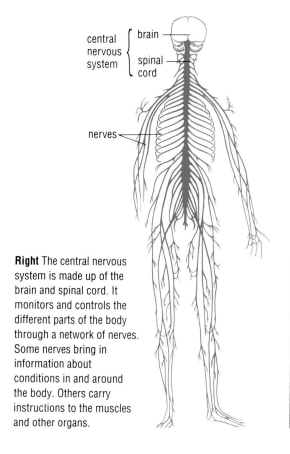

central
nervous { brain
system { spinal
cord

nerves

Right The central nervous system is made up of the brain and spinal cord. It monitors and controls the different parts of the body through a network of nerves. Some nerves bring in information about conditions in and around the body. Others carry instructions to the muscles and other organs.

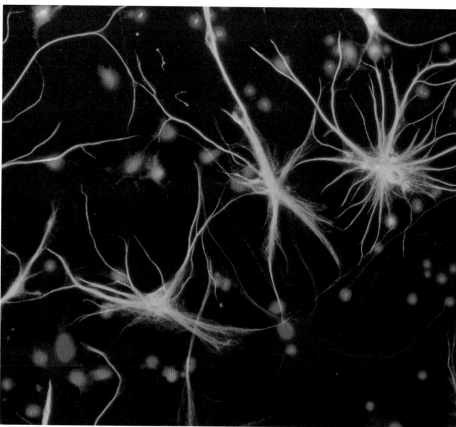

Your body also has internal sensors, such as those which detect changes in glucose and carbon dioxide levels in the blood.

Sensors send their signals along nerves to the central nervous system. There, they are processed. Then signals are sent back along another set of nerves, called motor nerves. These signals might make you move an arm or leg, or blink your eyes.

You have conscious control over some movements; for example, you can decide to nod your head or wiggle your fingers. However there are some actions which happen automatically – reflex actions. Reflex actions include blinking your eyes, and dropping something hot when you pick it up.

Not all of your body's changes are controlled by nerve impulses. Some instructions are carried round the body by chemical messengers called hormones. Hormones are chemicals produced by the endocrine glands and put into the bloodstream. For example, a hormone from the pituitary gland affects the rate at which you grow. And a hormone called insulin from glands in the pancreas affects how quickly your liver changes glucose into glycogen.

REFLEX ACTION
You can watch one of your muscles give a reflex action. Sit on a chair or stool. Cross your legs so that one is resting just above the knee of the other. Ask a friend to tap the higher leg just under the kneecap with the bottom of a spoon. If the tap is in the right place, your leg will automatically kick upwards, and there is nothing you can do to stop it! The muscle movement is completely automatic.

REACTION TIME
It takes time for nerve impulses to travel to and from the brain. That is why there is a brief delay before you react to things which you see.

Here is a test to find your reaction time. Ask a friend to hold a ruler at one end so that it hangs vertically. Put your finger and thumb either side of the other end, but without touching it. Tell your friend to let go of the ruler without giving you any warning. Watch the ruler closely. As soon as it drops, try to catch it between your finger and thumb. See how far along the scale you have caught it. The further it falls, the slower is your reaction time. Here are some distances, with corresponding reaction times in brackets (10/100 s means 10 hundredths of a second, and so on):

5 cm (10/100 s)	20 cm (20/100 s)
10 cm (14/100 s)	25 cm (23/100 s)
15 cm (17/100 s)	30 cm (25/100 s)

Above Nerve cells and their supporting cells in the spinal cord, magnified 900 times. The nerve cells are shown in red and pink, with faint nerve fibres coming from them. The green and blue parts are cells which support the nerve cells and supply them with the substances they need.

A SENSE OF BALANCE

It is difficult to make a doll or model figure stand up, but real people do not normally have this problem. They have a sense of balance. Some people have an especially good sense of balance. They can walk on stilts or tightropes, or do somersaults on narrow beams.

Even standing on flat ground, you are still balancing. Sensors detect any tiny movements and send signals to your brain. The brain sends motor signals to your feet and toes so that they adjust their push on the ground.

The balance sensors are situated in your inner ears. In each ear, there are three fluid-filled tubes called the semicircular canals, arranged so they can detect movement in three directions. Each canal has a bulge at one end which contains a blob of jelly. When you move your head, fluid flows past the blob and makes it move. The blob pulls on tiny hairs. These pull on a nerve which sends signals to the brain.

Next to the semicircular canals is a larger fluid-filled bulge called the ear sac. This too contains a blob of jelly, but the blob has tiny bits of chalk in it to make it heavier. If you tilt your head, the weight of the blob makes it change position. This time, the signals from the nerve tell your brain whether you are upright or not.

Sometimes, the signals from the semicircular canals do not quite match those from your eyes – perhaps because your body is being rocked about. The confusion in the brain can make you feel sick. Travel sickness may be caused in this way.

Above For work like this, you need a very good sense of balance! To maintain balance, the brain is constantly processing information from the eyes and from the semicircular canals in the inner ears, and sending instructions to the muscles in the arms, legs, feet, and back.

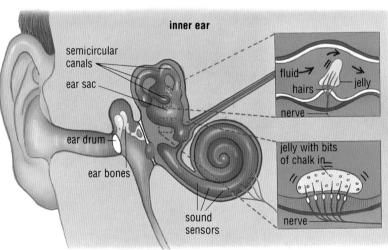

Left The organs of balance are situated in the inner ear. They are the semicircular canals and the ear sac. Sensors (nerve endings) in the semicircular canals detect a flow of fluid when your head moves. Sensors in the ear sac detect whether your head is upright. They do so by sensing the position of a blob of jelly and chalk.

EXTREME CONDITIONS

The human machine is designed for warm, tropical conditions. It cannot naturally cope with the lower temperatures found in areas far north and south of the Equator. Fortunately, humans have found a way round this problem: we wear clothes to keep in our body heat. But some environments are so harsh and extreme that special suits are needed to keep us alive and active. For example, space suits and deep-sea diving suits must maintain the correct pressure and temperature, as well as supplying air and removing the gases breathed out.

COMPARISONS

The human machine has been around in more or less its present form for several million years. Cars have existed for a much shorter time – not much more than 100 years.

In some ways, humans and cars are similar. Both consume fuel and oxygen, and both produce carbon dioxide and water. But the human machine has self-repairing parts which last longer, and it does not need costly roads. When the going is really tough, the human machine can get through.

	Car	Human
Engine(s)	Petrol or diesel engine	Muscles
Fuel	Petrol or diesel fuel	Any food, which is then converted to glucose
Gas required for engine(s) to work	Oxygen	Oxygen
Waste materials produced	Carbon dioxide, water (+ carbon monoxide, unburnt fuel, and oxides of nitrogen, unless catalytic converter is fitted)	Carbon dioxide, water, biodegradable organic waste
Load-carrying ability (typical)	1000 kg	20 kg
Energy needed to travel 1 km on level ground (typical)	2500 kJ	100 kJ
Maximum speed (typical)	160 km per hour (100 mph)	25 km per hour (15 mph)
Ability to cross ground	Smooth surface normally required, but some types can cross rough ground up to 45° steep	Can cross extremely rough and mountainous ground, climb trees and cliffs, and also cross water
Servicing and maintenance	Major service required at least once a year; some parts (e.g. tyres) need replacing regularly	Largely self-repairing; occasional health checks needed, and sometimes medical treatment
Lifespan (typical)	10 years	75 years

Left How the human machine compares with the car. Humans may be slower and less powerful, but they are far more versatile, less fussy about their fuel, and they last longer. Their engines are less polluting, but unfortunately their activities cause a great deal of pollution in other ways.

Below The human machine can only operate in extreme conditions like this if protective clothing is worn. Here, a firefighter is wearing an aluminium suit which can withstand the flames, but even this cannot offer protection against intense heat for more than a few minutes.

ENERGY FOREVER

O ur food supplies us with energy. Our transport and industries rely on energy from oil and other fuels. Without energy, nothing would ever get done. But what is energy? Where does it come from? And what happens to it when we have used it?

*I*f you have to ride a bicycle uphill, it can be very hard work. Pushing the pedals round tires you out. People say that it 'uses up energy'. But pushing does not always use up energy. If you rest a bicycle against a fence, there are forces pushing on the fence and also on the ground. But the fence and the ground do not get tired out! That is because there is no movement. It seems that energy is only 'used up' when a force makes something move.

WHAT IS ENERGY?

Energy is what makes things move. Food has energy because your body can use it to make your muscles move. Fuels have energy because engines can use them to produce motion. Batteries have energy because they can make electric motors spin round.

Heat is a form of energy. This may seem puzzling because an electric fire does not appear to move when it gets hot. In fact, there is movement, but you cannot see it. The atoms in any solid are always vibrating. If the solid is heated up, its atoms vibrate faster. This means that billions of tiny forces are giving the atoms extra speed.

Scientists measure energy in joules (J). A joule is about as much energy as you would need to lift this book about 10 cm. Lifting more books would require more energy. Lifting them over a greater distance would take more energy still.

Whenever a force moves something, scientists say that work is done. The bigger the force and the further it moves, the more work is done. This means that there is a link between energy and work. If something has energy, it can do work. Like energy, work is measured in joules. In lifting this book about 10 cm, you would be doing about one joule of work.

So, energy is not really a 'thing' at all. An energy value in joules is a 'bank balance' of work that can be 'spent' in the future. The work may produce motion which you can see, like an aircraft taking off. Or it may produce motion which you cannot see, as happens when an electric fire heats up and its atoms move faster.

Left By burning fuel, a large power station like this can supply about 2 million joules of energy every second. The clouds from the wide cooling towers are just steam, but waste gases from the tall chimney pollute the atmosphere and add to global warming.

Right Even on the flat, a cyclist has to spend energy to overcome frictional forces such as air resistance. But uphill cycling takes even more energy because there is the force of gravity to overcome as well. Eventually, all energy that is spent ends up as heat.

Forms of Energy

Energy can exist in many different forms, but whatever form it takes, it can be used to make things move. There may be large forces producing motion you can see, or small forces producing motion you cannot see, like the movements of atoms or their particles.

These are the main forms of energy (with examples of things that have them): kinetic energy (anything moving); potential energy (anything stretched, compressed, or held above the ground); heat energy (things which can cool down); chemical energy (food, fuels, batteries); radiant energy (light, sound); electrical energy (electric currents); nuclear energy (nucleus of an atom).

Below Energy can exist in many different forms. It can change from one form to another, but can never be lost or destroyed. If things have energy, they can make things move. However, the movements may be too small to see – for example, atoms vibrating faster.

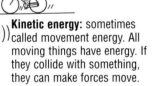

Kinetic energy: sometimes called movement energy. All moving things have energy. If they collide with something, they can make forces move.

Potential energy: this is stored energy which things have because of their position or what has been done to them. A rock balanced on a cliff has potential energy. A stretched rubber band also has potential energy. If the rock falls, or the rubber band springs back, the stored energy is released.

Heat: everything is made of atoms which are constantly on the move. If something cools down, its atoms move more slowly. The energy given out is called heat.

Chemical energy: this is stored energy which can be released by chemical reactions. Foods, fuels, and batteries store chemical energy. For example, burning is a chemical reaction which releases energy from fuel.

Radiant energy: light, heat radiation, X-rays, and sound are all examples of radiant energy. Many types of radiant energy, travel in the form of waves.

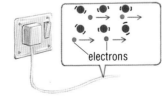

electrons

Electrical energy: this is the energy carried by an electric current. A current is a flow of tiny particles called electrons.

Nuclear energy: this is energy stored in the nucleus (the centre) of the atom.

APPLES AND ENERGY

When Isaac Newton sat under an apple tree, so the old story goes, an apple fell on his head. This is one way of getting energy from an apple. Another, and better, way is to eat it. The chemical energy an apple stores is about 100,000 times more than its kinetic energy when falling.

In general, the chemical energy stored in foods and fuels is on a much larger scale than the potential and kinetic energies of the things standing or moving around us. This influences industrial societies in how they decide to obtain their energy. For example, to replace one fuel-burning power station, it would take 500 giant, wind-driven generators. This is because fuels are a much more concentrated source of energy than moving air.

Changing but Keeping

Energy can change from one form to another. Think about the energy changes which occur before and after you eat an apple. The apple tree has absorbed energy radiated from the Sun. As the apple grew, some of this was stored as chemical energy. When you eat the apple, its chemical energy is stored in your body. You release this energy by a chemical reaction called respiration (see page 67). As a result, you can move your muscles. So some of the chemical energy is changed into kinetic energy.

You can think of this process as an energy chain, with energy being changed into different forms as it passes along the chain. However, at each stage of the chain, some energy is wasted as heat. Even the kinetic energy you have when you move about is eventually changed into heat, as friction from the ground and the air finally slows you down.

Scientists have studied many energy chains. As a result, they have discovered a law about energy: it can change into different forms, but it can never be made, and it can never be lost or destroyed. This is called the law of conservation of energy. Conservation means 'keeping'. The law has this name because it tells you that the same total amount of energy is kept all the way along a chain.

Everything that happens in the Universe is part of an energy chain. We often talk about 'using energy', but we never really use it up. We just pass it on in some other form. Eventually, it ends up as heat, but this becomes so spread out that it can be impossible to detect or use.

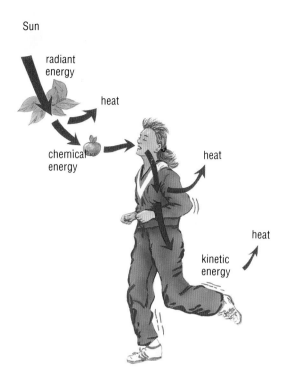

Sun

radiant energy

heat

chemical energy

heat

kinetic energy

heat

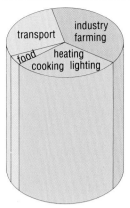

transport
industry
farming
food
heating
cooking lighting

Left The taller block shows how energy is used for each person in an industrialized country. The volume of the block represents the amount of energy.
Below The shorter block shows how it is used for each person in a developing country. People in industrialized countries use far more energy and are much more wasteful with it.

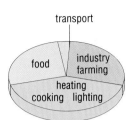

transport
food
industry
farming
heating
cooking lighting

Left This energy chain shows how energy passes from the Sun to a plant, to food, and then to a person. The energy changes form several times. However, the total amount of energy is unchanged. At every stage, some energy is wasted as heat. Eventually all the energy ends up as heat.

SUPPLYING THE ENERGY

Industrial societies need a huge amount of energy to run their factories, homes, and transport systems. Much of this energy comes from burning oil, coal, and natural gas. The majority of power stations use these fuels, and most cars, buses, and trucks run on petrol or diesel fuel, both of which are made from oil.

Oil, coal, and natural gas are extracted from the ground. They are called fossil fuels because

Below Niagara Falls, on the US–Canadian border. Water from the river falls more than 45 m, changing potential energy into kinetic energy. Some of this energy is then converted to electrical energy in a hydroelectric power station.

they were formed from the remains of plants and tiny sea creatures which lived on Earth many millions of years ago. The decaying remains became buried and then crushed. More and more mud built up above them and eventually turned to rock, which trapped the fossil fuels underneath.

The Earth has only limited supplies of fossil fuels. Once gone, there will be no way of replacing them. At present rates of use, there is probably enough oil and natural gas left to last 50 years or so, and enough coal to last about 300 years.

Apart from supply problems, fossil fuels have a heavy environmental cost. When they burn, they pollute the atmosphere. Some pollutants can be removed by, for example, catalytic converters on cars and desulphurization units in coal-burning power stations. However, even the cleanest exhaust gases still contain plenty of carbon dioxide gas. In the atmosphere, carbon dioxide traps the Sun's heat, rather like the glass in a greenhouse. This adds to global warming, which is also called the greenhouse effect.

Below Most power stations use heat to generate electricity. The heat comes from burning coal, oil, or gas, or from a nuclear reactor. In most cases, the heat is used to make steam to turn turbines which drive generators. However, combined-cycle gas turbines also have a generator that is turned by the shaft of a jet engine.

Unfortunately, power stations that rely on heat for their energy actually waste more energy than they deliver. This is not poor design. There are scientific limits to the percentage of heat that can ever be used to produce motion (see page 159). Much of the wasted energy is lost as heat through the cooling system.

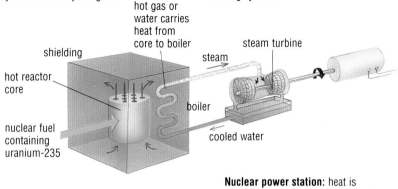

Nuclear power station: heat is released by the fission (splitting) of uranium-235 nuclei in the reactor core. The heat is used to make steam in a boiler. The steam turns a turbine which drives the generator.

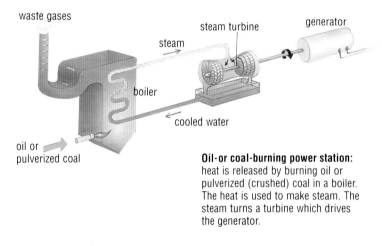

Oil- or coal-burning power station: heat is released by burning oil or pulverized (crushed) coal in a boiler. The heat is used to make steam. The steam turns a turbine which drives the generator.

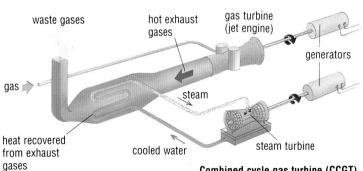

Combined cycle gas turbine (CCGT) power station: gas is used as the fuel for a gas turbine (jet engine). The shaft of the engine turns one generator. Heat from the jet exhaust is used to make steam to drive another generator.

Right Today, the world's oil supplies are running out, and they cannot be replaced because the processes which form this valuable liquid take hundreds of millions of years. This diagram gives you some idea of how fast supplies are dwindling. At the present rate of use, even allowing for more finds, there may only be enough oil left to last for another 50 years.

In nuclear power stations, the heat to raise steam for the turbines comes not from burning fuel, but from fission in a nuclear reactor (see page 101). Power stations like this do not produce large amounts of polluting gases. However, they are expensive to build, and expensive to shut down at the end of their working life. They need extremely high safety standards, and also produce radioactive waste which is difficult to dispose of safely.

There are some alternatives to fossil fuels and nuclear power. Hydroelectric schemes generate electricity using the potential energy of water behind a dam. Aerogenerators (generators driven by windmills) use the kinetic energy of the wind. Solar panels absorb the radiant energy from the Sun and use it to heat up water.

One advantage of these alternative energy sources is that they are renewable – when the energy has been delivered, there is always more to take its place. However, one disadvantage is that none can challenge oil as a convenient and concentrated source of energy for vehicles. Electricity from power stations can be used to charge up batteries in electric cars, but manufacturers are reluctant to make electric cars because they cannot offer the performance of fuel-burning vehicles.

Right These aerogenerators (wind-powered generators) are part of a large wind farm in California, USA. With a scheme like this, there are no burning fuels to pollute the air, but noise levels are high, and hundreds of generators are needed to match the output of a conventional power station.

Below This solar-powered car travelled nearly 3000 km across Australia at an average speed of 65 km/h. Banks of solar cells on its back and sides absorbed enough of the Sun's energy to charge the batteries for its electric motor.

Without good insulation, houses waste energy. The walls and roof account for nearly half the energy lost. Draughts account for about a third. Heat losses and draughts can be reduced, but with people living in the house, there must be regular air changes.

WASTE OR SAVE?

In industrialized countries, people tend to be very wasteful with energy. However, there are some ways that savings can be made.

Transporting people by car takes twice as much energy per person as transporting them by bus. If a car is only carrying one person, the figure rises to eight times. So encouraging people to use public transport is one way of saving energy.

Fuel-burning power stations waste more than a half of their energy as heat. Production of this heat is unavoidable, but it can be used to supply the surrounding district with hot water for heating systems.

Household rubbish is often dumped in landfill sites, such as old quarries. But it can be used as a source of energy. Rotting waste gives off methane gas, which can be collected and used as a fuel. Some power stations can burn waste directly as a fuel.

Below Some of the ways in which insulating materials are used in a modern house. Usually the insulation stops heat getting out, but with a refrigerator or freezer it has to stop heat getting in.

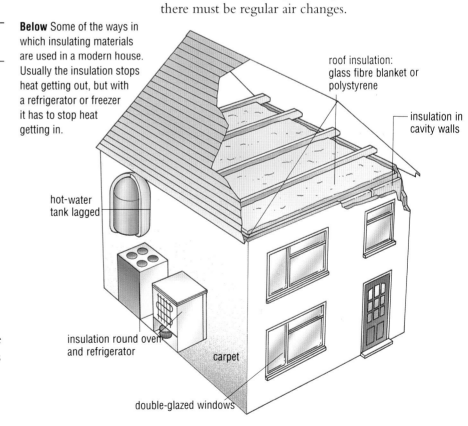

roof insulation: glass fibre blanket or polystyrene

insulation in cavity walls

hot-water tank lagged

insulation round oven and refrigerator

carpet

double-glazed windows

ENERGY FROM THE SUN

In one way or another, nearly all of our energy has come from the Sun. Plants absorb the energy in sunlight, so their energy comes from the Sun. Animals, including humans, feed on plants or on animals which have fed on plants, so their energy also comes from the Sun. Fossil fuels contain energy from the Sun which was trapped by plants many millions of years ago. Even the energy from wind and water originally came from the Sun. Winds arise because the Sun heats some parts of the Earth more than others, and this makes air move. In hydroelectric schemes, where lakes are filled by rainwater, the rain got into the air in the first place because the Sun's heat made water evaporate from rivers, seas, and oceans.

WHERE DOES THE SUN GET ITS ENERGY?

The Sun has been shining for 4500 million years. Humans have been relying on its heat and light for over a million years. But only during the last century has the secret of its energy source been discovered.

By the middle of the 19th century, scientists had measured the Sun's heat output. From geological evidence, they had also realized that the Earth was probably many hundreds of millions of years old. The Sun must have been heating the Earth for all this time. How could it have been pouring out energy for so long? No known process could explain it; if the Sun burnt its fuel, like a fire, its chemical energy would have long since run out. Science had to come up with some new energy source!

By the early 1900s, researchers were investigating the recently discovered phenomenon of radioactivity. In time, it became clear that the nucleus of an atom could release energy, and that this might be the source of the Sun's energy. Today, we know that the Sun gets it energy from nuclear fusion (see page 102). Deep in its core, hydrogen nuclei combine to form helium nuclei, releasing huge amounts of energy as they do so. Nuclear energy has kept the Sun shining for 4500 million years – and should keep it shining for another 6000 million.

How the world gets its energy

Solar panels absorb energy radiated from the Sun and use it to heat water.

Solar cells use the energy in sunlight to produce small amounts of electricity.

Energy in food We get energy from the food we eat. The food may be from plants, or from animals which fed on plants.

Plants as fuels Wood is still an important fuel in many countries. When wood is burnt, it releases energy which the tree once took in from the Sun. In some countries, sugar cane is grown and fermented to make alcohol, which can be used as a fuel instead of petrol.

Energy from waste Rotting animal and plant waste can give off methane gas (the same as natural gas) which can be used as a fuel. Marshes, rubbish tips, and sewage treatment works are all sources of methane. Some waste can also be used directly as fuel by burning it.

Batteries Some batteries (e.g. in a car) have to be given energy by charging them with electricity. Others are manufactured from chemicals which already store energy. But energy is needed to produce the chemicals in the first place.

The Sun The Sun radiates energy because of nuclear reactions deep inside it. Its output is equivalent to that from 400 million billion billion electric fire elements. Just a tiny fraction reaches the Earth.

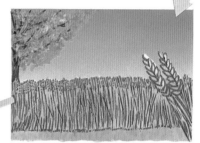

Energy in plants Plants need energy to grow. They take in energy from sunlight which falls on their leaves and use it to turn water and carbon dioxide from the air into new growth. Animals eat plants to get the energy stored in them.

Fossil fuels Coal, oil, and natural gas are called fossil fuels. They were formed from the remains of plants and tiny sea creatures which lived on Earth many millions of years ago. The world's industrial societies rely on fossil fuels for most of their energy. In many power stations, the heat from burning fuels is used to change water into steam. The steam turns turbines which drive electrical generators.

Fuels from oil Oil is a mixture of substances which are used to produce other fuels including: petrol, kerosene (paraffin), jet fuel, central-heating oil, diesel fuel.

IMITATING THE SUN

Scientists and engineers are now trying to design fusion reactors which can be used as an energy source on Earth. However the technical problems are immense. For fusion to start, atoms must collide at very high speeds, which means heating gas to a temperature of 100 million °C or more. The superhot gas, called a plasma, cannot be held in any ordinary container, so it will have to be trapped by a strong magnetic field. In the Sun, fusion happens at 'only' 15 million °C, but the Sun uses a different fusion process which would not give enough energy if scaled down to the conditions possible on Earth.

Fusion reactors will have many advantages over today's nuclear power stations. Some of the hydrogen they need can be extracted from sea water. Their main waste product, helium, is not radioactive, so there is no long-term storage problem with nuclear waste. Also, the reactors have built-in safety: if a fault develops, fusion stops automatically.

One day, fusion reactors may meet much of the world's energy needs. Until then, existing energy resources must be managed carefully so that supplies do not run out and pollution is kept to a minimum.

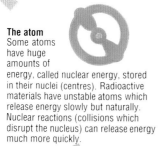

The Moon The gravitational pull of the Moon (and to a lesser extent, the Sun) creates gentle bulges in the Earth's oceans. As the Earth rotates, different places have high and low tides as they pass in and out of the bulges.

The atom Some atoms have huge amounts of energy, called nuclear energy, stored in their nuclei (centres). Radioactive materials have unstable atoms which release energy slowly but naturally. Nuclear reactions (collisions which disrupt the nucleus) can release energy much more quickly.

Geothermal energy Deep underground, the rocks are hotter than they are on the surface. The heat comes from radioactive materials naturally present in the rocks. It can be used to make steam for heating buildings or driving electrical generators.

Tidal energy In a tidal energy scheme, an estuary is dammed to form an artificial lake. Incoming tides fill the lake; outgoing tides empty it. The flow of water in and out of the lake is used to turn generators.

Nuclear power In a reactor, nuclear reactions release energy from nuclei of uranium atoms. This produces heat which is used to make steam for drving electrical generators.

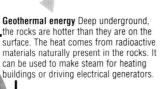

Earth's weather systems These are en by heat radiated from the Sun. Hot sing above the Equator maintains

e energy Waves are caused by the (and partly by tides). Waves cause a up-and-down movement on the ce of the sea. This movement can be to drive electrical generators.

Hydroelectric energy An artificial lake forms behind a dam. Water rushing down from this lake is used to turn generators. The lake is kept full by river water which once fell as rain or snow.

Wind energy For centuries, people have been using the power of the wind to move ships, pump water, and grind corn. Today, huge windmills are used to turn electrical generators.

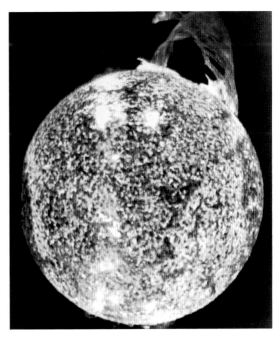

Above The Sun is powered by nuclear fusion deep in its core. Its energy output is equivalent to 20,000 billion billion electric hot plates, and it has enough hydrogen fuel left to keep shining for another 6000 million years.

HOT STUFF

We need heat to stay alive, yet too much is dangerous for us. Fortunately, humans have discovered how heat travels, how to produce it, and how to get rid of it when it is not wanted. But heat has a natural tendency to spread out, and that causes problems when we want to harness its energy.

*F*irewalkers can run across red-hot coals without burning their feet. Is it the power of the mind? Possibly not. Scientists think that it may be because very little heat comes out of the coal. However, this is not an idea to test for yourself!

Scientists have ideas about firewalking because they think they know what heat is and how it behaves. In this chapter you will be discovering some of the secrets of heat.

HOT AND COLD

Imagine two identical spoons, one standing in a hot drink, the other in a cold drink. The spoons look the same, but they certainly do not feel the same. So what is the difference?

Materials are made of atoms, and these are often in clumps called molecules. Atoms and molecules are constantly on the move. In solids and liquids, for example, they vibrate. They do not all vibrate at the same speed but, on average, the hotter something is, the faster its atoms move. So, the atoms in a hot spoon are vibrating faster than in a cold one.

To measure the level of hotness, scientists use a range of numbers called a temperature scale. Depending on which country you are in, temperatures may be given in degrees Celsius (°C), sometimes called 'degrees centigrade', or in degrees Fahrenheit (°F).

The colder something becomes, the slower its atoms move. However, temperature cannot go on falling forever because there is a limit to how slowly the atoms can move. We now know that the lowest possible temperature is -273°C (-459°F). This is called absolute zero.

Nothing has ever been cooled to absolute zero, though scientists have got to within a few millionths of a degree of it. The science of very low temperatures is called cryogenics.

Left When firewalkers run across hot coals, there are several reasons why their feet do not get burnt: they only touch the coals for a fraction of a second; coal is a poor conductor, so it lets heat out slowly; and there is cold water or wet grass to cool the feet at the end of the run. Even so, firewalking is extremely dangerous because of the risk of something going wrong.

FIXING THE ZERO

Minus temperatures, like -273°C, arise because of the way in which the zero is chosen on the temperature scale. On the Celsius scale, 0°C is the temperature of melting ice, so anything colder than melting ice needs a number lower than zero. In other words, it needs a 'minus' number.

Scientists often use the Kelvin temperature scale. This has its zero at absolute zero, so all Kelvin temperatures have positive values. For example, water freezes at 273 K, which is the same as 0°C and 32°F.

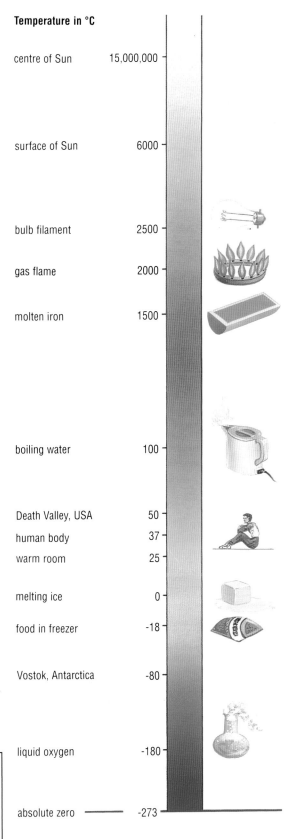

Temperature in °C

centre of Sun	15,000,000
surface of Sun	6000
bulb filament	2500
gas flame	2000
molten iron	1500
boiling water	100
Death Valley, USA	50
human body	37
warm room	25
melting ice	0
food in freezer	-18
Vostok, Antarctica	-80
liquid oxygen	-180
absolute zero	-273

Above Typical temperatures on the Celsius scale. On this scale, ice melts at 0°C and water boils at 100°C under normal conditions. The scale is sometimes called the 'centigrade' scale because there are 100 ('centi') degrees ('grades') between the melting point of ice and the boiling point of water.

Right Heat is the energy which flows from one thing to another because of a temperature difference. Here, atoms in the hotter block are moving faster. They transfer some of their energy to the slower atoms in the colder block. Without the temperature difference, there would be no heat flow.

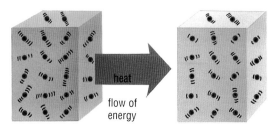

higher temperature

atoms move faster

heat

flow of energy

lower temperature

atoms move slower

WHAT IS HEAT?

Scientists often say that heat is a form of energy. This is a useful idea, but it does not really explain very much. It is much easier to say what heat is not!

Heat is not the same as temperature. A kettleful of boiling water is at the same temperature as a spoonful of boiling water, but it contains more heat and would give you a much nastier scald. Heat is not an invisible substance, although people once thought it was when they realized it could flow.

To understand what heat is, think about a hot spoon cooling in air. As the atoms in the spoon are moving, they have energy. When the spoon cools, its atoms lose energy and slow down. The atoms around it gain energy and speed up. So, there is a flow of energy from the hot spoon to the cooler air. 'Heat' is the word used to describe the energy transferred. Heat is not really a 'thing' at all!

Below These columns of steel have just come out of a foundry. They are still glowing red-hot at a temperature of over 1000°C. As in other solids, the atoms in the steel are vibrating. But when the atoms lose energy, their vibrations will become less and the temperature will fall.

BIGGER AND BIGGER

There is another difference between a hot spoon and a cold spoon. A hot spoon is slightly bigger than a cold one – though by such a small amount that you would never notice.

Most materials expand when heated. For example, if a teaspoon is put in boiling water it becomes about 1/10 mm longer! The bigger vibrations of the atoms cause the expansion. The more the atoms vibrate, the more they push each other apart.

Engineers have to allow for expansion when building large structures. For example, if you look at motorway bridges, you will see that tiny gaps have been left in the concrete at the ends for expansion.

HEAT ON THE MOVE: CONDUCTION

If you leave a metal spoon in a hot drink, the whole handle soon becomes hot, though only a part of it is in the liquid. This is because heat flows along the spoon. The metal is a good conductor of heat.

Solids conduct heat because atoms vibrating faster at one end pass on some of their energy to their neighbours and make them vibrate faster, and so on through the material.

Metals are the best conductors of all. This is because they have tiny particles called electrons moving freely between their atoms. These 'free electrons' have escaped from the atoms, and can carry energy quickly from one part of the metal to another. An electric current is also a flow of free electrons. That is why metals are good conductors of electricity as well as heat.

Liquids are usually poor conductors of heat, and gases are even worse.

flow of heat by conduction

higher-temperature end

lower-temperature end

Above Heat is travelling along this bar by conduction. Fast-moving atoms at the hottest end of the bar gradually pass on energy to their slower-moving neighbours.

HEAT ON THE MOVE: CONVECTION

Hot air rises. In a room with a heater, hot air will rise above the heater and cooler air will move in to take its place. The result is a circulating current of air called a convection current, which quickly carries heat around the room. Air is a poor conductor of heat, but it can transfer heat very rapidly by convection.

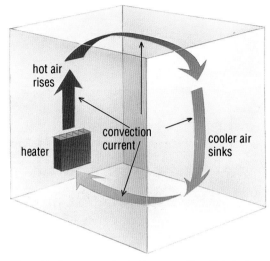

Above Most rooms are heated by convection. Hot air rises above a heater. Cooler air flows in to take its place. In this way, all the air in the room is gradually warmed up. Even so-called radiators work by convection.

Convection can take place in liquids as well as gases. If you watch the movement of peas in a pan of boiling water, you will see how the heat makes the water rise and fall in circulating currents.

Sometimes, natural convection currents arise in air. These are called thermals. They are produced when the Sun heats up things like rocks or buildings, and these warm the air above them. Soaring birds use thermals to carry them upwards. So do gliders. By flying from one thermal to another, both can stay airborne for hours.

Convection drives the Earth's wind and weather systems. Regions near the Equator receive most heat from the Sun. Hot air rising above the equator sets up huge circulating currents in the atmosphere. The Earth's rotation affects the movement of air in these cells, causing belts (zones) of wind around the Earth. In Britain, for example, winds tend to blow in from the south-west.

Above Hang-gliders can be carried upwards by thermals (rising currents of hot air). However, the problem for the pilot is to find a thermal.

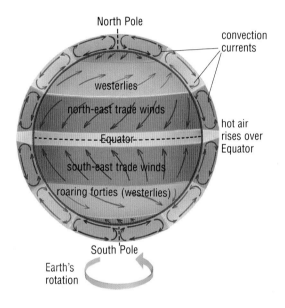

Left Hot air rising above the Equator sets up convection cells in the atmosphere. These, together with the Earth's rotation, give the Earth its wind belts. In each belt, there are prevailing winds – winds which tend to keep blowing in the same direction.

HEAT ON THE MOVE: RADIATION

There is empty space between the Earth and the Sun, so there is nothing to carry heat by conduction or convection. Yet the Sun's heat still reaches us. This is because the Sun radiates its energy in the form of waves which can travel through empty space. They are called electromagnetic waves and include infrared and light waves. (You can find out more about them on pages 171–175.) If we absorb these waves, their energy makes us hot. People sometimes call them 'heat radiation', or just 'radiation' for short.

Above The Hubble Space Telescope in orbit above the Earth. The shiny foil is necessary to protect the telescope from the Sun's heat radiation.

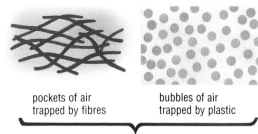

pockets of air trapped by fibres

bubbles of air trapped by plastic

insulating materials

Above Many materials are good insulators because they trap tiny pockets or bubbles of air. Air, on the other hand, is a very poor conductor of heat.

Above Penguins need very good insulation to protect them from the intense cold of Antarctic winters. They have to rely on a thick layer of body fat as well as their feathers which trap air to keep warm.

Some surfaces are better at absorbing heat radiation than others. If a black car and a white car are left side by side in a car park on a sunny day, the black car becomes hotter inside than the white car. This is because black is a better absorber of radiation than white. White reflects much of the radiation that strikes it. Shiny surfaces are the best reflectors of all, and therefore the worst absorbers. Poor absorbers of heat radiation are also poor at giving it off. For example, a shiny kettle or saucepan retains heat better than a black one.

Insulating materials that rely on trapped air include fur, feathers, wool, fibreglass, and plastic foam. Materials like this stop heat entering or escaping, so they can be used to keep things cool as well as hot.

CUTTING THE FLOW

Very poor conductors of heat are called insulators. They include materials like cork, rubber, plastics – and air.

Air is one of the best insulators of all. However, it must be trapped in tiny pockets or bubbles, otherwise it will circulate and carry heat by convection.

HOLDING HEAT

If a material takes in heat, its temperature rises. However, some materials are better at storing heat than others – in other words, they are better reservoirs of heat. Water is especially good; much more heat is needed to warm up water than the same weight of rock, concrete, or metal. And this heat can be given out again when the water cools down. But being a good storer of heat is not the same as being a good conductor of heat. Water, for example, is a poor conductor.

Right When water heats up, it absorbs nearly 10 times as much heat as the same weight of steel for the same temperature rise. That is one of the reasons why water is used as a heat carrier in car cooling systems and in central-heating systems.

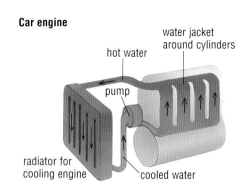

Car engine

water jacket around cylinders

hot water

pump

radiator for cooling engine

cooled water

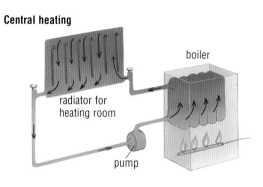

Central heating

boiler

radiator for heating room

pump

Water is often used as a heat carrier. The coolant in a car engine is mainly water. It passes through a metal jacket around the cylinders in the engine and carries waste heat to the radiator. Water is also used in central-heating systems to carry heat from the boiler to the radiators.

The Earth's oceans act as a huge heat store which affects the climate. They warm up more slowly than the land, and they cool down more slowly as well. That is why the sea can still be warm in autumn even when land temperatures are low.

BODY HEAT

You depend on your body heat. Without it, your 'engines' (muscles) would not work properly, nor would all the other vital chemical reactions needed to maintain life. Your fingers and toes do not necessarily need to be warm, but it is important that the temperature of the central part of the body stays close to about 37°C. This central part is called the core.

The body has several automatic systems for keeping its temperature steady, including sweating, shivering, and changing the blood flow near the skin. However, sometimes you have to help the process by putting on extra layers of clothing – or taking them off again. If you are 'running your engines' (moving your muscles), this generates heat for the body.

Humans are not the only creatures to maintain a steady body temperature. All other mammals (the furry animals) do, and so do birds. Animals like this are called homoiothermic or 'warm-blooded'.

The 'engines' (muscles) of warm-blooded animals are always ready for action and can work rapidly. However, warm-bloodedness is very expensive on energy. Most of the food we eat is used to produce body heat and maintain our body temperature. Much less is used to produce movement.

Other animals do not have automatic temperature control. They are poikilothermic, or 'cold-blooded'. Examples include fish, amphibians (such as frogs and newts), and reptiles (such as snakes and lizards.)

Below The main ways in which the body gains and loses heat. Humans need to maintain a core temperature of about 37°C. For this to stay steady, the body's heat gains must exactly match its heat losses.

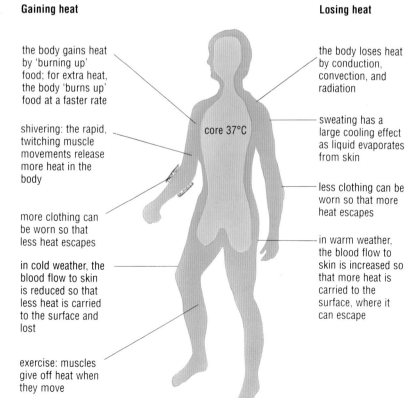

Gaining heat

the body gains heat by 'burning up' food; for extra heat, the body 'burns up' food at a faster rate

shivering: the rapid, twitching muscle movements release more heat in the body

more clothing can be worn so that less heat escapes

in cold weather, the blood flow to skin is reduced so that less heat is carried to the surface and lost

exercise: muscles give off heat when they move

core 37°C

Losing heat

the body loses heat by conduction, convection, and radiation

sweating has a large cooling effect as liquid evaporates from skin

less clothing can be worn so that more heat escapes

in warm weather, the blood flow to skin is increased so that more heat is carried to the surface, where it can escape

Right Like other reptiles, this agamid lizard does not have automatic temperature control. However, it cannot be active if its body temperature is too low. To warm itself up, it must move out of the shade and bask in the sunshine.

'Cold-blooded' is not really a true description of these animals because they still need warm bodies for their muscles to work quickly. But they have to control their body temperature by moving about. For example, lizards may move into the sunshine or back into the shade. When their bodies cool down, they move more slowly. However, they need much less food than warm-blooded animals of a similar size. Crocodiles, being cold-blooded, only need a meal every few weeks, whereas lions, which are warm-blooded, have to spend most of their time hunting for food.

BIG OR SMALL?

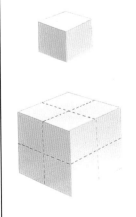

Size affects how well an animal keeps its body heat. To find out why, compare the two blocks of warm metal on the left. The big block is equal to eight small ones joined together, so it holds eight times as much heat. However, it has only four times the surface area from which to lose its heat, so it cools down more slowly. Check the areas for yourself. The small block has six grey squares over its surface, the large block has 24.

Now think of a small animal and a large one – say, a mouse and an elephant. They are rather like the small block and the big one! Being smaller, the mouse tends to lose heat more quickly. That is why some small mammals hibernate in winter. They allow their body temperature to drop so that their life systems run more slowly, and less energy is needed to keep them alive.

KEEPING COOL

If you spread some water on the back of your hand, the water soon evaporates. It changes into a gas called water vapour. As the water evaporates, your hand is cooled. This is because energy is needed to change water into vapour, and the water takes the energy (heat) from your hand. If you blow on your hand when it is wet, this speeds up the evaporation, so your hand feels even colder than before.

Your body uses evaporation to keep cool. When your blood temperature rises more than about 0.5°C above normal, you start to sweat – a liquid (mainly water) starts to come out of tiny holes in your skin. As the sweat evaporates, it draws heat from your body.

Cooling by evaporation can be a problem. If someone's clothes get wet on a cold, windy day, the cooling effect can chill their body very quickly. In severe cases, the core temperature may start to fall. This dangerous condition is called hypothermia. If climbers and hill-walkers are injured, they are especially at risk because they may no longer be able to move about to keep warm.

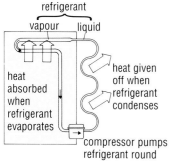

refrigerant
vapour — liquid

heat absorbed when refrigerant evaporates

heat given off when refrigerant condenses

compressor pumps refrigerant round

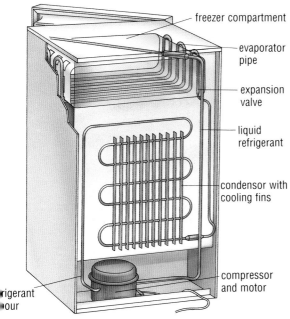

- freezer compartment
- evaporator pipe
- expansion valve
- liquid refrigerant
- condensor with cooling fins
- compressor and motor

rigerant
our

Refrigerators use the cooling effect of evaporation. They contain a liquid which evaporates in a pipe in the freezer compartment, absorbing heat as it does so. It turns liquid again in the pipework at the back of the refrigerator. Overall, heat is taken from inside the fridge and given out at the back.

SPREADING AND WASTING

Heat has a natural tendency to spread out. If you mix hot and cold water, the heat spreads to give warm water. However, warm water will not naturally 'unmix' into hot and cold; once the fast and slow molecules have become mixed up, it is very difficult to separate them. It is rather like trying to 'unmix' billions of assorted buttons: the task is not impossible, but it wastes a great deal of energy. Changing warm water into hot and cold is not impossible either. You could cool one half inside a refrigerator and warm the other half on the pipework at the back. However, running the refrigerator would waste energy.

Right When hot water and cold water are combined, the faster and slower molecules become mixed up. The process can only be reversed by wasting energy. This natural tendency of heat to spread out causes problems for engineers. It is impossible to build a fuel-burning engine which does not waste energy.

Left In this refrigerator, a motor-driven compressor drives the refrigerant round. The liquid refrigerant turns to vapour when it passes through the expansion valve. This produces the cooling effect. The vapour turns back to liquid in the condenser.

Below A comparison of the efficiencies of different engines. All of these engines waste more energy than they can deliver in the form of motion. The wasted energy is released as heat, which is why engines need cooling systems.

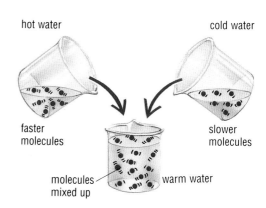

hot water — faster molecules
cold water — slower molecules
molecules mixed up — warm water

Scientists have another way of looking at the mixing–unmixing problem. They say that things have a natural tendency to move from order to disorder. Think of what happens when you rub your hands together and movement energy is changed into heat. Moving each hand gives all its molecules extra motion in the same direction, so the motion is ordered. As your hands warm up, the molecules vibrate faster, but in all directions at random. The motion has become disordered.

Changing movement energy into heat is easy because ordered motion is being changed into disordered motion. However, reversing the process and changing heat into movement energy can only be done by wasting energy.

Engines burn fuel. They change heat into movement energy, so they must waste some energy as heat. A typical car engine has an efficiency of only 25 per cent: only 25 per cent of the fuel's energy is changed into movement energy. Like other engines, it wastes more energy than it delivers. Careful design can reduce the problem, but not solve it. If heat is used to produce motion, then some energy has to be wasted.

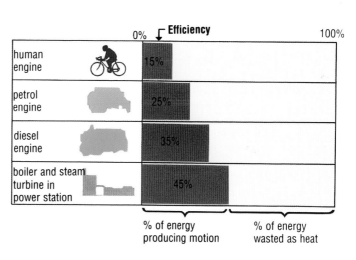

0% Efficiency 100%

human engine	15%
petrol engine	25%
diesel engine	35%
boiler and steam turbine in power station	45%

% of energy producing motion — % of energy wasted as heat

SHOCKING BEHAVIOUR

*T*housands of years ago, people found that amber had strange properties when rubbed. Today, the secrets revealed in amber allow you to watch television, speak to people on the other side of the world, and receive heat and light at the touch of a switch.

The Ancient Greeks experimented with amber, a natural fossilized yellow resin. They found that, when rubbed, it attracted tiny fragments of cloth and dust. You can try similar experiments yourself with more modern materials. For example, if you rub a plastic pocket comb vigorously in your hair, then bring the comb close to some tiny bits of paper, it will pick them up. And if you rub a balloon against your sleeve, the balloon will stick to the wall. Rubbing amber, plastic, and other materials gives them an electric charge. The very word 'electric' comes from the Latin word for amber, *electrum*.

Lightning is one of the most spectacular effects of electric charge. It is caused by the build up of charge on clouds. In the middle of the 18th century, Benjamin Franklin carried out the very dangerous experiment of flying a kite into a thundercloud. He did this to show that lightning was the result of the same kind of electricity as that produced by rubbing things together.

Electrically charged objects will only pick up very light things, whereas magnets can pick up quite heavy chunks of metal. So for thousands of years, the electric effects remained little more than a source of entertainment, while magnets were put to use, for example in compasses.

WHERE CHARGE COMES FROM

All atoms have clouds of electrons, which are particles of negative (–) electricity (see page 98). The electrons move round a nucleus. This has the same total charge as all the electrons, but its charge is positive (+). Normally, the positive and negative charges balance out and the whole atom is electrically neutral. But in many materials, some outer electrons are only loosely bound to their atoms. If two things rub together, loose electrons may become detached and be transferred from one object to the other.

Below Lightning flashes over a town in the USA. To make this picture, the camera shutter was left open for several minutes so that successive flashes were all recorded on the same film.

Above The worker inside the cage is quite safe, despite the electrical discharges from the 2.5 million volt van de Graaf generator. Faraday showed that no electric field, and hence no shocks or flashes, can happen inside a metal cage.

If a polythene rod is rubbed with a duster, the polythene becomes negatively charged. On the other hand, if perspex is rubbed with a duster, the perspex becomes positively charged. In each case, the duster ends up with the opposite charge to the rubbed material.

Electric charges exert forces on each other. A positive charge and a negative charge exert a pull on each other (attract) but two negative, or two positive charges, push each other away (repel). When a negatively charged rod is held close to an object, negative charges on the object are pushed away to the opposite side, and positive charges are attracted to the side nearest to the rod. The charge on the rod and the charge on the object then attract each other and the object sticks to the rod. This process is called electrostatic induction, and the object is said to be in the electrostatic field of the rod.

Michael Faraday showed that frictional electricity and current electricity from a battery are the same. He also showed that electric fields could not exist inside a metal box (now called a Faraday cage).

THUNDER AND LIGHTNING

Thunderstorms usually occur during very hot weather when thermals arise. Thermals are upward-moving currents of hot air and they can carry water droplets at high speed up into the clouds. As the droplets and ice crystals swirl around, they become charged electrically. Tiny, positively charged ice crystals are blown up to the top of the cloud, and negatively charged hailstones fall to the bottom.

A charged rod attracts a small object because the charge on the object is rearranged by electrostatic induction. In the same way, the charged thundercloud exerts forces on the earth and electrostatic induction takes place. As a result the negative charge on the underside of the cloud induces a positive charge on the earth and an intense spark (lightning) then jumps between the two. The discharge heats the air and makes it expand, causing the noise of thunder. But sound travels much more slowly than light, which is why you hear the thunder after you see the flash.

As a result of the transfer, one object has more electrons than normal, so it gains negative (-) charge. The other has fewer electrons than normal, so overall it is left with positive (+) charge. Charges produced in this way are sometimes called 'frictional electricity'. Which object becomes negative and which becomes positive depends on the relative ease with which the electrons can move on the surface of the two materials.

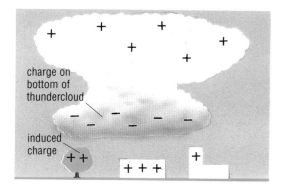

Above Negative charge on the bottom of a thundercloud induces positive charge on the surfaces beneath. Lightning occurs if charge is pulled across the gap.

Right A thundercloud builds up, as hot air carries water droplets rapidly upwards.

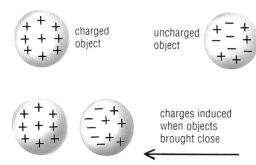

Above How a charged object induces charge on something which is uncharged. The charged object repels like charges, but attracts unlike ones. So the charges in the nearby neutral (uncharged) object become separated.

Metals can be charged by rubbing, but because a metal conducts electricity so well, the charge immediately runs away through the body of the experimenter. Frictional electricity is therefore more usually seen with materials that do not conduct electricity, like glass, resins, plastics, and rubber. Materials like this are called insulators. As electricity does not move on them, it is often known as static electricity. Michael Faraday called it 'ordinary' electricity, but nowadays we use electric power so much that current (moving) electricity is more 'ordinary'.

Sometimes, when you pull off a jumper, you can hear the crackling of electrical discharges and, in the dark, see tiny sparks. The use of fabric conditioner in the rinse after washing helps prevent this. It makes the material conduct electricity, so the charge leaks away.

EVERYDAY SHOCKS

If you wear shoes with rubber or synthetic soles and walk across a dry carpet, you may receive a shock when you touch a metal doorknob. This is because your body has become charged by the rubbing action of the soles on the carpet.

Sometimes, you get a shock when you step out of a car and touch the handle to close the door. Usually, this is because you are wearing woollen or cotton clothes which have rubbed against a synthetic material on the seat. Your body becomes charged, and if your shoes have insulating rubber or synthetic soles, the charge can leak away only when you touch the handle. To avoid this, try touching something metallic on the inside of the door while getting out of the car. Then the charge, which is developed most strongly as the two materials separate, is dispersed before it has time to build up enough to give a shock.

SERIOUS SHOCKS

Although the shocks just described may be unpleasant, they are not dangerous, but frictional electricity can cause serious accidents. For example several supertankers have exploded when their oil tanks were being cleaned out with powerful water jets.

ELECTROSTATIC EXPERIMENT
Turn on a tap to produce a smooth stream of water a few millimetres in diameter. Rub a plastic comb or the body of a cheap ballpoint pen vigorously with a cloth and hold it close to, but not touching the stream. Electrostatic attraction will produce a kink in the flow.

At one time, the sparks from charge which had built up on an aircraft could occasionally cause explosions. Nowadays, these hazards are better understood, and precautions can be taken to prevent them. For example, the rubber in aircraft tyres contains a conducting material which disperses any charge. And aircraft wing tips have discharge electrodes fitted. When an aircraft becomes charged, the charge becomes concentrated on these spikes and is 'sprayed off'.

Precautions must be taken when fuel tanks are being filled because the friction in the fuel flow can be enough to create a large charge. That is one reason why petrol pumps are made of metal.

PUTTING CHARGE TO WORK

Frictional (static) electricity is put to good use in a variety of ways. Factories have tall chimneys because it is important to keep the smoke and fumes well away from people. But the particles of soot, ash, and other solid matter in the smoke do eventually come down again. By using electrically charged plates in the chimney, about 98 per cent of the solid material can be removed before it reaches the top. This is called electrostatic precipitation. In the USA, about 20 million tonnes of ash are removed by this method every year.

Above A lightning conductor being fitted to the top of a tall building. The conductor is made of thick copper to carry the heavy current that would run down it if it was struck by lightning. There are sharp spikes at the top, and a large metal plate buried in the ground.

The charges arise because of friction between the droplets in the water jet. The effect is similar to that produced by the uprush of water droplets in a thundercloud. In conditions like this, small sparks can occur despite the damp surroundings, and these can ignite the petrol vapour and air mixture left behind when a tank is emptied.

In aircraft, charge can be picked up by flying through thunderclouds, or by the friction of the wheels on landing.

Right Smoke pouring from the chimney of a paper pulp mill in the USA. This kind of pollution can now be prevented by installing electrostatic precipitators which attract the solid particles out of the smoke as it goes up the chimney.

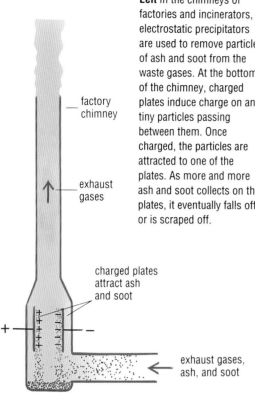

Left In the chimneys of factories and incinerators, electrostatic precipitators are used to remove particles of ash and soot from the waste gases. At the bottom of the chimney, charged plates induce charge on any tiny particles passing between them. Once charged, the particles are attracted to one of the plates. As more and more ash and soot collects on the plates, it eventually falls off or is scraped off.

factory chimney

exhaust gases

charged plates attract ash and soot

+ —

exhaust gases, ash, and soot

Cars and aircraft are usually painted by spraying them. However, during spraying, as much as 25 per cent of the paint never reaches the surface being painted unless something is done to reduce the waste. By deliberately putting electric charges on the spray gun so that the droplets of paint become charged, the droplets are attracted to the object being painted and stick much more effectively to its surface. The saving in the cost of the paint is far more than the cost of the charging equipment.

The same technique is sometimes used with dry powders. Powdered plastic material can be sprayed onto a metal, using charges to make it stick. When the metal is heated, the plastic melts and forms a thin, continuous coating.

Photocopiers also use electric charges and dry powders. A lens forms an image of the picture or text to be copied. The pattern of dark and light parts is then transferred to a piece of paper as a pattern of charged and uncharged areas. When black powder is sprinkled over the paper, it sticks to the charges and not elsewhere. The powder is then sealed onto the paper by heating. This technique of copying is called xerography. It is also used in some fax machines.

CHARGES ON THE MOVE

When a lightning flash occurs, a huge amount of energy is released. It can be enough to set buildings on fire and melt metals. When effects like this are produced, it is the movement of the charge that is important. If charges are moving, the flow of charge is called an electric current.

Once a lightning flash has occurred, it takes a little while for the charge to build up to a sufficiently high level for another flash to occur. But suppose that you could keep the charge building up and discharging steadily, without breaks. Then you would have a continuous flow of charge. That is exactly the effect produced by a battery – though with nothing like as much energy as lightning. It is also the effect produced by the generators in a power station.

To produce an electric current, a supply of energy is needed. This is usually obtained from chemical reactions (as in batteries) or from motion (as in generators). It can also be produced directly from light or heat radiation. This happens in the solar cells which provide electric power for satellites and other space vehicles.

Above In electric arc welding, a very large current is passed between the work and the welding rod. So much heat is generated that the rod melts. The liquid metal can join pieces of metal together or repair holes. The welder wears a helmet to protect the eyes from the dazzling light produced, and also to ward off flying drops of white hot, liquid metal.

ANIMAL ELECTRICITY

Our bodies are run by electricity. Like all animals, we have brains which monitor and control different parts of the body by receiving and sending electrical signals (nerve impulses) through the nerves. Usually, the charge involved is very small. However, a few animals can link up nerve impulses and make enough charge to stun or even kill their prey. For example, the electric eel produces a voltage of up to 600 volts, enough to kill other fish, or give a person a really nasty shock.

PUSHING CHARGE ROUND

Here is a model which may help you understand what the words 'voltage' and 'current' mean.

Suppose you have two containers, connected together by a tube, and you pour water into one of them. The water will run through the tube until the level is the same in both containers. If you now raise one container above the other, water will flow through until the levels are the same again.

The greater the difference in the water levels, the faster the water will flow. The rate at which the water flows corresponds to the current – the rate at which 'loose' electrons will flow in a metal wire.

Below A water model of what happens in an electric circuit. The difference in water level in the two containers represents the battery voltage. The flow of water through the connecting pipe represents the current. The greater the voltage (difference in level), the greater the current (flow).

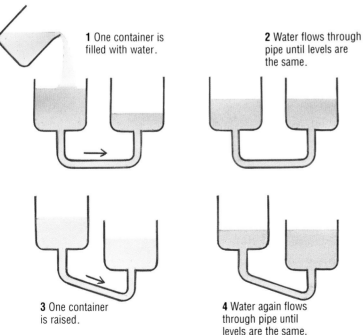

1 One container is filled with water.

2 Water flows through pipe until levels are the same.

3 One container is raised.

4 Water again flows through pipe until levels are the same.

The difference in water levels, which causes the flow, corresponds to the voltage. The bigger the voltage, the bigger will be the current flowing.

The batteries in torches and portable radios usually have a voltage between about 1.5 and 9 volts. The exact value depends on the materials used and how many compartments there are in the battery. The mains supply to a house has a voltage between about 100 and 240 volts, depending on the country.

CELLS AND BATTERIES

The first electric cell was made by an Italian scientist called Alessandro Volta in about 1800. In one of his experiments, he moistened some blotting paper with salty water and sandwiched it between a piece of copper and a piece of zinc. He found that, when the copper and zinc were connected, a current flowed through the wire linking them. Although he did not know it at the time, a chemical reaction was removing electrons from the copper plate and causing extra electrons to collect on the zinc plate. The voltage which drove the current round was named '1 volt' after him. Today electrical measurements are made differently, and the voltage of a simple cell like Volta's is in fact 1.1 volts.

To produce a bigger current, a higher voltage is needed. Volta achieved this by making a pile of alternate copper and zinc plates with moist blotting paper between each. The result is called Volta's pile.

Strictly speaking, a single unit with one plate of each metal is known as a cell. A pile such as Volta's is called a battery of cells. However, nowadays we tend to call all chemical sources of electricity 'batteries', whether they consist of many cells or just one. For example, a car battery (12 volts) is made up of 6 cells, giving 2 volts each. A torch battery (1.5 volts) is just a single cell.

MAKING YOUR OWN CELL
You can make a cell for yourself by sticking a piece of zinc and a piece of copper into a lemon or orange. The juice has the same effect as the salty water in Volta's cell. The cell, which will have the same voltage as Volta's, should light a 1.5-volt torch bulb dimly for a short time.

BATTERIES FOR ALL

There are many different kinds of battery, but all have two things in common. There are always two different elements (for example zinc and copper, carbon and copper, zinc and mercury), and there is always a liquid in between (salt water in Volta's cell). This liquid is called the electrolyte. Sometimes it is in the form of a paste so that it cannot be spilt.

The reason why two different elements are needed is similar to that for using two different materials when producing static electricity by rubbing. The electrons have more freedom to move in one material than in the other, so there is a tendency for them to transfer from one to the other. In a cell, the two plates are conductors of electricity, and so is the liquid between them. Electrons 'liberated' by the chemical reactions can go on flowing round and round as long as there is a continuous path for them. This path is called a circuit. The flow can be stopped by means of a switch which breaks the circuit.

The batteries used in torches, pocket calculators, portable radios, and hearing aids have damp paste between their plates. They will go on producing a flow of electricity as long as the chemical action continues.

In cheap batteries, a zinc container forms one plate and a carbon rod the other. After a time, the zinc container is dissolved, so when batteries like this are made, they are completely sealed in an outer jacket to stop the paste running out and corroding anything near it. Long-life alkaline batteries use the same plate materials as a zinc-carbon cell, but they have a different electrolyte. The tiny 'button' batteries used in watches and cameras often have zinc and mercury, or zinc and silver oxide, as their two plates.

Some batteries are rechargeable. When run down, they can be revived by forcing a current through them in the opposite direction. These batteries usually have nickel and cadmium as the two elements. Batteries like this should only be recharged with a special charger which gives the right voltage, and you should never try to recharge an ordinary battery.

Above In town, this car is powered by an electric motor, which causes no pollution. Out of town, it is powered by a small diesel engine. This also drives a generator which recharges its batteries.

Batteries in cars and electric vehicles are often 'wet'. They have a liquid in them and should be used only in an upright position. Their plates are normally lead and lead oxide, and they can be recharged many times before they wear out. Modern car batteries are often sealed, but they still contain a liquid, usually dilute sulphuric acid.

Electric cars are quiet, and produce no direct atmospheric pollution (though the power stations that supply the electricity for the chargers do pollute the atmosphere). Research is being done to find rechargeable car batteries that are much lighter in weight than those already available. It seems likely that batteries using plastic plates may one day be used.

Below This giant electromagnet is being used to move and sort scrap metal. When the current is switched on it, attracts iron, steel, and other magnetic materials, but not non-magnetic materials like aluminium, brass, and copper. When the current is switched off everything is dropped.

SIMILAR BUT DIFFERENT

A charged object, like a rubbed comb, is surrounded by an electric field whose effects you can see on tiny pieces of paper or specks of dust. A magnet is surrounded by a magnetic field which can be made visible with iron filings. In some ways, electric and magnetic forces are similar, but in other ways they are different. Here are some examples.

Magnetic forces tend to be far stronger than electrical ones. But, just as an electric charge on one body can produce a redistribution of charge on another – the effect called induction – so a magnet can produce a redistribution of magnetism on another piece of magnetic material. Any object can become electrically charged, but only magnetic materials like iron and steel and special alloys can become magnetized.

Electric charges are positive and negative; magnetic poles are north and south (see page 95). Like charges repel and opposite charges attract. But, while like magnetic poles repel and opposite magnetic poles attract, north and south poles can never exist separately. If you break a magnet, new north and south poles will appear at each side of the break.

LOOKING FOR LINKS

Electricity and magnetism are closely linked. If an electric current is passed through a coil of wire, it behaves like a magnet. And if there is a core of magnetic material inside the coil, the material become magnetized. This idea is used in an electromagnet.

If a magnetic field passes through a coil of wire, and the field changes in some way (for example, by getting stronger or weaker, or by moving) then an electric current is generated in the coil. In effect, a current starts flowing in order to compensate for the change in the field. By producing its own magnetic field, it tries to put things back as they were before the change occurred.

Electric motors and generators (dynamos) use the two effects described above – that a current produces a magnetic field, and that a change in a magnetic field produces a current.

Left These engineers are installing a generator in a large power station in Mexico. The part shown is called the stator, which does not move. Later, the rotor will be installed inside the stator. The rotor is a powerful electromagnet which is spun round at high speed. The moving magnetic field generates current in the coils in the stator.

These effects, which were discovered by Faraday, are also used in transformers, which change voltage in power supply systems and in electronic equipment such as televisions and radios. Transformers work using alternating current (AC), the type of current generated for the mains supply. Unlike the current from a battery, AC flows forward, backwards, forwards, backwards, and so on, changing direction at a rate which gives 50 forward surges per second in most European countries; 60 in the USA.

In a transformer, two coils are wound around the same iron core. When an alternating current is passed through one coil, it sets up a rapidly changing magnetic field in the core. This generates an alternating current in the second coil. So power is passed from one coil to the other, although there is no electrical connection between them. The link is entirely magnetic.

The output voltage depends on the number of turns in each coil. It may be more than the input voltage, or less. However, increasing the voltage does not give you something for nothing. Although the charge is given more 'push', the flow is reduced – in other words, there is less current. When power is transmitted by overhead lines, the voltage is stepped up by transformers in order to reduce the current. It is stepped down again before being supplied to consumers.

MOTORS AND GENERATORS

In a simple electric motor, a current makes a coil magnetic so that it is pulled round by a magnet and into line with the field. The motor has a rotating switch which automatically reverses the current every half turn so that the coil is then pulled round another half turn and so on.

The process also works in reverse. If the coil of a motor is turned, a voltage is generated. In other words, the motor becomes a generator (dynamo). The idea is simple, but we rely on the principle for nearly all our electricity.

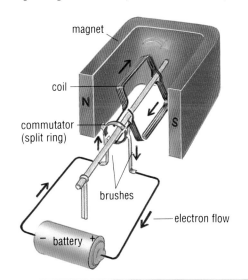

Left A simple electric motor. With current through it, the coil becomes an electromagnet which is pulled round by the magnetic poles either side. Each half turn, the commutator changes the current direction so that the coil is pulled round another half turn.

QUICK AS A FLASH

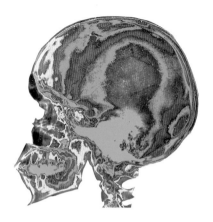

*L*ight is just one member of a whole family of
radiations known as electromagnetic waves. Other
members include radio waves, ultraviolet, and X-rays.
Apart from light, our eyes cannot detect these radiations,
but we can make use of their effects.

THE SPEED OF LIGHT

*F*or thousands of years, people did not realize that light takes time to travel from place to place. Early experiments to measure its speed all reinforced the theory that light travels instantaneously. Now, with more accurate measurements, we know that its speed is 300,000 km per second through empty space. Light normally travels in straight lines. But if it could move in circles, it could travel nearly eight times round the Earth in a second!

ELECTROMAGNETIC RADIATION

Anything that spreads out from its source can be called 'radiation', so light is a form of radiation. But what is light? The easiest way to think about this is to imagine the magnetic field surrounding a magnet. If the magnet is wobbled, waves of magnetism will travel outwards just as waves will travel along a rope if you wobble one end.

When a magnetic field varies, it creates an electric field which varies as well – rather as a moving magnet generates a current in the coils of a dynamo. So, a vibrating magnet sends out waves which are partly electric and partly magnetic. These are known as electromagnetic waves.

Light is a series of electromagnetic waves produced, not by big wobbling magnets, but by movements in atoms. But there are other members of the electromagnetic family as well. They are radio waves, microwaves, infrared, ultraviolet, X-rays, and gamma rays. They all travel through space at the same speed as light, but they differ from each other in the rate at which the wobbles occur. This can vary from a few times a second for some radio waves, up to a hundred million, million, million times a second for some gamma rays.

The rate of vibration (wobble) is called the frequency. It is measured in hertz (Hz). A frequency of 1 Hz means one vibration per second – so one wave is being sent out every second. 1 kilohertz (kHz) means 1000 waves per second, and 1 megahertz (MHz) means 1,000,000 waves per second.

Left Straight-line beams of light from modern lasers, seen against the background of the Great Pyramids at Giza which were built about 2600 BC. The Ancient Egyptians knew that light travels in straight lines. They used this fact to arrange rows of posts to make lines for measuring their buildings and fields.

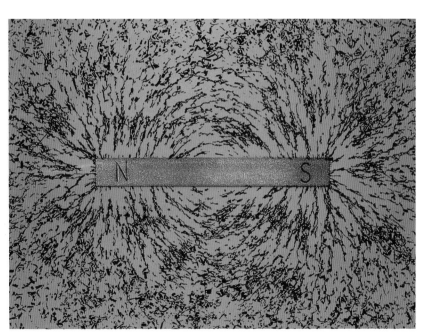

Left The magnetic field around a bar magnet is shown using iron filings. Each filing becomes a magnet because it is near the bar magnet, and the attraction between opposite poles of the tiny filings makes them line up. The lines of force seem to radiate out from the magnetic poles of the bar. Any variation in a field like this causes electromagnetic waves.

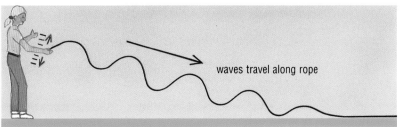

waves travel along rope

Left Making waves run along a rope by moving one end rapidly up and down.

Right In the spectrum of white light, different colours have different wavelengths. Waves of red light are the longest, and are rather more than twice as long as those of violet. Over 3000 waves of violet light would fit into only 1 mm.

Colour	Wavelength in millionths of a millimetre
violet	380–420
blue	420–490
green	490–575
yellow	575–590
orange	590–650
red	650–760

Below The full range of electromagnetic waves is called the electromagnetic spectrum. It ranges from radio waves (which have the lowest frequencies and the longest wavelengths) to gamma rays (which have the highest frequencies and the shortest wavelengths). Light is the only type of radiation that our eyes can detect.

When dealing with waves, it is sometimes more convenient to talk about wavelength rather than frequency.

Imagine that someone is moving a stick up and down in a pond so that ripples are sent out across the surface of the water. The wavelength is the distance from the crest of one wave to the next.

Now imagine that the stick is moved up and down at a faster rate. More waves are sent out every second, so the wave crests are closer together. In other words, a higher frequency produces a shorter wavelength.

In the electromagnetic family, radio waves have the longest wavelengths and gamma rays have the shortest.

LIGHT AND SIGNALS

Light is rather special. All members of the electromagnetic family have their own particular properties, but light is the only radiation which we can detect directly. Our eyes have evolved to be sensitive to light and can form images with it (see page 22).

Most animals see about the same range of frequencies as humans. However, some insects can also see part of the ultraviolet spectrum and some snakes can detect infrared. They must see these other waves as new colours – being human, we cannot possibly imagine what these new colours look like!

Light has other uses apart from sight. Photography and television are really extensions of the seeing process. But light is also used for communication.

Years ago, blazing beacons were lit on land to signal the approach of an enemy. Later, sailors began to use flags to communicate with other ships. Of course, that system depended on light from the flag reaching the person watching. Signalling could also be done with lamps which were covered or uncovered in a sequence which flashed out signals in Morse code.

Nowadays, telephone conversations can be sent long distances using tiny beams of light travelling through strands of glass.

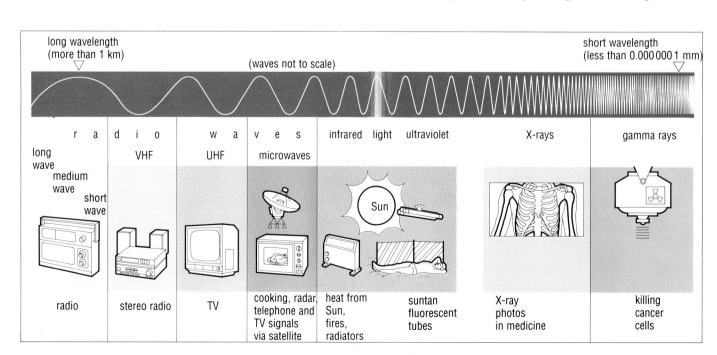

First, a microphone changes the sound into electrical signals. These are coded into pulses which represent a series of numbers, called digital signals. The signals are converted into light pulses by a tiny laser and fed along an optical fibre – a strand of glass no thicker than a human hair. The light pulses bounce back and forth from the walls of the fibre and cannot escape. When they reach their destination, they are converted into electrical signals. After decoding, the signals go to a telephone earpiece. There, they make a metal plate vibrate so that it gives out a copy of the original sound.

Thousands of optical fibres can be put in one cable. Also, by chopping up different speech signals into very short bursts, many conversations can be sent together down the same fibre. In this way, a single cable can carry many thousands of telephone conversations at the same time.

In an optical fibre system, the basic light beam is called the carrier. Signals are sent by modulating (varying) this beam. In radio communication radio waves are the carrier. The carrier is then modulated by varying either the 'size' of the waves (amplitude modulation, or AM) or the frequency (frequency modulation, or FM). Each radio station transmits programmes using its own carrier frequency, marked on your receiver in kHz or MHz.

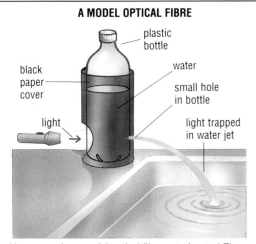

A MODEL OPTICAL FIBRE

plastic bottle

black paper cover

water

small hole in bottle

light

light trapped in water jet

You can make a model optical fibre out of water! The diagram above shows you how.

The experiment works best in the dark. Shine the torch beam into the bottle through the large hole and towards the small hole. You should see part of the light beam trapped inside the jet of water. The jet of water is behaving like a large optical fibre.

LASER LIGHT

Lasers produce a narrow, intensely bright beam of light. Tiny crystal lasers are used in CD players, in bar-code readers, and in optical fibre communication systems. Larger gas-filled lasers are used by surveyors for making accurate alignments. At the heart of a gas-filled laser, there is a tube rather like the tubes in a neon advertising display. To understand how a laser works, it helps to think about the light from a neon tube, and how this compares with the radio waves sent out from a transmitter.

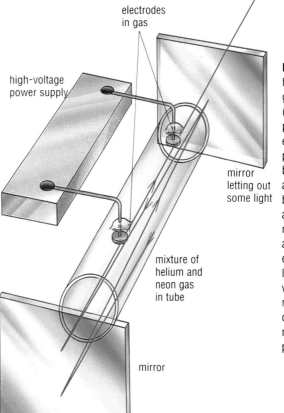

laser beam

electrodes in gas

high-voltage power supply

mirror letting out some light

mixture of helium and neon gas in tube

mirror

Left The main parts of a helium–neon laser. In the glass tube, atoms in the gas (which is at a very low pressure) are excited by the electric discharge from the power supply. The atoms begin to give off light. And as the light is reflected backwards and forwards along the tube by the mirrors at each end, more and more atoms become excited. They all give off light waves which are in step with each other. The intense, narrow beam of light is let out through one of the mirrors which is only partly reflecting.

In a neon tube, a discharge of electricity 'excites' atoms in the gas so that these give out light waves. The gas appears to glow without interruption, but each atom is sending out random bursts of waves.

A transmitter sends out radio waves by making a current flow to and fro in an antenna (aerial). However, the waves are sent out in a continuous stream rather than in random bursts like light.

Producing radio waves is rather like moving a stick regularly up and down in water, whereas producing light waves is like throwing in a handful of pebbles. The basic principle of a laser is to persuade a large number of atoms to emit (send out) their radiation in step, so that the waves are more like a constant stream of radio waves than a series of random bursts.

The lasers used in school laboratories are normally the helium–neon type. In a laser like this, there is a tube filled with a mixture of helium and neon gas at low pressure. The gas starts to give out light when an electric discharge is put through it. At the ends of the tube, there are mirrors which reflect the light up and down the tube millions of times every second. This has the effect of putting all the emitted waves in step with each other. One of the mirrors is only partly silvered, so the laser light can get out. It is intensely bright and travels in a narrow beam which does not expand. Nowadays, lasers can be made to produce light of almost any wavelength, including infrared. The light output of a small helium–neon laser is about $1/1000$ watt.

RADIO AND MICRO WAVES

Marconi was the first person to use radio waves to send information. It was a simple signal that switched on a bell on the other side of his laboratory. That was in 1894. Speech transmission was not developed until 1906. By the 1920s, radio stations were broadcasting news and music to radio sets in the home. These early broadcasts used what are now called long waves. Provided the transmitter was powerful enough, and the receiver sensitive enough, they could be heard more or less anywhere in the world. At first this was a surprise because no one expected them to reach beyond the horizon – after all, light travels only in straight lines. However, the Earth is surrounded by layers of charged particles called the ionosphere and these layers reflect long waves. The waves can travel many thousands of kilometres round the Earth, bouncing between the ionosphere and the ground, until they are picked up by a receiver.

Low frequencies (in other words, long wavelengths) are not capable of transmitting high quality sound, so VHF (very high frequency) signals are used for this. But VHF signals are not reflected very well by layers in the ionosphere, so their range is limited. Even higher frequencies, called UHF (ultra–high frequency) are needed to transmit the detail required for television pictures. Again, these are limited in range.

Microwaves are used for satellite communication because they pass easily through the ionosphere. Microwaves are also used in radar. The position of an aircraft or ship can be worked out by measuring how long it takes a pulse of microwaves to be reflected back to the dish which sent the signals. The information is displayed in map form on a screen.

Most radio waves are stopped by water, but very low frequencies (very long wavelengths) will travel underwater. These frequencies are used for communication between submarines and aircraft flying above them.

WAVES FOR COOKING

Many years ago, radio engineers found that objects heat up when placed in a powerful beam of radio waves. Nowadays, this principle is used in microwave ovens.

Microwaves affect the water in food. They penetrate right through the food, making the molecules vibrate so rapidly that all the food becomes hot very quickly. In an ordinary oven, the outer layers of food insulate the inner parts, so it takes much longer for the heat to reach the middle.

HEAT IN THE DARK

Infrared radiation lies beyond the red end of the light spectrum. People sometimes call it 'heat radiation' because it makes you hot when you absorb it. An electric iron does not glow in the dark, yet if you put your hand some way away from the flat surface, you can feel the heat. The human eye is not sensitive to infrared, so it can be used where it is important that no light is seen – in burglar alarm systems for example.

Right In the dense smoke of a fire or under the rubble from a collapsed building, it is difficult to find people who may be trapped. Using an infrared camera, firefighters can see through the smoke and debris.

Far right Although the infrared camera picture is not in colour, there is no doubt that this is the body of someone who needs rescuing.

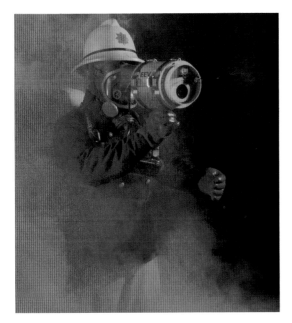

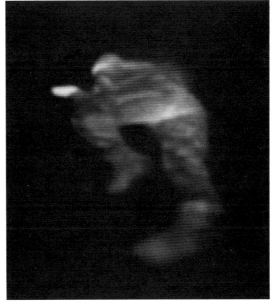

Above Dandelions, which look yellow in sunlight, appear quite different in ultraviolet light. Their centres absorb ultraviolet, but the florets round the outside reflect it strongly, and look bright to insects whose eyes are sensitive to the radiation.

Infrared is not affected by mist, fog, or clouds, so TV cameras that are sensitive to infrared can be used to 'see' through clouds as well as in the dark. With cameras like this, rescue workers can see through dense smoke. Infrared cameras can also detect small differences in temperature on the human body, so they can reveal tumours or other medical problems.

TV remote controllers use infrared pulses to send channel, volume, and other information to a TV set.

BEYOND THE VIOLET

In some stage performances, when the ordinary lights are turned off, the dancers or puppets on stage seem to glow in bright colours even though there is no visible light shining on the stage. This effect is produced by lamps which give out invisible ultraviolet. People in the entertainment business sometimes call it 'black light'. It makes special dyes in the costumes glow.

Far left This photograph is taken with ordinary light. The gold snuff box is inlaid with a pattern of diamonds of many different sizes.

Left When the snuff box is illuminated by ultraviolet light, the diamonds fluoresce with a beautiful blue light. Fluorescence is a glow produced when other radiation is absorbed.

The dyes in the costumes are similar to those in highlighter pens and vivid posters. They are fluorescent. That is, they absorb the ultraviolet radiation and convert its energy into visible light. 'Whiter than white' washing powders use the same effect (see page 86).

There is ultraviolet radiation in sunshine. It gives white-skinned people their suntans, but too high an exposure can cause skin cancer. Ultraviolet can also damage people's eyes. It has the same effect as intense light but because you cannot see it you do not close your eyes or turn away.

High in the Earth's atmosphere, there is a special type of oxygen called ozone. It protects us by absorbing some of the Sun's ultraviolet radiation. Natural processes are continually making new ozone and destroying old, but the ozone layer seems to be getting thinner and developing holes. This may be because people are releasing too many ozone-damaging chemicals into the air.

Below An X-ray photograph showing the hip joint between the femur and the pelvis. X-rays pass through bone much less easily than through flesh. On the photograph, this makes bone appear paler than the flesh and the background. The X-rays are stopped almost completely by the steel rod inserted into the bone and the screws fastening it, so these parts appear white.

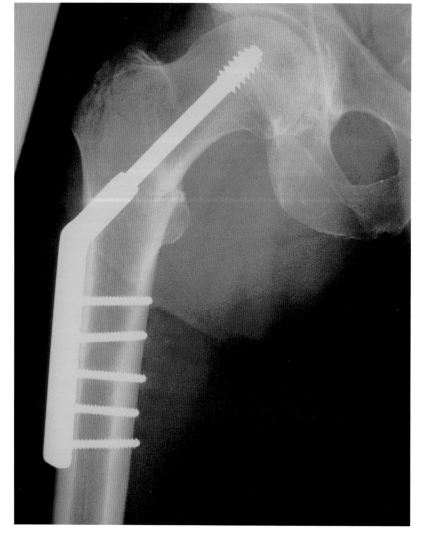

MORE USES OF ULTRAVIOLET

Scientists can use the fluorescence of materials to analyse them. Just as white light can be broken up into a spectrum by a prism, so ultraviolet can be broken up. But the prism has to be made of quartz. The spectrum is photographed, its different wavelengths measured, and the whole pattern used as a 'fingerprint' to identify the material.

Ultraviolet can speed up the setting of some plastics. Dentists use it to harden fillings. A thick optical fibre carries the ultraviolet light to the right part of the tooth.

X THE UNKNOWN

X-rays were discovered by Wilhelm Röntgen by accident, in 1895. Some unused, wrapped photographic plates were being stored near an electric discharge tube. When developed, they had blackened as if exposed to light. Invisible rays must have been coming from the tube. They were named X-rays because nobody knew what they were. Soon, X-rays were being used to take shadow photographs of bones. This was possible because the X-rays were absorbed by bone but could pass through flesh.

X-rays belong to the electromagnetic family, and have shorter wavelengths than ultraviolet. Even shorter wavelength X-rays will pass through bone, and also through metals.

SEEING SECTIONS

Using X-rays and computer technology, it is possible to produce an image which shows a section through a human body – just as if the body had been sawn in two! The technique is called computer-assisted tomography. The equipment is known as a CAT scanner, and an X-ray tube is mounted on a circular frame which surrounds the patient. As the X-ray tube moves round the patient, a detector also moves so that it is always on the opposite side. Signals from the detector are sent to a computer which works out what each section looks like. A section can be taken anywhere across the body.

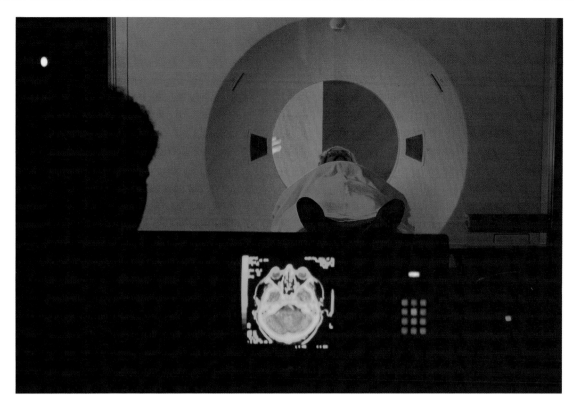

GAMMA RAYS

Gamma rays come from radioactive materials. They have the highest frequencies (and shortest wavelengths) of all electromagnetic waves. They are the most harmful, and the most penetrating. Both gamma rays and X-rays are used to examine chunks of steel to look for cracks caused by stress.

In hospitals, concentrated beams of gamma rays are used to kill tumours. Much weaker gamma rays can also help doctors find out what is wrong with a patient. For example, the thyroid gland naturally absorbs iodine, so if tiny traces of radioactive iodine are put into the body, the thyroid will give off gamma rays. By studying these, doctors can tell whether the gland is normal or diseased.

PARTICLES OR WAVES?

In the 17th century, Sir Isaac Newton thought that light was a stream of tiny particles which he called 'corpuscles'. Later experiments showed that light belongs to the whole family of electromagnetic waves. But other experiments showed that these wave radiations must be particles.

So, electromagnetic radiations sometimes behave like waves and sometimes like particles. This may sound confusing, but the world of atoms and electrons is very different from the normal-sized world you are used to. The difficulties start if you expect things on the atomic scale to behave in the same way as they do on the normal scale.

Here is another way of looking at the problem. Imagine that you have travelled back 500 years in a time machine. You meet some people and try to explain to them what a car is. They listen to your explanation and then discuss it. Some say that a car is a type of horse because you give it 'food' (fuel) and it goes by itself. Some say that it is a type of carriage because it has seats and can get you from place to place. But a car is neither a horse nor a carriage. It is a car! It is the same with waves and particles. Electromagnetic radiation may sometimes behave like waves and sometimes like particles, but really it is neither. It is electromagnetic radiation.

Scientists have a name for these particles of electromagnetic wave energy. They call them photons. The higher the frequency of the radiation, the more energy each photon has. That is why X-rays and gamma rays are much more dangerous than light. Their photons deliver far more energy.

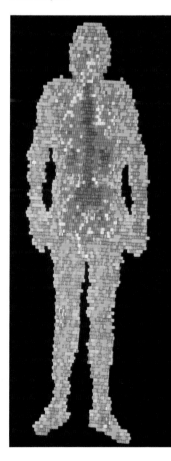

TIME ON YOUR HANDS

Over the centuries, people have devised more and more accurate ways of measuring time. Today, the need for accuracy is greater than ever. However, time itself remains one of the biggest mysteries of all. And one person's time can be quite different from another's.

For centuries, people's ideas about time depended on the way the Sun moved across the sky. At midday, the Sun was at its highest point. One day was the time it took the Sun to reach its highest point again. Of course it was not really the Sun that was moving; it only appeared to move because the Earth was rotating once per day.

We now divide the day into 24 smaller units called hours, but our modern hours are rather different from those of 600 years ago. Before mechanical clocks came into use in the 14th century, an hour was one twelfth of the period of daylight. In summer, daylight lasted longer than in winter, so summer hours were longer than winter ones!

With the arrival of mechanical clocks, hours became fixed. As clocks became more accurate, time could be measured in smaller units – minutes and seconds. Today, some scientific clocks can measure time in picoseconds (million millionths of a second).

Clocks may use the same length hour, but they are not all set to give the same time. That is because the Sun appears to be at its highest point in the sky at different times depending on where you are on the Earth's surface. For example, when it is midday in London, England, it is midnight in Wellington, New Zealand.

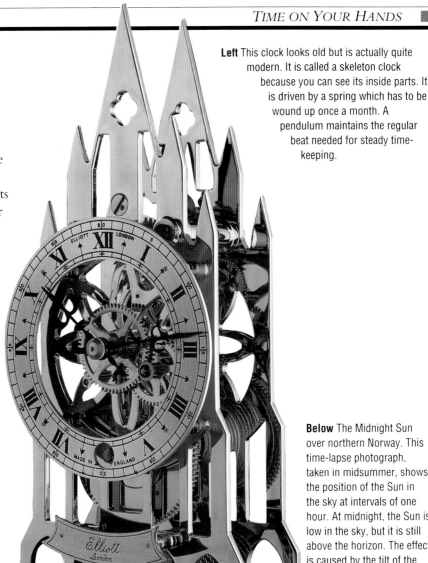

Left This clock looks old but is actually quite modern. It is called a skeleton clock because you can see its inside parts. It is driven by a spring which has to be wound up once a month. A pendulum maintains the regular beat needed for steady time-keeping.

Below The Midnight Sun over northern Norway. This time-lapse photograph, taken in midsummer, shows the position of the Sun in the sky at intervals of one hour. At midnight, the Sun is low in the sky, but it is still above the horizon. The effect is caused by the tilt of the Earth's axis.

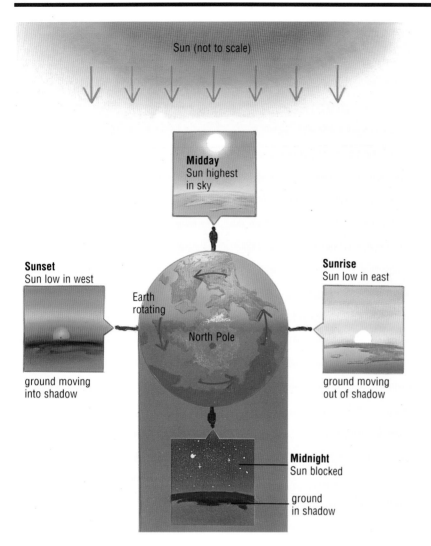

Sun (not to scale)

Midday
Sun highest
in sky

Sunset
Sun low in west

Earth
rotating

North Pole

ground moving
into shadow

Sunrise
Sun low in east

ground moving
out of shadow

Midnight
Sun blocked

ground
in shadow

Above The position of the Sun in the sky depends on where you are standing on the Earth's surface. That is why different places around the world need their clocks set to different times. In the diagram above, it is early morning for one person, midday for the second, late evening for the third, and midnight for the fourth.

Before the 1880s, everyone used their own local time. In Britain, for example, clocks in London were about 10 minutes ahead of those in Bristol. When railway timetables were first introduced, this made life difficult. So, in 1880, Britain adopted the average time at the Greenwich Observatory as its standard. It is still called Greenwich Mean Time (GMT).

Since 1884, the world has been divided into internationally agreed time zones. In most cases, you alter your watch by one hour when passing from one zone to the next.

SHORT SEPTEMBER

In England, in 1752, people went to bed on 2 September and woke up the following day on 14 September. This was because 11 days had been omitted from the calendar for that year by Act of Parliament. The change was needed to bring England's calendar into line with those of other European countries, whose dates were a closer match with the seasons.

---

61 SECONDS IN 1 MINUTE

Nowadays scientists use a very accurate definition of the second as the starting-point for all time measurements. The definition is based on the natural frequency of light waves emitted by certain atoms of caesium gas, and the instrument used for the measurements is called an atomic clock. Defining a second in this way may sound complicated, but it gives a result that never varies. The frequency of the light waves is not affected by temperature or any other factor which can alter the timekeeping of other clocks.

Accurate time measurements show that the speed of the Earth's rotation varies slightly. We are all used to leap years, when an extra day is added to the calendar so that it does not go out of step with the seasons. Sometimes, 'leap seconds' have to be added as well to correct for slight changes in the length of the day. For example, the very last minute of 30 June 1994 was made 61 seconds long so that July would start a second later!

Sometimes, time signals are given on the radio to mark the hour. Normally, you hear six bleeps in succession, but when a leap second is added, there are seven bleeps.

NAVIGATING WITH TIME

As a sailor, finding your position north or south of the Equator is relatively easy. It can be calculated from the angle of the Sun above the horizon at midday. But finding a position east or west is much more difficult, and it relies on good timekeeping:

Imagine that you are somewhere in the Atlantic Ocean. When you left Greenwich, you set your clock. Now, it says 12 noon, but the Sun has only just risen. Indeed, you have to wait another 6 hours before it is midday locally and the Sun is at its zenith in the sky. You can use this information to calculate how far round the globe you are. Compared with Greenwich, your midday seems to be 6 hours late. As the Earth does one turn in 24 hours, it must have rotated a quarter of a turn (90°) in 6 hours. So you must be 90° west of Greenwich.

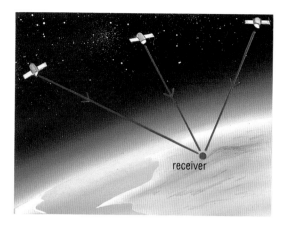

Above In the Global Positioning System (GPS), the receiver calculates its position by comparing the arrival times of synchronized signals from different satellites.

Right An artist's impression of a Navstar satellite, which forms part of the Global Positioning System. Eventually, up to 26 satellites like this will be in orbit around the Earth.

Of course, to calculate your position, you must be sure that your midday really is 6 hours behind that in Greenwich. But you may have left Greenwich a month ago! What if your clock is running fast or slow? An error of just 5 minutes on the clock could affect your calculated position by as much as 130 km.

It was navigation problems like this that first prompted the search for better ship's clocks. In 1772 John Harrison won a £20,000 prize for making an accurate clock, called a chronometer, that could keep time to within half a minute a year. That is more accurate than most modern digital watches.

Today, ships can navigate using the Global Positioning System (GPS). This is a ring of satellites which circle the Earth in geostationary orbits (their motion matches the Earth's rotation so that they stay in fixed positions above the ground). GPS also depends on very accurate timekeeping. The satellites transmit synchronized radio signals which can be picked up by a small receiver below. In the receiver, a tiny computer compares the arrival times of the signals from different satellites. Knowing the speed of the signals, and their time separation, it can calculate a position to within a few metres.

Right The further west you go, the more delayed the Sun's apparent movement across the sky seems to be. By measuring the time delay, navigators can work out how far west they have travelled.

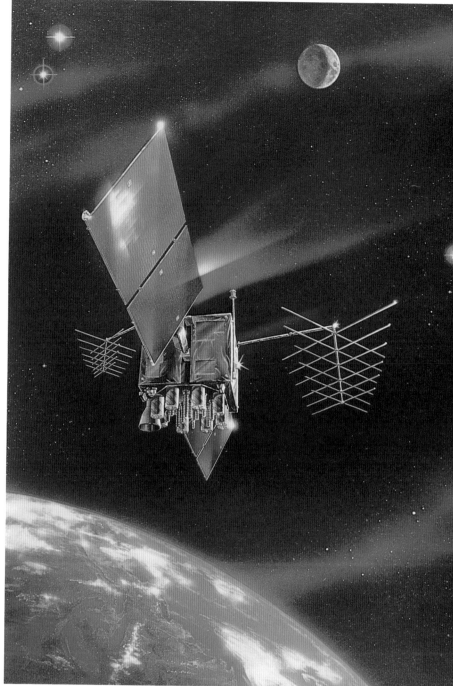

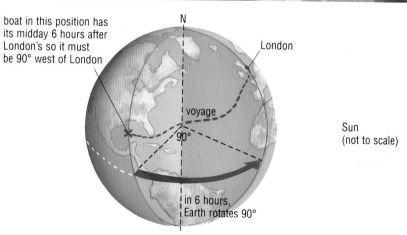

boat in this position has its midday 6 hours after London's so it must be 90° west of London

N

London

voyage

90°

Sun (not to scale)

in 6 hours, Earth rotates 90°

Right Is the train travelling past the trees, or are the trees travelling past the train? According to the theory of relativity, it makes no difference because all motion is relative. When Einstein was travelling towards Oxford on a train, it is said that he asked the guard: 'Does Oxford stop at this train?'

RELATIVITY AND TIME

In 1905 Albert Einstein proposed his theory of special relativity. This reached some rather dramatic conclusions about the nature of time. However, the theory was not put forward for that reason. It came about in an entirely different way.

Einstein started with two basic ideas. The first was that all speeds are relative: they only tell you how fast something is moving relative to something else. A train may be travelling in a straight line past a platform at 100 km/hour, but inside the train everything behaves as if the platform is travelling past the train, and any scientific experiments carried out in the train give exactly the same results as they do outside. The second idea was based on some very surprising experimental evidence: relative motion seems to have no effect at all on the speed of light.

Light always appears to pass you at the same relative speed (about 300,000 km/second) – even if you are rushing towards the light source or away from it.

Einstein linked his ideas mathematically and arrived at certain conclusions. One was that relative motion affects how we view other people's measurements of distance and time (and therefore speed). At ordinary speeds, the effects are far too small to detect. But if you could look into a rocket travelling past you at nearly the speed of light, any clocks inside would appear to be running slow. However, to the people in the rocket time would be normal.

This result did away with the idea that there is any such thing as absolute time. Each person has their own time, and people's times can be different depending on how they are moving relative to each other.

Another of Einstein's conclusions was that mass is a form of energy, or, to put it another way, energy has mass. As things gain or lose energy, they also gain or lose mass. Einstein expressed this idea in a famous equation, $E = mc^2$ (c stands for the speed of light). In the equation, c^2 is such a big number that energy changes in everyday events produce no detectable changes in mass. However, when scientists first studied nuclear reactions, they measured mass changes which made them realize that huge amounts of energy might be released under some circumstances. This discovery ultimately led to the development of the atomic bomb and other forms of nuclear power.

In 1915 Einstein published his theory of general relativity. This extended his earlier ideas to include the effects of gravity and acceleration on space and time.

Below Astronauts falling towards a black hole – a collapsed star whose gravitational pull is so strong that even light cannot escape. To the astronauts, time is normal. But to a distant observer, their time will slow and then stop altogether as they enter the black hole.

Scientists are using the theory of general relativity to develop their ideas about collapsed stars called black holes.

At the edge of a black hole, gravity is so strong that even light cannot escape. Gravity also affects time. If you could pick up time signals from some astronauts falling towards a black hole, their time would go slower and slower until, as they entered the black hole, it would stop altogether. However, to the astronauts time would be normal. In reality, falling into a black hole would not be a pleasant experience for the astronauts, because the increasing gravitational pull as they approached it would stretch out their bodies like spaghetti!

When carrying out high-energy experiments, nuclear physicists have to allow for the effects of relativity. In particle accelerators, protons, electrons, and other particles can be accelerated to speeds approaching that of light. The extra energy they gain actually makes them heavier – exactly as predicted by Einstein's equation. Being heavier, they are more difficult to accelerate, and extra force is needed to keep them moving round their circular track. Time is also altered. Some particles which have a very short life can be observed for much longer because their time appears to be going slow. The effect is called time dilation.

One consequence of the theory of relativity is that the speed of light seems to be a sort of universal speed limit. Nothing can ever travel faster than light. As things get faster, their mass increases, so more and more energy is needed to make them go even faster. There is not enough energy in the Universe to make any ordinary matter travel as fast as light.

ARROWS OF TIME

Why does time go forwards and not backwards? Why can we remember yesterday but not tomorrow? These are just two of the questions that people have asked about time. Scientists have reached some conclusions, but many mysteries remain.

Here is a problem which may help you understand more about the direction of time. If a snooker table (or a pool table) were photographed at three different times during the early stages of one game, could you tell which photograph was taken first, which next, and which last? You probably could. That is because you would expect the arrangement of the balls to be more and more disordered as time passed. So the direction of time seems to match the change from order to disorder. But this raises another question: why does order tend to become disorder?

Right The same snooker table at three different stages in the early part of a game. The pictures are not in the correct sequence. Can you tell which came first, which next, and which last? The arrangements of the balls give clues about the likely direction of time, because there is a natural tendency for order to become disorder.

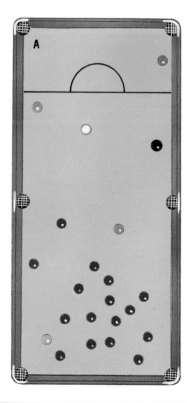
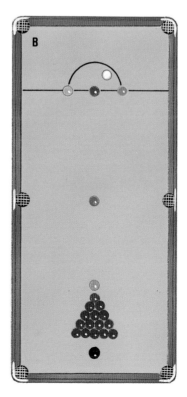
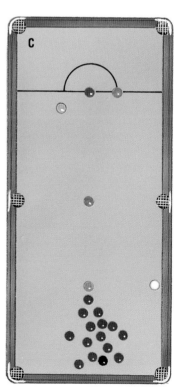

To answer this question, think about the balls on the snooker table. They can be in an ordered arrangement, as at the start of the game, or in a disordered arrangement. However, there are billions of times more possible disordered arrangements than ordered ones (see page 92). Just think of all the ways the balls could be arranged on the table. Each time a player takes a shot, this produces another arrangement. But the chances of it being an ordered arrangement are remote. So the passing of time tends to change order into disorder.

Thermodynamics is the study of heat. When heat spreads, the motion of atoms and molecules becomes more and more disordered (see page 159). As the tendency for order to change into disorder is connected with the spread of heat, it is sometimes called the thermodynamic arrow of time. Our brains also follow this tendency. We put our thoughts in order, but to do this our brains need energy, and this means that they produce waste heat. Overall, they put more disorder into the Universe than order, so they are governed by the thermodynamic arrow of time. That is why we can remember the past but not the future.

Scientists are also interested in another arrow of time. They call it the cosmological arrow, and it came from the Big Bang.

TIME AND THE BIG BANG

Most scientists now think that the Universe was created about 15 billion years ago in a gigantic explosion called the Big Bang. An incredibly hot, dense ball expanded rapidly from almost nothing As it grew bigger and bigger, the stars and galaxies were created from the matter and energy within it.

The Universe is still expanding. It will probably go on expanding for at least another 10 billion years, and may expand forever. The expanding cosmos (the Universe) also gives a direction to time. This is the cosmological arrow, and its direction matches the thermodynamic arrow.

The Big Bang was the beginning of time as we know it. It is meaningless to ask whether there was time before the Big Bang because the rules of science break down at that point.

Big Bang (15,000 m) — JAN 1

Solar System (Sun and planets) formed (4500 m) — SEPT 13

first simple life on Earth (3500 m) — OCT 7

first land plants and animals (400 m) — DEC 22

first dinosaurs (220 m) — DEC 26

last dinosaurs (65 m) — DEC 30

first humans (5 m) — DEC 31 9.00 pm

present — DEC 31 12.00 pm

Left This chart shows the dates on which certain events would have happened if the whole of time since the Big Bang were compressed into one year – 'm' stands for 'million years ago'. On this scale, our Sun will keep shining until about the end of May of the following year (6000 million years into the future), and the Universe will keep expanding at least until the end of August (10,000 million years into the future). It may go on expanding forever.

We have no way of knowing whether time existed before the Big Bang. Indeed, some scientists now think that time does not need a starting-point. They have developed a mathematical model in which time is rather like the surface of a sphere, such as the Earth. You can start a journey at one point, say the North Pole, but the surface itself has no beginning or end.

TRAVELLING THROUGH TIME

The space we live in has three dimensions: we can move up and down, left and right, and backwards and forwards. Our position can also change with time. That is why time is called the fourth dimension. Together, the four dimensions make up space-time.

There are many directions in which we can move through space, but we only seem to be able to travel in one direction through time – into the future.

So is travel into the past impossible? Certainly there are strong arguments against it. If you could travel backwards in time, you might influence the future – for example, by preventing your parents from meeting. This means that you would not have been born, so your journey would have been impossible in the first place. Another argument says that if time travel were possible, someone in the future would have discovered it. As we have never seen any visitors from the future, it must be impossible.

Examples like this seem to rule out time travel, but that is not necessarily the case. Scientists working with the equations of general relativity have pointed out that 'tunnels' through space-time, called wormholes, are a theoretical possiblity. Wormholes could produce time dilation effects. Under some circumstances, it might be possible to make a journey from one point in space to another, return through a wormhole, and arrive at a slightly earlier time than you left. However, no one has yet discovered a wormhole or any means of creating one. And if wormholes do exist, they are likely to be highly unstable. At present, we must accept that there is no return ticket for our journey through time.

Below A wormhole is a tunnel connecting different parts of space-time (shown here as a two-dimensional sheet). Some scientists have suggested that wormholes might be used as time machines, but so far wormholes are only theoretical. Nobody has ever found one.

Above Building a time machine is much easier in Hollywood than in real life. For the moment, we cannot control the speed or direction of our journey through time.

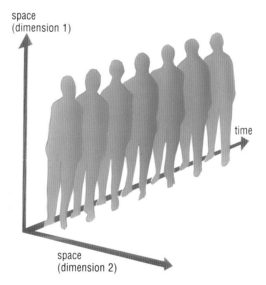

Left We are travelling through space-time, even when standing still. This chart shows two space dimensions and one time dimension. In reality, we exist in four-dimensional space-time.

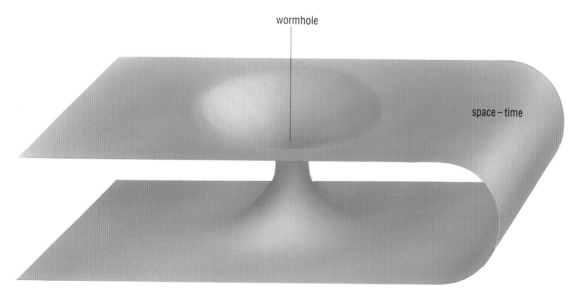

GLOSSARY

acids Chemicals that are corrosive and neutralize alkalis. They turn litmus paper red and have a low pH value.

alkalis Chemicals that are corrosive and neutralize acids. They turn litmus paper blue and have a high pH value.

alloy Mixture of a metal with other substances (often metals). For example, brass is an alloy of copper and zinc.

analogue information Information represented by something which can change continuously, such as the position of a pointer, or the strength of a current.

atom The smallest particle of a chemical element. It consists of a nucleus of protons and (in most cases) neutrons, with electrons speeding around it.

bacteria Microscopic single-celled organisms.

Big Bang The starting point of our Universe, according to modern theory. It may have occurred about 15,000 million years ago.

binary System of counting which uses only two digits, 0 and 1.

biodegradable Able to be decomposed by microbes (such as bacteria).

carbohydrates Foods such as sugars and starch which are compounds of carbon, hydrogen, and oxygen.

cell (electric) A two-terminal device which supplies electricity. It is often called a battery, though a battery really means a collection of cells.

cell (living) The smallest living unit in an animal or plant. In most cases, it contains a nucleus which controls its activity.

chain reaction (fission) Process in which neutrons split nuclei, such as uranium, which release more neutrons, which split more nuclei... and so on.

chemical reaction Process in which substances combine chemically to form a new substance: for example, hydrogen burning in oxygen to form water.

chromosomes Thread-like bits in the nucleus of a cell which contain the genetic information.

compound New substance formed when two or more chemical elements combine. For example, sodium chloride (common salt) is a compound of sodium and chlorine.

conductor A material which heat or electricity can flow through.

convection The transfer of heat by a moving gas or liquid: for example, hot air rising.

corrosion Damage to a surface, especially of metals, by chemical action: for example, the rusting of iron.

CRO (cathode ray oscilloscope) Equipment which can be used to show the pattern of signals, such as sound waves.

current (electric) A flow of charge, usually of electrons.

digital information Information represented by a series of specific numbers.

DNA (deoxyribonucleic acid) Substance in cells which carries genetic information in the form of a chemical code. There is a strand of DNA along the entire length of each chromosome.

electromagnet An iron bar with a coil around it, which becomes magnetic when an electric current flows in the coil.

electromagnetic waves A family of waves made up of radio waves, micro-waves, infrared, light, ultraviolet, X-rays, and gamma rays. Different members of the family have different wavelengths.

electron A tiny particle from the region of an atom outside the nucleus. It has a negative (-) electric charge. A flow of electrons is called a current.

electron microscope A microscope which uses electrons instead of light to form the image.

element A substance containing only one type of atom. There are about 100 different elements and everything is made from them.

energy Something has energy if it can make things move – though sometimes the movements are too small to see, like heat energy making atoms vibrate faster.

enzyme Any chemical from a living thing which changes the speed of a chemical reaction without being used up itself.

evaporate To change from liquid to vapour (gas). When clothes are dried, the water evaporates to become water vapour.

fission (nuclear) Splitting of heavy atomic nuclei to form two lighter ones. Energy is released in the process.

fluoresce To give off light because radiation has been absorbed. Fluorescent paints absorb the ultraviolet in sunlight and give off extra light.

force A push or pull. It is measured in newtons (N).

frequency The number of vibrations per second or the number of waves sent out per second. It is measured in hertz (Hz).

fusion (nuclear) The combining of very light atomic nuclei to form a heavier nucleus. Energy is released in the process.

gamma rays Highly penetrating electromagnetic waves similar to X-rays. They are given off by some radioactive materials.

gene A section of DNA in a chromosome. It carries information about an inherited characteristic.

germ Any microbe that causes disease.

half-life The time taken for half the atoms in a radioactive sample to decay (i.e. for half the unstable nuclei to break up). It is also the time taken for the radiation from a radioactive sample to halve in strength

hormone Any chemical produced in the body of a plant or animal which controls how an organ works. For example, insulin is a hormone which controls how quickly the liver removes glucose from the blood.

indicator A chemical which changes colour to indicate how acid or alkaline a solution is. Litmus is an indicator.

infrared radiation Invisible electromagnetic waves with wavelengths longer than light (but shorter than microwaves). Much of the radiation that warms you from a fire is infrared.

insulator Anything which prevents the flow of heat or electricity.

ion An atom which has either lost or gained at least one electron so that it is positively (+) or negatively (-) charged.

isotopes Different versions of the atoms of one element. They have the same numbers of electrons and protons, but different numbers of neutrons.

joule (J) Unit for measuring energy. You would need about one joule of energy to lift this book 10 cm upwards.

mass The amount of matter in something. It is often measured in kilograms (kg).

membrane A thin, flexible sheet – for example, the 'skin' around a living cell.

microbe Any microscopic organism. For example, bacteria are microbes.

microwaves Radio waves of very short wavelength. They are used for communication, radar, and cooking.

molecule A group of atoms bonded together so that they act as a single particle. The number of atoms in a molecule can be from two to many thousands.

neutron One of the particles in the nucleus of an atom. It has about the same mass as a proton but no electric charge.

organism Any living thing: for example, an animal, plant, or microbe.

photosynthesis Chemical process in which plants use the energy in sunlight to turn carbon dioxide and water into food (glucose sugar). It also produces oxygen.

pitch How high or low a musical note sounds to the ear. Sounds are produced by vibrations. The higher the frequency, the higher the pitch of the note.

polymer A chemical compound with long-chain molecules formed from repeating units of shorter molecules. The shorter molecules are called **monomers**.

pressure How concentrated a force is. As force is measured in newtons, pressure is measured in newtons per square metre, also called pascals (Pa).

proteins Substances used in building the bodies of all living things. They have chain-like molecules formed from carbon, hydrogen, oxygen, and nitrogen – and often sulphur as well.

proton A positively (+) charged particle in the nucleus of all atoms. A hydrogen atom has a single proton as its nucleus.

quantum theory The theory that quantities such as energy can only exist in 'packets'. Each packet is a quantum. It cannot be broken into smaller amounts.

radiation Anything that radiates from its source. It could be waves, such as light or sound, or it could be a beam of invisible particles, such as neutrons.

refraction The bending of a beam of waves as they pass from one material to another: for example, a beam of light bending as it passes from air into water.

respiration Chemical process in which living cells release energy from their food. If the reactions use up oxygen, respiration is **aerobic**. If no oxygen is used up, respiration is **anaerobic**.

solution A mixture in which one substance has dissolved in another.

solvent A liquid used to dissolve something: for example, water dissolving sugar, or cleaning fluid dissolving grease.

synthetic Material produced by chemical processes in a factory, rather than occurring naturally. For example, nylon is a synthetic material.

transformer A device which can step voltage up or down. It only works with alternating current (AC).

ultrasound Any sound that is of such high frequency that it is beyond the range of human hearing. Sounds like this are also called **ultrasonic** sounds.

ultraviolet radiation Invisible electromagnetic waves with wavelengths shorter than visible light (but longer than X-rays). They are present in sunlight and can damage your skin and eyes.

vacuum A completely empty space with no air or other gas in it at all.

virus A tiny microbe which can invade and take over living cells.

voltage A measure of how strongly electric charge is being pushed round a circuit by a battery or mains supply.

wavelength The distance between the crests of one wave and the next.

weight The downward force of gravity on something. Scientists measure weight in newtons because it is a force. However, in everyday language 'weight' is used for mass, which is measured in kilograms.

X-rays Highly penetrating electro-magnetic waves. They are similar to gamma rays but have longer wavelengths.

Converting measurements

	Metric		UK/US equivalent
length	1 millimetre (mm)		= 0.039 in
	1 centimetre (cm)	= 10 mm	= 0.394 in
	1 metre (m)	= 100 cm	= 39.4 in
			= 1.094 yd
volume	1 cubic centimetre (cm³)		= 0.061 in³
	1 millilitre (ml)	= 1 cm³	= 0.035 fl oz (UK)
			= 0.036 fl oz (US)
	1 litre (l)	= 1000 ml	= 1.76 pint (UK)
			= 2.11 pint (US)
			= 0.22 gallon (UK)
			= 0.26 gallon (US)
weight*	1 gram (g)		= 0.035 oz
	1 kilogram (kg)	= 1000 g	= 2.21 lb
	1 tonne (t)	= 1000 kg	= 0.98 ton

Bigger or smaller

To make units bigger or smaller, prefixes are put in front of them:

micro (μ)	= 1 millionth	= 0.000 001
milli (m)	= 1 thousandth	= 0.001
kilo (k)	= 1 thousand	= 1000
mega (M)	= 1 million	= 1 000 000

For example
1 micrometre		= 1 μm	= 0.000 001 m
1 milligram	= 1 mg	= 0.001 g
1 kilometre	= 1 km	= 1000 m
1 megatonne		= 1 Mt	= 1 000 000 t

* In the strict scientific sense, these units of 'weight' are units of mass.

INDEX

If there are several page references, look at the one in bold (e.g. **87**) first. Page numbers in italics (e.g. *110*) refer to illustrations.

A
absolute zero 153
absorption of colours 23–25
absorption of food 138
acceleration 106–109, *110*
acid 28, **87**
aerofoil 114
air
  atoms present in 65
  for diving 125
  as an insulator 156
  pressure from 113–117
airship *121*
alimentary canal 138
alkali 28, **87**
alloys 53–54
alpha particles 98–99
alphabets 45
alternating current (AC) 169
alternative energy 148
aluminium **54**, 77, 79
amber resin *61*, 161
amoeba 59
analogue 46–47
aqualung 124
Archimedes' principle 120
atmosphere
  atoms present in 65
  carbon dioxide in 68
  oxygen in 67
  pressure from 113
atoms 49, 53
  in living things 57, **65**, *66*
  structure of 98–99

B
bacteria *49*, **57**, *73*
  in recycling 68, 69, 73
balance, sense of 142
balloons *119*, 120–121
base *see* alkali
bases (in DNA) 61–62
batteries *150*, 166–168
bee dance 43
bends (diving) 125
beta particles 98–99
bicycle 130–131
binary numbers 46–47
Big Bang 104, 184
biodegradable 73
birds, flight of 114–115

black holes *181*, 182
boiling 51
bones 59, **135–136**
bosons 105
brain 7–10, 140, *141*
buoyancy 118–123
burning 100, *101*
  fuels 68, 147, *148*, 150

C
canning food *74*, 75
car
  electric *167*
  petrol/diesel 143
  solar-powered *149*
carbohydrates 139
carbon 49, **50–51**, 55
  atoms, structure of 98
  in living things 65, 66, **68**
carbon cycle 68
carbon dioxide
  in atmosphere 65, 67, **68**
  molecules 66
carrier (signal) 173
CAT scanner 18, 176
cells, electric 166
cells, living 56–62, *141*
cellulose 58, **66**
Celsius scale 153
cement 86
centrifuge 109
chain reaction 101
chance 88–93
  games of 93
chemical
  combinations *see* compound
  energy 146, *147*
chemicals (household) 87
chlorophyll 58, **66**
chromosomes *61*, 62, *63*
clay 55
coal
  burning of 147, *148, 150*
  formation of 68, **147**
cold-blooded 157–158
colloids 83
colour 20–29
  complementary 22
  primary 22
  printing 24–25
  secondary 22
  television 25–26
  wavelengths *172*
colour-blind 21
communication 40–47
compact disc (CD) 29, **46–47,** *126*
compass 95

complementary colour 22
compound **50**, 54–55
computer images 18, *19*
computers 46, 133
concave lens *15*
concrete 86, *87*
conduction of heat 154
cones (in eye) 23
convection 155
convex lens *15*
copper **50**, *53*, 54
copper sulphate 86
corrosion 79–81
cosmos 184
crystals *50*, *52*, 86, 99
cryogenics 153
current, electric 53, **166–169**

D
deceleration 107–109, *110*
detergents 85–86
diamond 49, **50–51**
digestion (human) 138
digital 46–47
diving, deep-sea 124
DNA 57, 58, **61–63**
drying food *74*, 75
dynamos *see* generators

E
ear 142
egg (ovum) 60, 93
egg white 83–84
Einstein, Albert 182–183
electric
  cells 166
  charge 97–98, **161–162**
  current 53, **166–169**
  forces **97**, 162
  forces between atoms 99–100
  motors and generators 168–169
electricity 53, **161–169**
electromagnet 168
electromagnetic
  force 104, 105
  radiation 170–177
  waves 170–177
electron microscope *16*, 17
electrons
  in atoms 53, 55, **98**, 105
  from batteries 166–167
  in heat conduction 154
  transfer during charging 161–164
elements 49–50, **53**
  in human body 65

energy 144–151
  conservation of 146
  in food 139–140
  forms of 146
  link with mass 182
  from the nucleus 101–102
  from the Sun 150–151
engines 159
enzymes 74
  for digestion 138
  in food 74
  in soap powders 86
evaporation 51
  cooling effect 158–159
expansion 154
eye 22

F

Faraday, Michael 162, 169
fats 139
feedback 10, **133**
fertilizers 70
Feynmann diagrams 105
field
  electric 168, 171
  magnetic 168, 171
fish, buoyancy of 122–123
fission, nuclear 101, *102*
floating 118–123
  in air 120–121
fluorescence *175*, 176
focus 16
food
  chains, webs, and pyramids 70–71
  energy in 139–140
  for human body 138–140
  preserving *74*, 75
forces
  electric **97**, 99–100
  fundamental 103–104
  gravitational 96–97
  magnetic 95–96
  magnifiers of 127
  nuclear **101–102**, 103–105
fossil fuels
  burning of 147, *148, 150*
  formation of 68, 147
Franklin, Benjamin 161
freezing food *74*, 75
frequency 32
  of electromagnetic waves 171–172
  of sound waves *39*
fundamental forces 103–104
fundamental particles 105
fusion, nuclear **102**, 150–151

G

g 106–111
gamma rays 98–99, *172*, **177**
gearwheels 128–129

generators 148, **168–169**
genes 42, **61**
genetic engineering 63
geothermal energy 151
germs 77
global warming **68**, 147
glucose 66–67
  fuel for human body 137–139
glues 84–85
gluons 105
gold 50, **53**, 80
GPS satellites 181
graphite 49, **50–51**
gravity **96–97**, 107
  effect on time 182
greenhouse effect **68**, 147

H

half-life 79, **99**
heat 145–146, **152–159**
  in human body 157
hertz (Hz) 32, 171
hologram 19
homoiothermic animals 157
hormones 141
hovercraft 113
human body 134–143
hydraulic machines 131
hydroelectric energy *147*, 148, **150** *151*
hydrogen *53*, 65
  structure of atoms *98*
hydrometers 122

I

ice crystals *52*
illusions 6–11
images 12–19, 22
incinerators 78, *165*
induction
  electrostatic 162, *163*
  magnetic 168
information
  passing on 40–45
  storing 45–47
infrared *172*, 174–175
insulation (heat) 149, **156**
ions 99
isotopes 98

J

joints 136–137
joule (J) 139, **145**

K

kilohertz (kHz) 171
kilojoule (kJ) 139
kinetic energy 146, *147*

L

lasers 19, *170*, **173–174**
  for digital signals 47
law, scientific 91
leaf structure *60*, 67
lenses 15, 22
leptons 105
levers 128
light
  bending (refraction) of 10
  reflection by mirrors 10
  speed of 10, **171**, 182
  wavelengths of 17
  waves 172–174
lightning *90*, 161, **162–163**

M

machines 126–133
  computer-controlled 133
  control of 132–133
  hydraulic 131
  pneumatic 131
  powered 132
magnetism **95–96**, 168–169, 171
magnifying 16–17
magnifying glass 15
Marconi, Guglielmo 174
mass **120**, 182
melting 51–52
mercury 54
metals 52–54
methane (from waste) *72*, 77, **78**, 149, *150*
microbes 73–77
microwaves 18, *172*, **174**
Midnight Sun *179*
minerals
  in bone 136
  in food 140
  for plants 66
mirage *14*
mirrors 13
molecule 50
  of water 50, 52, *66*, **100**
monomer *54*
Moon and tides *151*
mummification 76
muscle cells 60
muscles *135*, **136–137**
  storing energy 138
musical instruments 32–37

N

natural gas
  burning of 147, *148*, 150
  formation of 68, **147**
  from waste 77, 78
navigation 180–181
nerve cells 60, *141*
nerves 140–142

neutrinos 99, 105
neutrons 98
  in fission 101
  structure of 105
Newton, Isaac 21, 177
nitrates 69
nitrogen (in living things) 68
noise 32
nuclear
  energy **101–102**, 146, 150–151
  fission 101, *102*
  forces **101–102**, 103–105
  fusion **102**, 150–151
  particles 98, 105
  power stations 148, *151*
  radiation 98–99
  reactor 101
  waste **78–79**, 148
nucleus (of atom) 53, **98–99**
nucleus (of cell) 58

O

oil
  formation of 68, **147**
  as a fuel 147, *148, 150*
optical fibres *46*, 172–173
optical illusions 6–11
orbits 111
organic **55**, 70, 73
organisms 56
oscilloscope (CRO) 31
ovum (egg) 60, 93
oxygen
  in atmosphere *65*, 67
  liquid 51
  in living things 65, 66, **67**

P

particle accelerator *95, 104*
particles in atom **98–99**, 105
Pasteur, Louis 76
pasteurizing *74*, 76
paints, mixing 24
perception 7
persistence of vision 10
pH scale 87
pheromones 9
phloem tubes 66, *67*
photocopiers 165
photons **103**, 105, 177
photosynthesis *65*, **66–67**
pinhole camera 16
pitch 32–33
plastics 54
Plimsoll lines 121–122
pneumatic machines 131
poikilothermic animals 157
pollen 42
pollution 71, *85*, 147–148
polymers 54

potential energy 146
power stations 148, *150–151*
pressure
  from air 113–117
    changes in sound waves 31–32
  from water **119**, *124*, 125
primary colours 22
printing, colour 24–25
prism 21
probability 88–93
program (computer) 133
proteins 62
  in food 139–140
  molecules of 83–84
protons 98
  structure of 105
pulleys 129

Q

quantum theory 102–103
quarks 105

R

radar 18
radiation 16
  electromagnetic 170–177
  heat 155–156
  nuclear 98–99
radioactive decay 98–99
radio waves *172*, 174
rainbow 21
ramps 130
reaction time 141
recycling 77–78
reflex actions 141
refrigerating food *74*, 75
refrigerator 159
relativity, theory of 182–183
reproducing life 42, **62**
resonance 35
respiration 67
  aerobic and anaerobic 137
retina 22
robots *126*, 133
rods (in eye) 23
Röntgen, Wilhelm 176
rollercoasters 109
rotting 73–75
rubbish, household 73
rust 79–81
Rutherford, Ernest 99

S

sailing 116
salt (sodium chloride) 50, **54–55**, 99
satellites *111*, 181
scanning 17–18,
scanners **18**, 176, 177

scents
  from animals 44
  from flowers 42
screws 130
scuba 124
secondary colours 22
seeing 6–11
semicircular canals 142
senses 6–11
sensors (in body) 140–142
sewage 77
sharks, buoyancy of 123
shocks (electric) 163–164
signals, digital and analogue 46–47
simulators 108–109
skeleton, human 135–137
smell
  from animals 44
  sense of 9
soap 85–86
sodium hydroxide 87
solar
  cells *149, 151*
  panels 148, *151*
solution 83
sound **30–39**
  from animals 38–39
  electronic 37
  illusions 9–10
  from musical instruments 32–37
  waves **31**, 35
space–time 184–185
spectrum
  electromagnetic *172*
  light 21
sperm 60, 93
starch
  in food 138, 139
  in plants 66
static electricity 163
steel 54, *84*
  corrosion of 79–81
sterilizing (food and drink) *74*, 76
stomata *60*, 67
submarines 122
Sun, energy from 102, **150–151**
surface tension *100*
sweating 157, **158**
swim-bladder (in fish) 122–123
synthesizers 37
synthetic materials 54

T

tacking 116
television, colours on 25–26
temperature 153–154
thermals **155**, 162
thunder 162
tidal energy *151*
time 92, **178–185**
  travel 184–185

tornado *112*
touch, sense of 10
transformers 169

U

ultrasound 18
ultraviolet *172*, 175–176
upthrust 119–120
uranium 101, *102*

V

vacuum 113
vacuum cleaner 113–114
viruses 58
vitamins 139–140
Volta, Alessandro 166
voltage **166**, 169

W

warm-blooded 157–158
waste
  as an energy source 149
  nuclear 78–79
  organic 73
water
  in human body *65*
  molecules 50, 52, *66*, **100**
  vapour 51, 52
wave energy *151*
wavelength 17, **172**
waves
  electromagnetic 170–177
  sound **31**, 35
weight 120
weightlessness 110–111
welding 165
whales (humpback) *119*

wind
  belts 155
  energy 149, *151*
windmills 132, *151*
wings 114–115
wormholes 185

X

X-rays 18–19, *172*, **176**, *177*
xylem tubes 66, *67*

Y

yachts 116

Z

Z-particle *105*

Acknowledgements

Design and art direction: Julian Holland
Editorial coordination: Miranda Smith
Picture research: Caroline Wood

The authors and publishers would like to thank the following people for their help and advice in the preparation of this book: Professor Richard Gregory, Peter Mellett, Susan Pope, Professor David Pye, Dr C. P. R. Saunders and Nan Taylor. They would also like to thank the following for permission to reproduce photographs:

Allsport: p. 117, David Leah p. 134 (top), p. 134 (bottom), p. 136, Tony Duffy p. 137, David Leah p. 140.
Amblin/Universal (Courtesy Kobal): p. 185.
April Angold: p. 84 (top).
Ardea London: Jean-Paul Ferrero p. 119.
Aviation Picture Library: p. 18 (top).
Barnaby's Picture Library: p. 152 (bottom).
Bridgeman Art Library, London/Private Collection: p. 25 (top), Bonhams, London p. 121 (bottom).
J. Allan Cash Photo Library: p. 121 (top).
CERAM Research: p. 55.
Ciba Polymers: pp. 82-83.
Bruce Coleman Ltd.: C. B. & D. W. Frith p. 27 (bottom), Orion Press p. 41 (top), Kim Taylor p. 66, Kim Taylor p. 100, David Hughes p. 127.
Comstock Inc: p. 30 (top), p. 32 (top), p. 40 (bottom), p. 93 (bottom), p. 115, p. 130, p. 142.
© 1994 *M. C. Escher/Cordon Art*, Baarn, Holland. All rights reserved p. 11.
© *British Crown Copyright/MOD*. Reproduced with the permission of The Controller of Her Britannic Majesty's Stationery Office: p. 109 (bottom both photos).
EEV Ltd.: p. 175 (top left both photos).
Mary Evans Picture Library: Harry Price Collection, Univ. of London p. 7.
French Railways: p. 182.
W. J. Furse: p. 164 (top).
Giraudon: Musée d'Orsay, Paris p. 76 (bottom).
Sonia Halliday Photographs: p. 23.
Robert Harding Picture Library: Adina Tovy p. 30 (bottom), p. 32 (bottom), Gary White p. 35 (top), Ian Griffiths p. 36, Reg Wilkins p. 73 (bottom), Steve Bavister p. 108 (top).
Michael Holford: British Museum p. 44 (bottom), Statens Historiska Museum, Stockholm p. 79.
Hoverspeed: p. 113.
Kobal Collection: p. 86 (bottom).
Laurie Lewis: p. 34, p. 37.
Magnum Photos: Chris Steele-Perkins p. 13 (left), Jean Gaumy p. 52 (right), Philip Jones Griffiths p. 91, Erich Hartmann p. 93 (top), Hiroji Kubota pp. 118-119, Hiroji Kubota p. 147.
Mary Rose Trust: p. 76 (top).
NASA: p. 110, p. 144 (top), p. 151.
National Maritime Museum, London: p. 75 (top).
National Medical Slide Bank: p. 18 (bottom).
The Natural History Museum, London: p. 175 (bottom both photos).
Network: Mike Goldwater p. 33, John Sturrock p. 45, Christopher Pillitz p. 139, John Sturrock p. 155.
Nikon: p. 12 (top).
Oceaneering: p. 125.
Oxford Scientific Films: Peter Parks & Jonathan Watts front cover (bottom), Michael Fogden p. 9, Max Gibbs p. 20 (top), Warren Faidley pp. 20-21, Michael Fogden p. 27 (top), Toni Angermayer/Photo Researchers p. 41 (bottom), Robert Tyrrell p. 42, David Macdonald p. 43, Bruce Herrod p. 51 (bottom), Zig Leszczynski/Animals Animals p. 56 (top), Frithjof Skibbe p. 64 (bottom), P. J. Devries p. 69, Stephen Downer p. 70 (top), Avril Ramage pp. 74-75 (three photos), Jack Dermid p. 103, Tony Tilford p. 112 (top), Warren Faidley p. 112 (bottom), Tony Tilford pp. 114-115 (three photos), Stephen Dalton p. 128, p. 163.
OUP: Robert Watkins p. 6 (top), p. 47 (bottom), Chris Honeywell p. 13 (right), David Titchener p. 24, p. 88 (top), p. 126 (top).
Philips Lighting: p. 26.

Planet Earth Pictures: Peter Scoones p. 28, K. Ammann p. 44 (top), Jack Jackson p. 123 (top).
David Pye: p. 175 (top right both)
Rex Features: p. 8, Nils Jorgensen p. 77, p. 109 (top).
Phil Schermeister. © 1986 p. 6 (bottom).
Science Photo Library: Dr Jeremy Burgess front cover (top left), Dale Boyer/NASA front cover (top), D. Phillips front cover (centre), Claude Nuridsany & Marie Perennou back cover (top left), Dr Jeremy Burgess back cover (left), Tony Craddock back cover (bottom right), Claude Nuridsany & Marie Perennou spine, US Department of Energy p. 2, Michael Abbey p. 3, Pekka Parviainen pp. 4-5, David Nunuk p. 15, Hank Morgan p. 16, Biophoto Associates p. 17, Dr Arthur Lesk, Laboratory for Molecular Biology p. 19 (top), Philippe Plailly p. 19 (bottom), Peter Aprahamian p. 29, David Parker p. 40 (top), Will & Deni Mcintyre p. 46, Peter Menzel p. 48 (top), David Scharf p. 48 (bottom), Dr Tony Brain p. 49 (both photos), Dr Jeremy Burgess p. 50, Richard Megna p. 51 (top right), Vaughan Fleming p. 54, Chemical Design Ltd./Peter Visscher pp. 56-57, A. B. Dowsett p. 57, Richard Megna/Fundamental Photos p. 59, Petit Format/CSI p. 60, Vaughan Fleming p. 61, CNRI p. 63 (top), Philippe Plailly p. 63 (bottom), Claude Nuridsany & Marie Perennou p. 64 (top), Dr Jeremy Burgess p. 67 (top), Andrew Syred p. 67 (bottom), Adam Hart-Davis p. 70 (bottom), Astrid & Hanns-Frieder Michler p. 72 (top), David Nunuk p. 72 (bottom), Chris Bjornberg p. 73 (top), Astrid & Hanns-Frieder Michler p. 82 (top), Dr Mike Mcnamee p. 84 (bottom), Vanessa Vick p. 85, Martin Dohrn p. 86 (top), Gregory Sams p. 88 (bottom), Keith Kent p. 90, Marcelo Brodsky p. 92, © Tom Van Sant/Geosphere Project, Santa Monica p. 94 (top), Jack Finch p. 94 (bottom), David Parker p. 95, NASA p. 96 (top), Alex Bartel p. 96 (bottom), NASA p. 97 (top), Will & Deni Mcintyre p. 97 (bottom), Will & Deni Mcintyre p. 98, SEUL p. 102, Nick Wall p. 104, NASA p. 106 (top), NASA p. 111, David Nunuk p. 122 (top), Philippe Plailly p. 126 (bottom), Jack Fields p. 132, Brian Brake p. 133, Nancy Kedersha/UCLA p. 141, Martin Bond p. 144 (bottom), Peter Menzel p. 149 (middle), Heini Schneebeli p. 154, NASA p. 156 (left), Simon Terrey p. 160 (top), Peter Menzel p. 162, Ken Biggs p. 164 (bottom), Tommaso Guicciardini p. 165, Alex Bartel p. 168, Peter Menzel p. 169, Agfa p. 170 (top), Roger Ressmeyer, Starlight p. 170 (bottom), Sheila Terry p. 176, Elscint p. 177 (bottom), Phil Jude p. 179, GE Astro Space p. 181.
Tony Stone Images: Paul Chesley p. 12 (bottom), Mark Wagner p. 14, Jess Stock/Questech Ltd. p. 47 (top), Kristian Hilsen p. 52 (left), David Woodfall p. 78, Arnulf Husmo p. 87, Oli Tennent p. 116, David Higgs p. 122 (bottom), Donovan Reese p. 123 (bottom), Mark Wagner p. 131, Ulli Seer p. 145, Glen Allison p. 149 (top), Michelle Garrett p. 158, Ralph Wetmore pp. 160-161, Arnulf Husmo pp. 178-179.
Swatch UK: p. 178 (top).
Charles Taylor. p. 25 (bottom both photos), p. 35 (bottom).
Telegraph Colour Library: p. 152 (top), p. 156 (right).
TRH Pictures: Richard Winslade p. 114.
Volvo Car UK Ltd.: p. 108 (top), p. 167.
The Wilson Walton Group: p. 81 (both photos).
ZEFA: p. 38, p. 51 (top left), pp. 80-81, p. 101, p. 106 (bottom), p. 118 (top), p. 124, p. 143, p. 177 (top).

All artwork is by *Steve Seymour* (Bernard Thornton Artists) except for the following:
Brian Beckett: p. 43 (top left and right), p. 58 (left middle and bottom), p. 59 (top), p. 136 (top right).
Gillian Kelly: p. 59 (middle).
Frank Kennard: p. 22 (bottom), p. 60 (bottom right), p. 135, p. 136 (top left), p. 138, p. 141 (top left).
Oxford Illustrators Ltd.: p. 15 (left), p. 16 (right), p. 19 (middle and bottom), p. 22 (top), p. 58 (bottom right), p. 83 (top), p. 101 (bottom), p. 122 (bottom left), p. 128 (middle), p. 129, p. 130 (middle), p. 147 (top right), p. 149 (bottom), p. 159 (top left), p. 172 (bottom), p. 173 (right).
Jones Sewell Associates: p. 139 (top).
Peter Visscher. pp. 56-57.
Michael Woods: p. 60 (top).

40-564-1